Rooted and Grounded

Studies in Peace and Scripture: Institute of Mennonite Studies

Rooted and Grounded

Essays on Land and Christian Discipleship

EDITED BY

Ryan D. Harker
Janeen Bertsche Johnson

FOREWORD BY

Luke Gascho

PICKWICK *Publications* · Eugene, Oregon

ROOTED AND GROUNDED
Essays on Land and Christian Discipleship

Pickwick Publications
An Imprint of Wipf and Stock Publishers
199 W. 8th Ave., Suite 3
Eugene, OR 97401

www.wipfandstock.com

ISBN 13: 978-1-4982-3554-9

Cataloging-in-Publication data:

Harker, Ryan D., and Janeen Bertsche Johnson.

   Rooted and grounded / edited by Ryan D. Harker and Janeen Bertsche Johnson.

   xxv + 256 pp.; 23 cm

   ISBN 13: 978-1-4982-3554-9

   1. Land use—Biblical teaching 2. Bible. Old Testament—History and Criticism 3. Human Ecology—Religious Aspects—Christianity 4. Christian Life I. Title II. Series

BT 695.5 R55 2016

Manufactured in the USA.

Series Preface

Visions of peace abound in the Bible, whose pages are also filled with the language of violence. In this respect, the Bible is thoroughly at home in the modern world, whether as a literary classic or as a unique sacred text. This is, perhaps, a part of the Bible's realism: bridging the distance between its world and our own is a history filled with visions of peace accompanying the reality of violence and war. That alone would justify study of peace and war in the Bible. However, for those communities in which the Bible is sacred Scripture, the matter is more urgent. For them, it is crucial to understand what the Bible says about peace—and about war. These issues have often divided Christians, and the way Christians have understood them has had terrible consequences for Jews and, indeed, for the world. A series of scholarly investigations cannot hope to resolve these issues, but it can hope, as this one does, to aid our understanding of them.

Over the past century a substantial body of literature has grown up around the topic of the Bible and war. Numerous studies have been devoted to historical questions about ancient Israel's conception and conduct of war and about the position of the early church on participation in the Roman Empire and its military. It is not surprising that many of these studies have been motivated by theological and ethical concerns, which may themselves be attributed to the Bible's own seemingly disjunctive preoccupation with peace and, at the same time, with war. If not within the Bible itself, then at least from Aqiba and Tertullian, the question has been raised whether—and if so, then on what basis—those who worship God may legitimately participate in war. With the Reformation, the churches divided on this question. The division was unequal, with the majority of Christendom agreeing that, however regrettable war may be, Christians have biblical warrant for participating in it. A minority countered that, however necessary war may appear, Christians have a biblical mandate to avoid it. Modern historical studies have served to bolster one side of this division or the other.

Meanwhile, it has become clear that a narrow focus on participation in war is not the only way, and likely not the best way, to approach the Bible on the topic of peace. War and peace are not simply two sides of the same coin; each is broader than its contrast with the other. Since the twentieth century and refinement of weapons and modes of mass destruction, the violence of war has been an increasingly urgent concern. Peace, on the other hand, is not just the absence of war but the well-being of all people. However, the number of studies devoted to the Bible and peace is still quite small, especially in English. Consequently, answers to the most basic questions remain to be settled. Among these questions is that of what the Bible means in speaking of *shalom* or *eirēnē*—the Hebrew and the Greek terms usually translated into English as "peace." By the same token, what the Bible has to say about peace is not limited to its use of these two terms. Questions remain about the relation of peace to considerations of justice, integrity, and—in the broadest sense—salvation. And of course there still remains the question of the relation between peace and war. In fact, what the Bible says about peace is often framed in the language of war. The Bible very often uses martial imagery to portray God's own action, whether it be in creation, in judgment against or in defense of Israel, or in the cross and resurrection of Jesus Christ—actions aimed at achieving peace.

This close association of peace and war presents serious problems for the contemporary appropriation of the Bible. Are human freedom, justice, and liberation—and the liberation of creation—furthered or hindered by the martial, frequently royal, and pervasively masculine terms in which the Bible speaks of peace? These questions cannot be answered by the rigorous and critical exegesis of the biblical texts alone; they demand serious moral, theological, and historical reflection of the kind done in this volume.

Human activity has profoundly altered the environment, and may have damaged it irreparably. Accordingly, scholars across several disciplines describe our epoch, shaped decisively by human activity, as the Anthropocene. But environmental issues are entwined, always, with moral and political ones, and thus with issues of justice and peace. Concern for the environment, the earth, has its complement in care for the wellbeing of, and justice among, the creatures who inhabit it. Injustice, violence, and war have proved—they are proving even now—to be destructive of environments and societies, human and non-human alike. The issues are urgent and also contested, subject to disagreement and debate. *Rooted and Grounded* engages these issues from a shared perspective of deep conviction, while also reflecting different, sometimes conflicting philosophical and theological commitments. The commitments and their differences matter and call for further conversation.

Studies in Peace and Scripture is sponsored by the Institute of Mennonite Studies, the research agency of the Anabaptist Mennonite Biblical Seminary. The seminary and the tradition it represents have a particular interest in peace and, even more so, an abiding interest in the Bible. We hope that this ecumenical series will contribute to a deeper understanding of both.

Laura L. Brenneman, New Testament Editor
Ben C. Ollenburger, Old Testament Editor

Table of Contents

Contributors

Wilma Bailey (PhD, Vanderbilt University) is the Minnie Vautrin Professor Emerita of Christian Witness and of Hebrew Bible and Aramaic Scripture at Christian Theological Seminary in Indianapolis, Indiana.

J. Matthew Bonzo (PhD, University of Amsterdam) is Professor of Philosophy and the Director of the Institute for Christianity and Cultural Engagement at Cornerstone University in Grand Rapids, Michigan. He is co-author with Michael Stevens of *Wendell Berry and the Cultivation of Life: A Reader's Guide* (Brazos, 2008).

Steve Bouma-Prediger (PhD, University of Chicago) is Professor of Religion and Associate Dean for Teaching and Learning at Hope College in Holland, Michigan, and is the author of *For the Beauty of the Earth: A Christian Vision for Creation Care* (Baker Academic, 2010).

Nicholas R. Brown (PhD, Fuller Theological Seminary) is part-time Professor of Theological Studies at Loyola Marymount University in Los Angeles, California, and teaches part-time at Fuller Theological Seminary in Pasadena, California.

Winn Collier is a PhD candidate in Theology, Ethics, and Culture at the University of Virginia. Winn is pastor of All Souls Charlottesville in Virginia, and the author of three books, including *Holy Curiosity: Encountering Jesus' Provocative Questions* (Baker, 2008).

Ellen F. Davis (PhD, Yale University) is the Amos Ragan Kearns Distinguished Professor of Bible and Practical Theology at Duke Divinity School in Durham, North Carolina, and author of many books, including two that attend to agrarian themes: *Scripture, Culture, and Agriculture: An Agrarian*

Reading of the Bible (Cambridge University Press, 2008) and *Biblical Prophecy: Perspectives for Christian Theology, Discipleship, and Ministry* (Westminster John Knox, 2014).

Raymond Epp (MA in Peace Studies, Anabaptist Mennonite Biblical Seminary) is the Director of Menno Village Naganuma and a Mennonite Mission Network Associate in Hokkaido, Japan.

Luke Gascho (PhD, Nova Southeastern University) is the Executive Director of the Merry Lea Environmental Learning Center of Goshen (IN) College, and the author of various creation care resources for Mennonite Church USA, including *Creation Care: Keepers of the Earth* (Herald, 2008).

Ryan D. Harker (MDiv, Anabaptist Mennonite Biblical Seminary) is an adjunct instructor at Anabaptist Mennonite Biblical Seminary (Elkhart, IN) and the seminary's co-liaison to Blessed Earth's Seminary Stewardship Alliance.

Matthew Humphrey (MA in Theological Studies, Regent College, Vancouver) is Assistant Director of the Brooksdale Environmental Centre of A Rocha Canada (www.arocha.org), an international conservation organization outside of Vancouver, British Columbia, working to show God's love for all creation.

Elaine T. James (PhD, Princeton Theological Seminary) is Assistant Professor of Theology at St. Catherine University in St. Paul, Minnesota.

Loren L. Johns (PhD, Princeton Theological Seminary) is Professor of New Testament at Anabaptist Mennonite Biblical Seminary (Elkhart, IN) and is the author of *The Lamb Christology of the Apocalypse of John: An Investigation into its Origins and Rhetorical Force* (Wipf & Stock, 2014).

Hannah E. Johnson is a 2015 graduate of Bluffton University, Bluffton, Ohio, where she majored in Environmental Interpretation.

Janeen Bertsche Johnson (MDiv, Anabaptist Mennonite Biblical Seminary) is Campus Pastor, Director of Alumni Relations, and instructor at Anabaptist Mennonite Biblical Seminary (Elkhart, IN) and the seminary's co-liaison to Blessed Earth's Seminary Stewardship Alliance.

Ryan M. Juskus is a PhD candidate in Christian Theological Studies at Duke University, Durham, North Carolina, focusing on Christian political, economic, and environmental witness in global perspective.

Douglas D. H. Kaufman (MDiv, Anabaptist Mennonite Biblical Seminary) is pastor of Benton Mennonite Church (Goshen, IN), Conference Pastor for Leadership Transitions for Indiana-Michigan Mennonite Conference of Mennonite Church USA (Goshen, IN), and enrolled in the Masters of Theology program at Toronto (ON) School of Theology, pursuing a certificate in theology and ecology.

S. Roy Kaufman (MDiv, Anabaptist Mennonite Biblical Seminary) is a retired Mennonite pastor and author of *Healing God's Earth: Rural Community in the Context of Urban Civilization* (Wipf & Stock, 2014).

Richard J. Klinedinst (MA in Theological Studies, Anabaptist Mennonite Biblical Seminary; Juris Doctor, Indiana University) is lead attorney with the Indiana Department of Child Services.

D. Ezra Miller (MDiv, Anabaptist Mennonite Biblical Seminary) is a PhD candidate at Michigan State University.

Barbara Rossing (PhD, Yale University) is Professor of New Testament at the Lutheran School of Theology at Chicago and is the author of *The Rapture Exposed: The Message of Hope in the Book of Revelation* (Basic Books, 2005).

Laura Schmidt Roberts (PhD, Graduate Theological Union) is Associate Professor of Biblical and Religious Studies at Fresno (CA) Pacific University.

Rebecca Horner Shenton (PhD, Fuller Theological Seminary) lays the groundwork for careful, contextualized examination of farming and food from a Mennonite perspective in her dissertation, *The Cross and the Plow: Fertile Soil for a Mennonite Ethic of Food and Farming.*

Nathan T. Stucky (PhD, Princeton Theological Seminary) is the Director of the Farminary Project (http://farminary.ptsem.edu) at Princeton (NJ) Theological Seminary.

Adam M. L. Tice (MA in Christian Formation, Anabaptist Mennonite Biblical Seminary) is a hymn writer based in Goshen, Indiana. He has authored four books of hymns: *Woven into Harmony*; *A Greener Place to Grow: 50 More Hymn Texts*; *Stars Like Grace: 50 More Hymn Texts*; and *Claim the Mystery: 50 More Hymn Texts* (all with GIA Publications).

Patricia K. Tull (PhD, Emory University) is A. B. Rhodes Professor Emerita of Old Testament at Louisville (KY) Presbyterian Seminary and Network Education Director for Hoosier Interfaith Power and Light. She has authored numerous books, including many commentaries and *Inhabiting Eden: Christians, the Bible, and the Ecological Crisis* (Westminster John Knox, 2013).

Foreword

The declaration is quite captivating: *"Lord, you've been kind to your land!"* (Ps 85:1; CEB) From this brief statement we know that God's relationship with the land is profound. It is clear that God is the owner of the land, which is a reminder that we need to view the earth as a gift. It is also clear that to God the earth is much more than a possession—for God is kind, loving, and compassionate toward the land. The verse continues with the undergirding hope found in God's regenerative purposes for what is broken. God extends a steadfast love to the people and the land.

The Rooted and Grounded conference—and now this resulting book—pick up this chord in multifaceted ways. The presenters and authors extend a clarion call to view God's relationship with the land as a framework for our reflection and practice. The book is a timely piece for followers of Christ who seek a meaningful intersection between faith and environmental issues. The authors provide excellent lenses for examining biblical, theological, and historical constructs for holistic thinking and praxis.

I engage with the insights and learnings in this book from multiple vantage points: a child who grew up on a farm, a serious gardener, an educator, an academic director, a creation care leader and writer, and a student of biblical, theological, ethical, and ecological works. In my life and work, I have experienced many disconnects between land and faith, earth and following Christ, and soil and soul. The lack of understanding of the importance of the unity between these terms has caused brokenness in what should be seen as a whole. Repeatedly I have observed lack of kindness to the land—the earth.

A recent land story of mine illustrates the love, brokenness, and restoration cycle portrayed in Ps 85. Two years ago, my wife and I purchased an acre of land adjacent to our home. I developed a plan for planting an edible forest on this land that the previous owner had mowed for thirty years. After planting the nut and fruit trees, berry bushes, and vines, I started digging forty holes for the trellises for the grapes and kiwi. I looked with amazement and delight into the holes I was digging. Each of the two-foot-deep holes had a lovely profile of soil—ten inches of topsoil, three inches of small river stones, and then coarse sand. This rich prairie soil provides perfect conditions for this orchard that will mimic a healthy forest. I am doing this because I am committed to being kind to this land.

But there is a sad backstory regarding this parcel of land. This rich land was taken from the Potawatomi in a treaty signed in 1828. The earliest map marks my land as "Elkhart Prairie" and is next to the major trail that the Potawatomi traversed for centuries. As I work in this soil, I grieve over the injustices related to the "settling" of this landscape by Europeans. I ask questions. What have we done to the land? What have we done to our air? What have we done to our water? What are the injustices in which we have been complicit—knowingly or unknowingly?

I am often on my hands and knees in my land as I plant and nurture. This is also a time of prayerful communication for justice and peace to emanate from this parcel of ground. I am committed to being one of God's agents for change and restoration. I follow Jesus, the incarnate one, who embodies the peace and healing that is needed.

We each have stories of brokenness in our relationship with the land, and if we aren't aware of them, we need to search for them. Gaining an awareness of the injustices in our contexts aids in our truly becoming rooted and grounded. Psalm 85 articulates three relational responses that are also woven into the fabric of the essays in this book.

First, God grieves over our treatment of the land and calls us to repentance (Ps 85:2–7). The lament is strong in these verses. The people are returning to a place with conditions that are deplorable—fields that are damaged and dwelling places in ruin. It is clear that people have caused these conditions, even as we note God's forgiveness extended to them for wrongdoing (v. 2). The multigenerational impact of human actions is recognized (v. 5). The psalm registers multiple pleas to God: "Restore us!" (v. 4); "Bring us back to life again" (v. 6); and "Give us your salvation!" (v. 7). God has regenerative qualities and acts to which we appeal. Disciples of Christ need to join God as agents of change and restoration.

Second, God speaks peace for our role with the land and calls us to act generatively (Ps 85:8–9). Peace is proclaimed in answer to the earlier pleas. What a hope-filled message! Salvation is at hand! Similarly, Jesus frequently calls listeners to be wise, like a healthy tree or vine. The good news is that peace or shalom will bring wholeness—physically, relationally, and spiritually. In the Sermon on the Mount, Jesus illustrates his understanding and connection to the land (Matt 6:25–34). Here the great teacher and ecologist teaches peace and justice by pointing to birds, lilies, and grass.

Third, God enacts healing and the land yields a harvest (Ps 85:10–13). The last four verses portray a vision of great well-being. Here we have a confluence of love, truth, righteousness, and peace. This is God's salvation—completeness—which is the vision of the future. Walter Brueggemann writes the following regarding Ps 85:

> The future will be a gift of God's transformative, disruptive assertion . . . Insofar as shalom is a new order, it is a new order marked by the neighborly engagement of ground and sky, heaven and earth, God and people.[1]

Randy Woodley, professor at George Fox Evangelical Seminary, a Cherokee, states:

> Only by practicing shalom can humanity restore the Creator's intentions for this fragmented world. Wherever relationships are fragmented, it is by living out shalom that they can be made whole.[2]

Shalom is the core of Christian discipleship. Take up this book and read as a disciple of Christ committed to peace. Join with others in discussing the concepts of the compelling ideas contained within. Pursue ways to put the ideas into transformational practice. Pray for the restoration of the land and everything that lives on it.

Dr. Luke Gascho
Executive Director of Merry Lea Environmental Learning Center of Goshen College
Leader of Mennonite Creation Care Network

BIBLIOGRAPHY

Brueggemann, Walter. *Peace*. Understanding Biblical Themes. St. Louis: Chalice, 2001.
Woodley, Randy. *Shalom and the Community of Creation: An Indigenous Vision*. Grand Rapids: Eerdmans, 2012.

1. Brueggemann, *Peace*, 6.
2. Woodley, *Shalom*, 24.

Introduction

Ryan D. Harker and Janeen Bertsche Johnson

Psalm 85 begins with a petition: "Lord, you were favorable to your land; you restored the fortunes of Jacob . . . Restore us again, O God of our salvation."[1] This verse is grounded in both memory and hope—memory of the Lord's past faithfulness and hope for the Lord to again manifest that same faithfulness in a gracious act of restoration. In the face of the environmental crises facing our world today, how can the church remember the Lord's past faithfulness and have hope for coming restoration? What is the church's hope for the restoration of the land and of all creation? How is this hope grounded in the story of God's people, both in Scripture and in our tradition(s)?

These questions nourished the dream of a gathering called "Rooted and Grounded: A Conference on Land and Christian Discipleship." In our different roles in the church and at Anabaptist Mennonite Biblical Seminary (AMBS) in Elkhart, Indiana, we—Ryan and Janeen—had come to recognize that humanity's detachment from the land was causing both ecological and spiritual problems. We were encouraged that individuals and communities of faith had begun to imagine and embody alternative ways of living on the land, and we sensed a need to bring that imagination to the church and the academy. We desired to bring together scholars, farmers, environmental practitioners, church leaders, and anyone else interested in a biblical theology that forms us to be caretakers for the land and the life that depends on it. This desire was anchored in the basic affirmation that "the earth is the Lord's and all that is in it" (Ps 24:1).

---

1. All Scripture quotations in this introduction are from the NRSV Bible.

The Rooted and Grounded conference was held September 18–20, 2014 at AMBS. The conference featured three keynote addresses, over fifty papers and workshops, eight immersion experiences (visits to local sites), worship times, storytelling, and many opportunities for conversation among the 170 participants from across North America and the world.

Out of the conference, this book was born. Here we have collected the three keynote addresses by S. Roy Kaufman, Ellen Davis, and Barbara Rossing; seventeen of the conference papers; and three "interludes," which represent workshops and worship from the conference.

Like the conference out of which this volume grew, this book is an interdisciplinary look at the intersection of land and discipleship. The conference emerged out of the growing conviction among the editors and organizers of the conference that the way we read our Bibles and the way we theologize affects how we live on the land. Likewise, the way we live on the land affects how we read our Bibles and the way we theologize.

As an interdisciplinary contribution to the scholarly and ecclesial conversation on creation care, this book covers a broad spectrum of perspectives and approaches. It is divided into three sections: biblical reflections, theological reflections, and historical reflections. Such a division, while helpful, has its shortcomings, not least because each contribution, regardless of its placement in the volume, is in conversation with the Bible, church tradition, and contemporary theology. Regardless, we hope that the categories facilitate smoother navigation of the book and deeper reflection on the ideas therein.

Part one, *Biblical Reflections*, consists of contributions that engage deeply with the biblical text—from Gen 1 to the Apocalypse to John—seeking to learn from the text how to imagine our life on the land. These essays model the kind of engagement with the text that the church desperately needs in order to navigate a faithful existence on the land and to honor the Creator and the gifts of creation.

Part two, *Theological Reflections*, is a diverse assembly of perspectives on several different topics—from watershed discipleship to eschatology and virtue ethics. Several authors also interact extensively with the work of Wendell Berry. Together, these pieces model original, patient, and critical engagement with key issues in the church's thinking about land and discipleship.

Finally, part three, *Historical Reflections*, is a creative mix of articles that consider ways that our ecclesiastical and ethnic ancestors imagined their life on and in relation to the land. Though not every article is an engagement with Anabaptist/Mennonite history, this is certainly a dominant theme in this section of the book. These essays model a serious attempt to at once learn from our history and to think critically about it.

As the preface to this book indicates, *Rooted and Grounded* is the latest volume (no. 13) in the Studies in Peace and Scripture Series, initiated by the Institute of Mennonite Studies and published by various outlets. As such, *Rooted and Grounded* is something of an outlier for the series, which focuses on the issues of peace and violence in the Bible. While a significant number of this volume's contributions are explicitly biblical studies, most are not. And while peace is certainly a subtext for many of the contributions, this is not universally the case. Still, this book makes an excellent addition to the Studies in Peace and Scripture Series because any talk of the church's relationship with the land specifically and with creation in general must be grounded in the biblical vision of peace. Indeed, if the hope of the church is for God's promised renewal of all of creation, set forth by Jesus, then we simply must, like Ps 85, both remember and articulate afresh how a peace- and hope-filled life on the land is lived. We hope that this book makes a fresh and inspiring contribution to this excellent series.

Many individuals and institutions contributed to the Rooted and Grounded conference and this book. The editors would first like to thank the contributors to this volume both for their participation in the first Rooted and Grounded conference and for their enthusiastic support and involvement in this book project. AMBS gave its full support to the planning and hosting of the conference. The Seminary Stewardship Alliance, a coalition of seminaries working together at creation care, gave a generous grant and ongoing encouragement from former staff person Laura Leavell to make the conference possible. An additional grant came from the Institute for Ecological Regeneration of Merry Lea Environmental Learning Center of Goshen (IN) College. Katerina Friesen, Andrew Brubacher Kaethler, David Miller, Jamie Pitts, and Eric Vandrick (all from AMBS) and Luke Gascho (from Merry Lea) joined us on the planning committee for the conference; Julia Schmidt and Eric Vandrick served as student assistants. Barbara Nelson Gingerich, managing editor of Institute of Mennonite Studies, the research agency of AMBS, guided us as we began the book project. Heidi King served as our primary copy editor, and Sophia Austin and Lawrence Bottorf assisted with editing tasks. Joel Ickes also did most of the book's indexing. Our spouses, Brenna Harker and Barry Johnson, have given ongoing encouragement.

We offer this book to all who desire the restoration of the land that God created and entrusted to us. We invite readers to engage, discuss, and put these ideas from the Rooted and Grounded conference into practice with the hope from Ps 85:9 in mind: "Surely God's salvation is at hand . . . that God's glory may dwell in our land."

PART ONE

Biblical Reflections

1

Land as Kin

Renewing the Imagination

Ellen F. Davis

I remember with gratitude speaking at AMBS in February 2008, when I was writing my book *Scripture, Culture, and Agriculture*. That evening, people expressed a pained sense of loss, regret, even guilt because, as they said, Mennonites had forsaken their traditional agrarian heritage under the pressure of our urbanized culture and the illusion that staying "relevant" within that culture required leaving the farm behind. If that was true a few years ago, then the situation seems to have changed, and I celebrate with you the reclaiming of agrarianism—that invaluable element of the Mennonite heritage. Let us celebrate together by speaking again of the Bible as agrarian literature, indeed, as the only body of agrarian literature that rivals—in amplitude, scope, and subtlety—the new corpus of agrarian literature that has for fifty years now been emerging in strength largely in North America, largely in the Heartland—in what used to be called in our recent cultural benightedness "the fly-over states."

Let me be clear: the point I want to make is *not* that the work of Christian discipleship is to demonstrate the relevance of the Bible. Preachers and others generally cite its relevance when they are cadging a decorative or decorous phrase to ornament an argument that otherwise has nothing essential to do with the Bible—in a word, when "relevance" means Bible as convenient add-on. By contrast, my argument is that the substance of the

Bible can help us all, Christians and non-Christians alike, to grasp the full dimensions of both the problem we face and the hope we might have (or build). I hope to show that this ancient corpus may inspire fresh approaches to urgent matters; it might even inspire a renewal of our moral imagination.

I speak of moral imagination because the Bible is imaginative literature in the strongest sense. The imagination is the intellectual faculty whereby we reckon with anything that is not fully known to us, including God and the things of God such as nature—which, interestingly, is not a biblical word. What we call "nature," the Bible calls "the works of [God's] hands."[1] When people such as ourselves, who stand in biblically oriented religious traditions, say the Bible is inspired, at least part of what we mean is that it is or should be a primary shaper of our imagination about all manner of things, all dimensions of what it is to be human. But even those who don't hold to this claim might nonetheless find their thinking powerfully reframed by our witness to biblical representations of reality. Their perspective might be clarified were we to help them look through literary lenses that were carefully ground some 2,000 to 3,000 years ago. For as we know, what the Bible brings into sharp focus is what it is to be truly human, a uniquely knowing creature in a world we probe incessantly, manipulate, and alter. What the Bible tells us that our dominant culture does not, is that we do not and can never control the world.

Before continuing, I will make two short prefatory remarks:

1. First, the Old Testament/Hebrew Scriptures (the part of the Bible I know best) comes to us from a culture of farmers living in villages and small walled cities, where almost everyone, including in the cities, was directly involved in food production and processing.

2. The Bible mostly comes from a society in economic transition. (Maybe I should say "multiple societies in social and economic transition," since these texts emerged over a period of some 1,400 years, across the Eastern Mediterranean and east to Mesopotamia.) In many cases, the texts reflect severe economic straits. In an article recently published by the Land Institute in Salina, Kansas, economist Richard Levins wrote that in our own society "decision making power has in large part left the farm sector."[2] This is exactly the kind of situation that generated the classical prophetic movement in eighth-century Israel. The earliest prophets whose words are preserved—Amos, Isaiah, Hosea,

---

1. Ps 8:6 (Ps 8:7 Heb); 19:1 (19:2 Heb); 111:7, etc. (All Scripture translations in this essay are my own unless otherwise indicated.)

2. Levins, "Why Don't We Have Sustainable Agriculture Now?," 22.

Micah—all inveigh against what is happening to small farmers as local food production and consumption is yielding to commodity agriculture under crown control. Levins's concern is to come up with a farm bill that can counter "the shortcomings of unfettered corporate decision making."[3] Similarly, the prophets are pitting themselves against unfettered *royal* decision-making that is driving farmers off their own land or making them work it as serfs or slaves of a rising aristocracy (large landowners). There is no legal code in the Bible that does not give prominent attention to the problem of farmers falling into debt slavery; evidently it was a problem that Israel never managed to resolve once and for all. So in a very real sense, the biblical writers are giving us a mirror as well as a lens. They confirm our reality about how hard it is going to be, how hard it has always been, to "break the stranglehold," as Wes Jackson puts it, of "the powers controlling farm policy."[4] The Bible is imaginative literature, not fantasy literature; it is crucial to observe the difference.

In the following, I will hold up five biblical lenses or mirrors that might help us re-envision our humanity in relation to the land.

1. Gen 2:7: And the Lord God formed the human being [*adam*], dust from the fertile-soil [*adamah*].

   From an agrarian perspective, this verse from the second chapter of the Bible establishes our lineage. We are "descended," so to speak, as *adam* from *adamah*. This is a rare instance where a Hebrew pun works in English: we are human from humus. People and land are kin, and what is more, the fertile land comes first. Although "mother earth" is not a biblical phrase, I think the biblical writers would accept it as a metaphor, and this biblical image is akin to it. *Adamah* (fertile soil) is a feminine noun; the fertile soil is the original source of nurture from which human life derives and on which it utterly depends. I wonder if there is any connection between that understanding and the fact that the fifth of the Ten Commandments, beginning "Honor your father and mother," continues thus: "that your days may be long on the fertile soil (*adamah*) that the Lord your God is giving you" (Exod 20:12, cf. Deut 5:16). Certainly the biblical writers assume that "you" will live on the same fragile land your parents tended and preserved for you and your children.

3. Ibid.
4. Bontz, "Imagining Political Change," 25.

2. The Bible is relentlessly realistic about the human situation, and it is just one chapter later, in Gen 3, that things begin to fall apart. We should not be surprised that the first sin is an eating violation. At this point in the text, there is only one established limit on human conduct—they cannot eat from the tree of knowledge of good and evil—and the humans violate it. This evidently comes as an unhappy surprise to God. To me, one of the most poignant lines in the Bible is this one, from God's mouth to Adam's ear: "Who told you that you are naked?" And then in a flash, God knows what must have happened: "From the tree that I commanded you *not* to eat from it . . . you ate?!" (Gen 3:11).

   Of course, everyone wants to know if the biblical God meant humans to be permanently ignorant, since the tree of knowledge was forbidden to them. Philosopher Bill Vitek and biologist and farmer Wes Jackson have written perceptively on "the virtues of ignorance," and I will simply add here that the biblical writers do not make an idol of knowledge *per se*—which marks their intellectual culture as considerably more sophisticated than the one regnant in our own society. They value wisdom, not knowledge, and wisdom always involves practices that sustain life in community, such as caring for land and eating modestly, not gluttonously. (The book of Proverbs—the core wisdom text in the Bible—has a lot to say about both these things.) So how were the humans in Eden meant to gain wisdom? We are not told, but I imagine it would have been through evening walks with God; we are told in Gen 3:8 that God visited the man and the woman "in the breezy time of day." But these first humans, who were evidently arborists, tenders of orchards, chose the quick and dirty approach to knowledge, and the rest is history.

3. Now I am going to fast-forward from Genesis to the New Testament, to a very familiar scene—Jesus's feeding of the 5,000 (John 6:10–15 NIV)—but it might look a little different to you now. It is an image of what eating is supposed to look like in the kingdom of God.

   Jesus said, "Have the people sit down." There was plenty of grass in that place, and they sat down (about five thousand men were there). Jesus then took the loaves, gave thanks, and distributed to those who were seated as much as they wanted. He did the same with the fish. When they had all had enough to eat, he said to his disciples, "Gather the pieces that are left over ["the overflow"]. Let nothing be wasted." So they gathered them and filled twelve baskets with the pieces of the five barley loaves left over by those who had eaten. After the people saw the sign Jesus performed, they began to say, "Surely this is the Prophet who is to come into the world." Jesus, knowing that they intended to come and make him king by force, withdrew again to a mountain by himself.

The language of this story—as all of John's Gospel—is very condensed; you are supposed to see more than is said directly. So we are told that "there was plenty of grass in that place," and if you are thinking the way John is thinking, that is code; it is supposed to remind you of other "grassy" passages, such as Ps 23:

The Lord is my shepherd; I shall not be in want.

He makes me lie down in grassy pastures.

We all know the KJV's "green pastures," but the Hebrew is more concrete: we are talking about grass, food for sheep. The psalm is putting us in the sheep role, and from the perspective of the Psalms, that is a good role to be in. It means that God is looking out for you, providing for your basic needs: "I shall not be in want." Accordingly, we read in John's Gospel that Jesus gave the crowds bread and fish, "*as much as they wanted . . .* When they had all had *enough*" (italics added), he gathered up the leftovers, so nothing was wasted. You might say that Jesus was establishing an economy of sufficiency—enough, not too much. I think of Fritz Schumacher's notion of "the economics of permanence," the only economy that is compatible with wisdom. He cites Mahatma Gandhi's dictum: "Earth provides enough to satisfy every[one]'s need, but not for every[one]'s greed."[5] The same basic principles—sufficiency, no superfluity or waste—inform the story of God providing manna in the wilderness. Everyone collects just enough to eat for the day, and you cannot hoard extra (although they try, of course), because manna rots overnight.

I call this Gospel story an image of "prophetic feeding" because it is on the basis of this kind of food economy that the people recognize Jesus as a prophet (v. 14); likely they are remembering the great prophet Moses and the manna. But as John tells us, now they want to institutionalize the divine gift of food; they want to make Jesus king. In the Roman Empire, it was Caesar who claimed to be the source of food, with massive grain doles for the huge city of Rome. But to provide the city, the imperial court, and the Roman army with food meant stripping the provinces in Asia and Palestine where Jesus and his followers lived. So in wanting to make Jesus king, maybe "they"

5. Schumacher, *Small Is Beautiful*, 30–31.

are hoping to set up a competing imperial system and Jesus resists it. It is interesting that John does not specify who "they" are. There must be folks who would be glad to make a profit off the miracle man. Or maybe some of those who want to make Jesus king are people looking for a quick feeding fix because they feel the reality of food scarcity and are scared, like many in our society. We have lost confidence that we can have enough without overproducing, without hoarding, without laying waste to our land; in other words, we've lost the vision that communities can produce food within the limits of nature rather than industry producing food by violating those limits. This Gospel story speaks to our lack of confidence; it speaks of the daily generosity of God working through the created order and sometimes even through human hands and hearts. God's generosity is sufficient to meet our genuine need though not our greed, and that is the point of this story.

4. We'll move now to another image of God as Provider, one that gives some specific content to the idea of the daily generosity of God—the remarkable image of the Divine Farmer in Ps 65:

> For You, silence is praise, O God in Zion,
> and to You, vows are paid. O You who hear prayer,
> before You all flesh comes. Misdeeds—
> they are stronger than I am; our transgressions—
> it is You who atone for them.
>
> Privileged are those whom You choose and draw near
> to dwell in Your courts.
> May we be satisfied with the goodness of Your house,
> the holiness of Your temple.
>
> With awesome works, in righteousness, You answer us,
> O God of our salvation,
> the Confidence of all the ends of the earth,
> and of the remotest sea.
>
> He sets firm the mountains in his strength;
> He is girded with might.
> He silences the roar of the seas, the roar of their waves,
> and the din of nations.
> Those who inhabit the ends of the earth

feel reverent-fear at Your signs;
the reaches of morning and evening You make ring with joy.

You visit the earth and water it;
You abundantly enrich it—
God's stream, full of water—
You set their grain. Just so You set it:
drenching its furrows, settling its hillocks,
You melt it with showers; its growth You bless.
You crown the year with Your goodness,
and Your wagon-tracks drip ripeness.

The pastures of the wilderness are dripping,
and the hills are girdled with joy.
The meadows are clothed with the flocks,
and the valleys robed in grain.
They shout out; they even sing.

This is unlike any other image of God in the whole Bible—the Divine bending over the furrows to get the crop started at the beginning of the season, then driving the wagon home at harvest time with so much grain that it is falling off onto the wagon tracks; they "drip ripeness." Like any really good poem, this one says a lot in a short space, so let me expand a couple of points:

a. "He sets firm the mountains" (v. 7) and "You set their grain" (v. 10)—here we find the same verb. Thus, we are seeing two aspects of the same divine work: the macrocosmic work of creating the world and the microcosmic work of bringing forth bread from the earth. This poem gives a fairly detailed picture of what it takes to farm the steep, fragile, thin-soiled, semi-arid hill country of Israel and Judah. So I imagine ancient Israelite farmers hearing this and feeling personally addressed—encouraged, inspired, and yes, thrilled to recognize that in their daily work of setting the seed on the terraces and ensuring that the rainwater is caught and held, they are carrying out the work of God. Being a good farmer is *imitatio Dei.*

b. Note that this psalm begins with silence ("To you, silence is praise") and ends with the fields and valleys singing and

shouting for joy—sort of a *Fantasia* scene. It begins also
with a confession of sin: "[Our] misdeeds are stronger than
I am" (v. 4). From this progression—silence, confession of
sin, the audible jubilation of fields and valleys—I draw the
inference that the psalm reflects a historical moment such
as our own, when humans need to say less, engage in some
serious repentance, and listen— just listen—to how the other
creatures of God are offering their praise. This psalm has a
kinship with Wendell Berry's *Sabbath Poems*; it is "a timbered
choir" (his phrase for his own local woods) in a different
landscape. I'll cite at length from one of the 1984 Sabbath
Poems (II)—a poem that, like Ps 65, is marked with awareness
of divine generosity and burdened by the weight of our sin. It
is also a poem about silence and song.

> . . . . He steps
> Amid a foliage of song
> No tone of which has passed his lips.
> Watching, silent, he shifts among
>
> The shiftings of the day, himself
> A shifting of the day's design
> Whose outline is in doubt, unsafe,
> And dark. . . .
>
> . . . .
> . . . . Loss
> Has rectified the songs that come
>
> Into this columned room, and he
> Only in silence, nothing in hand,
> Comes here. A generosity
> Is here by which the fallen stand.
>
> . . . .
> Silent, the man looks at the loud
> World: road and farm, his daily bread.
>
> His beasts, his garden, and his barns,

His trees, the white walls of his house,

Whose lives and hopes he knows. He yearns

Toward all his work has joined. What has

He by his making made but home,

A present help by passing grace

Allowed to creatures of his name

Here in this passing time and place?

(Berry, *A Timbered Choir;1984–II*, 64–66)

Like our psalm, Wendell Berry's poem is creaturely; it is an expression of a farmer's humble, chastened search for a place in the
created order.

5. Berry's poem is about loss and the yearning for restoration by grace,
    and that moves me to one more biblical verse, one of my favorites,
    with which I shall conclude—Lev 26:42. It brings us back to the theme
    with which this essay began—namely, human kinship with the land.
    At this point in the biblical narrative, Israel is still at Sinai; the people
    have scarcely begun their forty years' wandering in the wilderness, let
    alone entered the land of promise. However, God is speaking of a fu-
    ture time when Israel will have sinned in the land and been punished
    for turning away from God; they will have been sent into exile, away
    from Canaan/Israel, into the lands of their conquerors. Yet after much
    suffering and loss, God will make good on this promise: "I shall re-
    member my covenant with Jacob, and yes, my covenant with Isaac,
    and yes, my covenant with Abraham I shall remember—and the land
    I shall remember."

    At least two things are notable here:

    a.   The land is not an "it," a thing, a commodity. Rather, it seems
         to be a covenant partner, like the descendants of Jacob,
         Isaac, and Abraham. So as the Bible envisions covenantal
         relationship with God, it is not a two-way relationship but
         a healthily triangulated relationship. All three partners are
         essential to God's design for the world.

    b.   Notice the order in which Israel's ancestors are named: Jacob,
         Isaac, Abraham. Do you hear what is surprising about this? It
         is reverse-order (from the usual "Abraham, Isaac, and Jacob").
         So we are moving back in time through the ancestral line:

Jacob, Isaac, Abraham . . . and the land. The land is the first ancestor from the perspective of Leviticus—that very green and very mystical book—and therefore the land is worthy of honor, possibly even above all other ancestors. "The land comes first," Wes Jackson writes, in the first modern agrarian essay I ever read, in a volume with the Bible-like title *Meeting the Expectations of the Land*.[6] The land is a covenant partner; it can expect things from us. "The land comes first"—principle informs every aspect of modern agrarian thought and practice. Funny—it is almost as though they got it from the Bible.

BIBLIOGRAPHY

Berry, Wendell. *A Timbered Choir: The Sabbath Poems 1979–1997*. Berkeley, CA: Counterpoint, 1998.

Bontz, Scott A. "Imagining Political Change." *Land Report* 108 (2014) 25.

Jackson, Wes, Wendell Berry, and Bruce Colman. *Meeting the Expectations of the Land: Essays in Sustainable Agriculture and Stewardship*. San Francisco: North Point, 1984.

Levins, Richard A. "Why Don't We Have Sustainable Agriculture Now?" *Land Report* 108 (2014) 21–24.

Schumacher, E. F. *Small Is Beautiful: Economics As If People Mattered*. New York: Harper & Row, 1973.

6. Jackson, Berry, and Coleman, *Meeting the Expectations*, 80.

2

Who Gets to Eat in the Garden of Eden?

Wilma Ann Bailey

For most of Christian history, interpretation of Scripture was entirely in the hands of a church hierarchy that was closely connected to the political entity of the day. This hierarchy was embedded in what we call state churches. Most people in those churches could not read. Translation and interpretation of Scripture was always determined by an elite whose goal was to shore up their own power and authority by using Scripture to keep the ordinary folk in line. Thus, the church handed us interpretations focused on obedience to those in authority and ignored texts that critiqued those authorities. Genesis 3—a text with much potential for challenging authoritative structures—was reinterpreted as being solely about disobedience. This established a pattern of hierarchy that mimicked the social structures in place at that time in Europe and early America: God over man, man over woman, humans over animals. That interpretation had devastating consequences, particularly for women and the natural world. Contrary to those traditional and accepted interpretations, Gen 3 is primarily about God's desire that the resources of the earth be shared.

In order to follow the logic of this story, we must briefly return to chapter 1 of Genesis. There God creates the human beings and gives them dominion over the living things on earth. Then, beginning in verse 29, God says,

> See, I have given you every plant yielding seed that is upon the
> face of all the earth, and every tree with seed in its fruit; you

shall have them for food. And to every beast of the earth, and to every bird of the air, and to everything that creeps on the earth, everything that has the breath of life, I have given every green plant for food.[1]

The green plants are given for the human beings and also for the animals, insects, birds, amphibians, everything that creeps on the earth. This is a critical statement for understanding Gen 3. The green plants are not just for the humans. They are for the animals, birds, and insects as well. Moreover, that simple statement conveys an important message about creation care. If God created the green plants for the animals as well as the humans, that has implications for what humans do to the earth. Humans dare not poison the grass that God created for nourishment for animals. Overusing pesticides and herbicides, and covering the plants with asphalt and developments, takes away the green plants that God intended for the animals. Now we turn to Gen 3.

Genesis 3 starts with a serpent. In Genesis, the serpent is classified as a wild animal.[2] "Now the serpent was more crafty than any other wild animal that the Lord God had made" (3:1). Many English translations assign a negative connotation to the serpent by translating the Hebrew word *arum* as "crafty" (NRSV, NIV, NASB) or "cunning" (NKJV). But the word *arum* can be translated in less negative ways—as "subtle" or "clever" as well. The problem is that the translators assume the serpent is an evil being and so they translate everything that the serpent says in a negative way. But the text does not suggest in any way that the serpent is evil or an evil being. It merely says that the serpent was one of the wild animals of the field.

Reading with the text makes sense of the opening question that the serpent puts to the woman: "Did God say, 'You shall not eat from any tree in the garden'?" That seems to be an odd way to open a conversation with a total stranger. There is no "Shalom" or "What is your name?" The opening question is about eating. Why would the serpent be interested in what the humans can or cannot eat? Because serpents eat too. The question for him is, Will this new being that God introduced into the garden compete with the animals for the food available there? The significance of the very real competition for food between animals and humans can be lost on twenty-first-century people who buy their food in a supermarket with little awareness of

---

1. Gen 1:29–30. All Scripture quotations in this essay are from the NRSV Bible.

2. In the first language of the Bible—Hebrew—the serpent is male. The attempted seduction of the female human by a male serpent is a significant subplot. It is not the female who seduces but the male. This is the opposite of what is typically encountered in fiction, myth, and the thinking of people in Western cultures.

where it comes from and what it took to bring the food to market. Farmers in ancient times, for example, knew that locusts could devour entire crops, causing famine and starvation in the human community. Humans were no match for locusts.

References to eating, food, and specific foods appear an astounding twenty-two times in the first twenty verses of this chapter, not counting additional references to fruit-bearing trees. Clearly there is a message here about food—a basic necessity for all living beings—and who gets to eat it.

The serpent's opening question presents the preposterous idea that the humans are not to eat from any of the trees of the garden. The woman corrects him, saying that they may eat from any tree in the garden except for one tree in the middle of the garden. She adds that God said that they must not touch the tree or they will die. No earlier text indicates that the humans may not touch the tree. As the story is told, this is something that the woman made up.

The statement about not touching the tree reveals something else: the woman has already been thinking about that tree. The serpent did not introduce the idea of disobeying God. The woman was probably already thinking about doing just that. Moreover, she is the one who introduces the idea of death. The serpent does not say anything about death until the woman mentions it. She says that if they eat from the fruit of the tree or touch it, they will die.

That is good news for the serpent! The serpent knows exactly what he needs to do. He has to get the woman to break that edict so that God will kill her. If the humans are dead, the serpent will have successfully eliminated competition for the food in the garden. And so, contradicting God, he assures the woman that she will not die. He says that the reason God does not want her and the man to eat the fruit of that particular tree is because God will feel threatened because the humans' eyes will be opened and they will be like God knowing good and evil. The serpent gives the woman three reasons why she should eat from the tree: (1) her eyes will be opened; (2) she will become like God; and (3) she will know good and evil (Gen 3:5). These reasons would appear to provide powerful motivation for breaking God's instructions. But the serpent's rationale does not work as intended.

According to verse 6, the woman decides to eat fruit from the tree but not for any of the reasons proposed by the serpent. She expresses no interest in having her eyes opened, in being like God, or in knowing good and evil. She has three reasons of her own for eating from the tree, none of which overlap with what the serpent said. Her reasons are: (1) the tree is good for food; (2) it is a delight to the eyes; and (3) it is to be desired to make one wise (Gen 3:6). Some people want to equate knowledge of good and evil with wisdom, but of course they are not the same. Knowledge alone does not cause one to make good decisions. Wisdom is the ability to do so.

The woman's logic is flawless. If the tree is beneficial, why not eat? The only problem is that God said, "Do not eat from that tree." No reason is given as to why the humans should not eat from the tree. Perhaps God is saving that tree for an animal that can eat only the fruit of that tree—the way pandas eat only bamboo and koalas eat only eucalyptus leaves. Maybe God just wants to remind the humans that God—not the humans—is the owner of the garden. And it is God who decides who gets to eat the fruit in the garden of Eden.

The serpent is right, probably much to his surprise. After eating from the tree, the eyes of the man and the woman are opened. But the only thing they see is that they are exposed and vulnerable. They try to cover themselves, but it is not enough to cover their embarrassment.

The couple tries to hide from God. God calls to the man and asks where he is. The man confesses that he was hiding because he was afraid. He was afraid, he says, because he was naked. Why would he be afraid of being naked rather than afraid of having disobeyed God? The text does not answer that question, but the next question that God asks is surprising. God does not ask the man, "Why did you disobey?" but rather, "Why did you eat?" "Have you eaten of the tree of which I commanded you not to eat?" The reference to eating occurs twice in God's question. The problem is not just that they disobeyed but that they disobeyed in a particular way. They attempted a coup, to seize from God control over access to the resources of the garden. The man blames God for having given him the woman who gave him the fruit that, he admits, he ate. The woman, in turn, blames the serpent for having tricked her, though we know that she did not in fact buy into his particular argument.

God then punishes each of the beings involved. Notice that two of the three punishments have to do with food and eating:

1. The serpent, who tried to get exclusive control of the fruit in the garden, is told that from now on he is going to eat dust, not fruit.

2. God repeats the original instruction given to the man about not eating from the tree. Again, the emphasis is on eating, not general disobedience. Humans have to eat. The punishment is that eating is going to be more challenging. The ground is cursed; it will still produce, but it will require hard work, and the toil will not always be rewarded.

3. Interestingly enough, the woman is the only one who receives a punishment not connected with food. Her punishment is related to

increased pain in childbearing. This suggests that women were not as exclusively associated with food in the past as we tend to think. It also suggests to me that in Gen 3 we have a combination of two stories—one focused on the man and one focused on the woman. In the dialogue with the serpent, God is referred to exclusively as God. When the consequence for the woman is announced in verse 16, God is the one who states it. But in the texts where the man is prominent (3:8–13), the title "Lord God" is used—the same language used in chapter 2 where the prohibition against eating from a particular tree is issued. In chapter 3, the man is confronted first, because he was the one who received the prohibition in chapter 2. The masculine singular "you" appears there (2:17). The woman was not prohibited from eating from the tree. Interestingly enough, the woman turns the masculine singular "you" into a plural "you" in Gen 3:3.

References to eating and food, in my mind, represent the resources of the garden of Eden and the resources of the earth. According to Gen 1, these resources are to be shared, not hoarded by one species or the other. Extrapolating from the text, this applies to peoples, nations, classes, and castes that attempt to control all of the resources and claim a right to decide who gets what, with the bulk of the resources going to the group(s) in control.

Unequal distribution of resources is the primary cause of unrest in the world. It is the cause of the rise of ISIS in the Middle East and Boko Haram in Nigeria, and the endless violence in the Congo. It is the reason why a wealth gap exists even in the United States. This was not always so. In fact, during the late nineteenth and early twentieth centuries—the time of the Rockefellers, Carnegies, Vanderbilts, Astors, et cetera—the large wealth gap that we have now did not exist in this country. It is a new phenomenon. Jobs not only for unskilled and semi-skilled people but also for professionals are being shipped overseas because the wealthy will make their money whether people here have jobs or not. Although our news reports point to youth becoming radicalized and following ISIS, when people in Turkish villages and Syrian villages were asked why young people are joining ISIS, they replied that it is because ISIS is employing them. Young people in villages with no employment and no hope for their future join ISIS because ISIS offers them a job.[3]

God insists that the resources of the earth do not belong to any one people, species, or nation. The resources belong to people and other living things of the earth. Sharing resources through a better tax system that

3. Yeginsu, "ISIS," September 15, 2014.

insists that the rich pay their fair share on their investment income would mean not only that everyone who needs a job would have one and that no one would go hungry or without medical care, but also that many of the social problems present in the world—from war to family violence—would decrease.

The story of the first man and first woman in Gen 3 is partly about God's insistence that the garden of Eden belongs to God—not to the animals represented by the serpent or to the humans. God's intent is that the resources in the garden and on the earth be shared. No one has a right to claim exclusive ownership of any of these resources.

BIBLIOGRAPHY

Yeginsu, Cylan. "ISIS Draws a Steady Stream of Recruits from Turkey." *New York Times*, September 15, 2014.

3

Rooted and Grounded

Yet Holding the Land Loosely in Trust

S. Roy Kaufman

Rural people are called to represent what God's rule of love should be in every diverse and unique local setting across the face of the earth and at every particular time. Rural people need to be mindful that they bear the divine image and are called to reflect God's character of love. They need to form a community that is just, egalitarian, and able to live harmoniously with all other local communities. Just as critically, they need to listen to the land and its life, to discover together both the constraints and the opportunities provided by the particular natural environment and historical moment in which they find themselves. In this way, humans may participate with God in the re-creation and healing of the earth and find productive and sustainable ways of living together on the land.

This mission accounts for the diverse agrarian cultures that have taken shape throughout history and around the world, each unique to their particular local environment and ethnic heritage. Together, these local cultures form the brilliant mosaic of "every tribe and language and people and nation" (Rev 5:9),[1] characterizing God's new creation in Christ. This is where land, community, and faith come together in creative missional intersection within the rural church.

1. All Scripture quotations in this essay are from the NRSV Bible unless otherwise indicated.

I studied at Associated Mennonite Biblical Seminaries (now Anabaptist Mennonite Biblical Seminary) in the late 1960s, a time of anti-establishment sentiments politically and ecclesiastically. I was not then considering pastoral ministry, being more intent on pursuing an academic career. So imagine my surprise to now find myself a veteran of thirty-eight years in the trenches of pastoral ministry in four rural congregations, all in the Great Plains of North America.

I say this to indicate my context. What I have to say grows out of these decades of service in pastoral ministry. What I'm sharing is what I've learned by living and walking with four struggling rural congregations and honed by years of learning how to have something redemptive and helpful to say to these local agrarian cultures and the people struggling in them. I've had to learn what the Bible has to say to rural people and congregations. It is what the Bible and these congregations have taught me that I share with you.

The authority from which I speak is not that of the academy but rather that of the church. It is the experience of the people in the pew that shapes what I say. Frankly, I'm glad and proud to speak for those folks. They've always been patient with me as I've tried to say something intelligible to them, to articulate their experience as agrarian folk in the light of the gospel.

I'm struck by the irony implicit in the title of this conference— "Rooted and Grounded." Rural people and communities need to be rooted and grounded deeply in the soil of their particular place in order to create healthy and sustainable agrarian cultures. Indeed, I would say that folks who aren't rooted and grounded and don't know where they are from or what it is that sustains their lives are seriously deficient in what it is to be human. I am deeply rooted in the soil of the Turkey Ridge valley of South Dakota, where I was born and where I now live. The irony arises from the fact that we live in a culture that does all it can to uproot and unground people. It is only in that state of loss of roots and groundedness that we become adequate consumers of the products that our culture requires us to buy in order for it to survive. In the normal state of affairs, agrarian cultures do very well at providing for themselves from the bounty of the land without becoming dependent on the money economy and the consumer mentality. So the dominant culture makes every effort to uproot and unground rural people.

This accounts for the ongoing disenfranchisement and dismantling of rural communities that I have observed firsthand throughout the years of my ministry. If one were inclined toward political plots, the systematic global dismantling of agrarian cultures and rural communities in the modern era would surely invite suspicion that this is intentional. I suspect it is simply a function of the convergence of a number of forces—the bureaucratic functioning of government agencies, the rapid increase in the size and influence of global corporations, and the simultaneous explosion of technological innovations. Together, these forces have effectively taken control of the agricultural enterprise in rural communities and, in the process, disenfranchised rural people.

It is ironic that the dominant culture seeks to uproot and unground the rural communities on which it depends for its welfare. It is doubly ironic that the institutional church does the same thing. For generations we have been taught as Mennonites to despise our heritage as *die Stille im Lande*, "the quiet in the land." Anabaptism began, the mythology goes, as a strong urban missionary movement but then lost its edge as it devolved into local, rural, agrarian Mennonite communities. This view overlooks the fact that the Anabaptist movement was born in the throes of the Peasant Wars of the 1520s in which some 100,000 peasants lost their lives in futile uprisings against the oppressive European nobility. Perhaps these agrarian Anabaptist communities, devoted to caring for the earth and living in nonviolent resistance to the oppression of the nobility, were far more missional than we have supposed!

But that's only the beginning of the church's critique of its rural past. Rural churches are castigated for their ethnic uniformity. It's time they became pluralistic and multiethnic, like their urban sister congregations, so the critique goes. We neglect to understand that *the formation of an ethnic agrarian identity is at the core of the missional life of rural congregations!* In *The First Urban Christians*, Wayne Meeks comments that "the conservatism of the villages preserved their diversity."[2] Intended perhaps as a criticism of rural life, this comment has crystallized for me the unique calling of agrarian cultures, which is to preserve the ethnic diversity of the human family.

It is the divinely ordained mission of rural congregations, as alternative communities of faith, to form and revitalize the unique agrarian culture of their local place. Rural congregations need, without apology, to own and know both their heritage of faith and the unique characteristics of their local natural environment. Of course, knowing one's roots should not devolve into an ethnocentrism that excludes other unique local communities. But if we don't know who we are and from where we have come, we have nothing of worth to share with other communities, nor are we then capable of learning anything of value from them.

Then there is the ultimate irony! The critics are right! Of course it's true that it's dangerous, if not flat-out wrong, to be rooted and grounded in the land! It's true that our faith calls us to be strangers and pilgrims and sojourners here on earth, particularly with respect to the markers of belonging

2. Meeks, *First Urban Christians*, 15.

most prized by the world—citizenship, landedness, power, wealth. It's true that, as with our lives, the more tightly we cling to the land, the more likely we are to lose it.

The issue is how we hold the land. Do we perceive it to be ours—a personal fiefdom to be managed for personal gain? Or do we perceive that we hold it in trust for the common good? Join me on a brief exploration of two texts that I have found most relevant for this question of our relationship—as rural people—with the land on which we live.

The first text is in Deuteronomy, purported to be Moses's farewell address to the people of Israel on the eve of their entry into promised land. That it might be a much later theological reflection on Israel's experience with landedness as God's people only increases its relevance, containing some measure of mature learning as to what the past centuries of landedness had to teach this faith community of Israel.

The first ten verses of Deut 8 contrast Israel's experience of landlessness in the wilderness with the landedness they are about to enter in promised land. The writer points out that in the scarcity of landless wilderness, the people of Israel learned to trust God's providence—that one does not live by bread alone "but by every word that comes from the mouth of the Lord" (Deut 8:3). Now the people of Israel are about to enter the bounty of promised land—"a land with flowing streams, with springs and underground waters welling up in valleys and hills, a land of wheat and barley, of vines and fig trees and pomegranates, a land of olive trees and honey, a land where you may eat bread without scarcity, where you will lack nothing, a land whose stones are iron and from whose hills you may mine copper" (Deut 8:7–9). Here, all the benefits of landedness are laid out!

The second part of Deut 8 then lays out the warning against the key temptation of landedness—that we will forget the Lord our God. "When you have eaten your fill and have built fine houses and live in them, and when your herds and flocks have multiplied, and your silver and gold is multiplied, and all that you have is multiplied, then do not exalt yourself, forgetting the Lord your God" (Deut 8:12–14). "Do not say to yourself, 'My power and the might of my own hand have gotten me this wealth'" (Deut 8:17). Because being landed requires our participation—agricultural labor and expertise—we are always in danger of forgetting God and supposing that the bounty we experience is the result of our activity.

The fact is that the same trust required to experience God's blessing in the scarcity of wilderness landlessness is also required to experience God's blessing in the landedness of promised land! Here is the great tension in being rooted and grounded. How can we engage our entire lives and creativity in making the land productive and responsive, which is what it means to develop a culture of the *agros* (field)—an agriculture—without imagining that we are its masters? How do we hold the land in trust, trustingly, as God's blessing and gift to the human family? Unless or until we are able to struggle toward an answer to these questions, we will risk losing the land and its bounty and move ever closer to that dystopian future so feared by the dominant culture of our time.

This same tension is explored in Mark 10, with an even clearer focus on the role of the community. In the catechesis for Christian discipleship in Mark 8–10, Jesus makes it abundantly clear that the Christian life involves self-denial and service to the rule of God's love: "If any want to become my followers, let them deny themselves and take up their cross and follow me. For those who want to save their life will lose it, and those who lose their life for my sake, and for the sake of the gospel, will save it'" (Mark 8:34–35). In Mark 10, reflecting on his encounter with the rich young ruler, Jesus extends the same principle to the land and the community of those who would follow him.

The rich young ruler comes to Jesus as a representative of the remaining landed element in the Galilean peasant population. He is respectful of Jesus but also communicates his sense of birthright and noblesse oblige. He is a righteous man, the best representative of the heritage he shared with Jesus, and one whom the text says Jesus "loved" (Mark 10:21). Yet he seems to have been, as so many of us rural agrarian folk are, possessed by the land. Challenged by Jesus to hold the land in trust for the welfare of his community, in which so many of his fellow Galileans were being dispossessed into dire poverty, the man was "shocked and went away grieving, for he had many possessions," or, we might suppose, much land (10:22). He cannot imagine that land of his as a communal rather than as a personal asset.

Jesus uses his encounter with the rich young ruler to warn his disciples about the dangers of wealth, which we can presume means the same as landedness. "How hard it will be for those who have wealth to enter the kingdom of God!" (Mark 10:23). Correctly perceiving that such a critique would cut a pretty wide swath, the disciples are doubtful, but Jesus reiterates the warning (10:24). Get that camel through the eye of the needle, if you can. That's easier than a wealthy person entering into the realm of God (10:25)! So the disciples throw up their hands and declare, "Then who can be saved?" (10:26b). But with God all things are possible (10:27)!

For once, the disciples seem to get the connection. Peter remarks, "Look, we have left everything and followed you" (10:28). Then we have in response what is among the most remarkable and astounding sayings attributed to Jesus Christ: "Truly I tell you, there is no one who has left house or brothers or sisters or mother or father or children or *fields*, for my sake and for the sake of the good news, who will not receive a hundredfold now in this age—houses, brothers and sisters, mothers and children, and *fields*, with persecutions—and in the age to come eternal life" (10:29–30; italics added).

Here we see Jesus implementing the surrogate family, or kin group, that for Jesus was constitutive of the new community that we now call the church at a congregational level. This surrogate kin group welcomes all who seek to come into God's realm of love, irrespective of their ethnic or familial identity. As Joseph Hellerman explains in *The Ancient Church as Family*, it is a kin group with God as parent and with all who join as siblings—brothers and sisters belonging as equals.[3]

What Jesus seems to be saying is that when we leave our biological families and give up the primary loyalty of our homes in order to come into God's realm of love, we receive a new family and a new home a hundredfold—the surrogate family of the new community formed by loyalty to God's realm. What Jesus envisions is a change of focus from self and family to the wider community in which we live. When we do this, we will find our home and family enlarged a hundredfold. We will find our lives to be more secure and more productive, despite the fact that our community will continue to face the depredations of the imperial culture in which all of our communities inevitably live.

But it's not just home and family that are multiplied when we enter God's realm! Those who leave fields for the sake of the gospel will receive fields a hundredfold in this age along with persecutions and, in the age to come, eternal life. These are *agrous*, the very same fields worked by agriculture in the agrarian culture. As in the third beatitude, it is not pie in the sky by and by for the poor. The meek, Jesus says, "will inherit the earth" (Matt 5:5)! What an astounding assertion! Those who choose to enter God's realm can expect to receive fields a hundredfold in this age!

This is no easy theology used to justify—as popular preachers might— the accumulation of personal wealth. It is simply a recognition that in the face of imperial powers decimating rural communities, it is much easier to hang on to some measure of control over the land when the community works together to subvert that imperial power. The alternative is what we currently experience here in North American rural communities, where one private landowner not only has to cope with the bureaucratic, corporate, technocratic powers but is also always in competition with his or her neighbor for more land. Little did we know how thoroughly being given title to the land would make us vulnerable and subject to the imperial powers of

3. Hellerman, *Ancient Church*, 64–68.

corporate, technocratic America! If we want to escape that trap, we can only do it together as communities seeking to live within God's realm of love! We can only do it by holding the land loosely, in trust and as a trust, as God's gift for the welfare of all.

These two forays into Old and New Testament texts demonstrate that the Bible is not only the product of agrarian cultures but also a document formative for agrarian culture. The Bible presupposes both the agricultural revolution that began some 10,000 years ago, and also the development of urban life and the reality of imperial civilization made possible by agriculture. The biblical story is God's answer not just to the reality of human sin but also to the exponential growth of human pride and power seen in the principalities and powers of urban civilization—idolatrous in relation to God, oppressive in human relationships, and exploitative of the earth. God's answer is the formation of local agrarian cultures, faith communities living on the land in resistance and as alternatives to the dominant cultures of urban civilization.

There fortunately are many models of traditional agrarian cultures that through long experience in living together on the land have learned to live sustainably and productively on the earth. But they are always tenuous and marginal, usually compromised, and always exploited, as with Israel's own story in the Old Testament. Still, these agrarian cultures of traditional peoples across the face of the earth, including the Israelites and Christian communities of rural America today, hold the promise of being able to shape a sustainable future for the human family and to bring healing to this earth of God's creating, now so badly disfigured by the exploits of urban civilization.

The key issue for any agrarian culture has to do with land tenure. Who controls the land, in terms of making the decisions about how the land will be used? Who benefits from the blessings of the land? Are these blessings the exclusive domain of individuals or institutional entities with vested interests in the land? Or do these blessings accrue for the community that lives on and works the land and, by extension, to all the communities of the human family? Do the blessings of the land serve the common good, or are they used as instruments of power and control by the few?

It would be nice if we could look to Scripture and find a universal prescription for land tenure. National claims of sovereignty over the earth were largely unknown in the sense that began to emerge in the colonial era, in which nation-states laid claim to every vestige of land on earth. With the blessing of the church in the late fifteenth century, nation-states began operating with the "Doctrine of Discovery"—that convenient fiction of European "civilization" that says, "We found it; it's ours!" Because of this fiction, the aboriginal peoples of the earth have been dispossessed from their lands. In this context, it would be important to explore the role of Mennonite agrarian communities in the colonization of the Ukraine and the Great Plains of the United States. We haven't come to terms with the realization repeated in Scripture with reference to promised land—that someone else was always there first! "At that time the Canaanites were in the land" (Gen 12:6).

The Old Testament does lay out a kind of land tenure policy. The people understood that the land was God's, as Lev 25:23 declares: "The land shall not be sold in perpetuity, for the land is mine; with me you are but aliens and tenants." When the people of Israel finally came into promised land and settled in the hill country of Palestine, the land was parceled out by tribe and clan and finally *bet-'av*, the "father's house."

Norman Gottwald asserts that these village settlements, or extended kinship groups living on the land, were the basic economic units in the Israelite social system. Each *bet-'av* "formed a self-sufficient unit in the sense that it produced the basic means of subsistence for all its members and consumed all, or nearly all, of what it produced."[4] In his classic study of land in the Old Testament, Walter Brueggemann pointed out that it was not that Israelite communities owned the land but that they were responsible for it, as a trust made to them. We see this understanding vividly played out in the conflict between King Ahab and Naboth in 1 Kgs 21. "It is the case not that the land belongs to [Naboth] but that he belongs to the land."[5] Naboth is not free to sell his land, not even to the king, not even at the cost of his own life. "The Lord forbid that I should give you my ancestral inheritance'" (1 Kgs 21:3). This is a strange and radical concept of land tenure, and perhaps it took root only fitfully in the agrarian cultures of early Israel. Still, it is remarkable to find this vestige of the ancient understanding still operative in the life of Naboth as late as the mid-ninth century BCE.

The land tenure patterns reflected in the Gospels of the New Testament are less clear. Perhaps something approximating private property had begun to be operative, particularly among those who actually claimed the land. Agrarian villages of Galilee likely lived upon the land as a kind of commons, as traditional cultures and peoples have always done throughout history. But as the dominant culture became more commodified in first-century CE Galilee, those with larger land holdings or better entrepreneurial skills or outside means (such as merchants), took advantage of the informal indebtedness that also marks every form of communal life, and they began to accrue estates at the expense of the indebted peasants. Hence the case of the rich young ruler we encountered in Mark 10.

4. Gottwald, *Tribes of Yahweh*, 292.
5. Brueggemann, *Land*, 93.

It doesn't matter what formal pattern of land tenure we live under. What does matter is the freedom and willingness of those who work the land to do so as a trust from God given for the good of all. What does matter is that those who work the land do so in the company of companions, a face-to-face communal arrangement to which all who belong are accountable and responsible. The gravest danger to agrarian cultures and rural communities is that the community will fail to cohere, that members of the community will allow themselves to be seduced by the brilliance of their work and the bounty of the land, and that together the community will forget the Lord their God (Deut 8:19). When communities lose their sense of dependence upon the Creator, they fail to hang together in any meaningful way and become a collection of self-interested individuals who are at the mercy of the powers of the dominant culture.

The oppressive powers of the dominant culture will always be out to exploit and disenfranchise and dispossess rural communities of their land—that's a given, fundamental reality that rural communities have always, do always, and will always have to confront. But the fact is that rural communities can and do and are able to confront these realities with some measure of success. Rural communities are amazingly successful at subverting the powers of government bureaucracy, corporate control, and technocratic initiatives so long as they are not bound by the demons of their own fear and greed, are not seduced by the dominant culture, or do not succumb to the fiction that the land is theirs to do with as they please. Land must be used for the common good of the community in response to the Creator who gifted the community with land.

In the Gospels, we see Jesus re-forming and re-vitalizing rural communities, creating what we later have come to call "the church," by engaging in two countercultural acts—casting out demons and exercising radical hospitality. As Ched Myers indicates in his commentary on the Gospel of Mark, Jesus performed the first of these acts by "binding the strong man"—Satan—thus releasing rural communities from Satan's power being exercised through the social, political, economic, and religious institutions of the dominant cultures. The most vivid example of this activity might be seen in the exorcism of the Gerasene demoniac in Mark 5:1–20. This man seemed to have been "possessed" by the demons of the Roman occupation of his homeland—the Legions! Released from the power of these demons, this healed man was sent home by Jesus as agent or catalyst of transformation for his entire community.[6]

6. Myers, *Binding the Strong Man*, 190–94.

The Gospels portray Jesus as the host in numerous ways. The picture that emerges is of Jesus and his band of itinerant followers making their way through the countryside of Galilee. When evening falls, Jesus gathers those around him, takes stock of what God had supplied from the bounty of the earth—whether through purchase or gathering or the generosity of others—and then seats everyone for the daily meal. Then we have that sacramental ritual repeated over and over again in the Gospels, whether at the miraculous feedings, the last supper, or the post-resurrection appearances. Jesus takes the bread, blesses it, breaks it, and gives it. And, as at the miraculous feedings, he keeps on giving until all are fed and sated.

These sacramental acts associated with eating are where land, community, and faith come together as the new creation of God, initiated through the life, death, and resurrection of Jesus Christ. So I conclude with the final words of Wendell Berry's essay, "The Gift of Good Land": "To live, we must daily break the body and shed the blood of Creation. When we do this knowingly, lovingly, skillfully, reverently, it is a sacrament. When we do it ignorantly, greedily, clumsily, destructively, it is a desecration. In such desecration, we condemn ourselves to spiritual and moral loneliness, and others to want."[7]

BIBLIOGRAPHY

Berry, Wendell. *The Gift of Good Land: Further Essays Cultural and Agricultural.* San Francisco: North Point, 1981.

Brueggemann, Walter. *The Land: Place as Gift, Promise, and Challenge in Biblical Faith.* Philadelphia: Fortress, 1977.

Gottwald, Norman K. *The Tribes of Yahweh: A Sociology of the Religion of Liberated Israel, 1250–1050 B.C.E.* Maryknoll, NY: Orbis, 1979.

Hellerman, Joseph H. *The Ancient Church as Family.* Minneapolis: Fortress, 2001.

Meeks, Wayne A. *The First Urban Christians: The Social World of the Apostle Paul.* New Haven, CT: Yale University Press, 1983.

Myers, Ched. *Binding the Strong Man: A Political Reading of Mark's Story of Jesus.* Maryknoll, NY: Orbis, 1988.

---

7. Berry, *Gift of Good Land*, 281.

4

Land and Community in the Book of Ruth

Elaine T. James

The book of Ruth is framed by issues of agricultural production and land care. The story begins with a breach in the health of the land: a famine (1:1) forces Elimelech and his family to leave Judah as agricultural refugees. The ramifications of this agricultural rupture are echoed in the death of Elimelech in Moab and the infertility and deaths of both his sons in rapid succession (1:3–5). The survivors—Naomi and her daughters-in-law, Orpah and Ruth—will need to find family and land again to reconnect those ruptured threads. The interest in the fields will continue throughout the story: when the two women return to Bethlehem, Ruth works there in the fields during the barley harvest. Much attention is given to acts of harvesting, eating, and threshing, and the plot will ultimately turn on the fate of a field that Naomi owns. In these ways, the story of Ruth is the story of how humans relate to their agricultural homes, and this implies a series of questions about the fields themselves: Are they healthy? Are they productive? Are they being cared for? This latter question about human responsibility to care for the fields is a reversal of the premise with which the story begins—namely, the question of whether the fields will be able to provide for the people. I will argue that one of the driving questions of the book of Ruth is how human life will be properly integrated with agricultural life. This question of care for the fields is only finally resolved at the birth of Obed, Ruth's son, whose name means "worker," or more technically, "tiller of soil." In the book of Ruth, ongoing care for the land must be provided by human caretakers, whose fates are intimately linked with the state of the fields themselves.

By acknowledging the plot's extension to issues of land, I have in mind something like what Aldo Leopold has memorably termed the "land-community": human stories are always necessarily situated within a broader fabric—a community that consists of soil, water, air, and other animate creatures, all bound together in relationships of interdependence.[1] Such an orientation acknowledges that the role of humans in the land community is properly that of "member and citizen," and as such entails a posture of respect for the sake of the whole.[2] This principle has also been emphasized by contemporary agrarians, who insist that land must be understood as a complex set of living relationships. As Wendell Berry articulates it, "A healthy community is a form that includes all the local things that are connected by the larger, ultimately mysterious form of the Creation."[3]

The book of Ruth opens with the setting, "In the days when the judges judged . . ." (1:1).[4] This evokes a particular economic and ecological landscape in which the social structure was family-based and decentralized. The model of land tenure is described in Num 16:14, where Dathan and Abiram demand an "inheritance *(nahalah)* of a field or vineyard." This suggests that an inheritance is a family's access to land for farming.[5] It is an ancestral farm, a *nahaalaah*, that will become crucial at the end of the story of Ruth. The archaeological record for hill country settlements like Bethlehem during this period corroborates this family-based agrarian model. With no evidence of public works or large-scale projects, the household would have been the locus of nearly all human activities.[6] The narrator's evocation of the period of the judges retrospectively locates the story in a family-based subsistence economy, where agricultural productivity was understood as a gift from YHWH (e.g., Deut 8:7–10; Josh 13:15, 24, 29; 15:1, 20; 16:5).[7] Reading Ruth in this light, the connections between land, people, and God emerge as principal concerns. This helpfully nuances prevailing interpretations that tend to read the story of Ruth as a story of the fate and agency of human characters. A banner example of this is Phyllis Trible's influential rhetorical analysis with the telling title, "A Human Comedy." In her reading, the story

1. Leopold, *Sand County Almanac*, 204.

2. A similar idea informs the *Earth Bible Project's* second guiding principle: "*Earth is a community of interconnected living things that are mutually dependent on each other for life and survival*" (Habel, *Readings*, 44; italics original).

3. Berry, "Conservation and Local Economy," 15.

4. All Scripture translations in this essay are my own unless otherwise indicated.

5. Dybdahl, *Israelite Village Land Tenure*. See also Habel, *The Land is Mine*.

6. Meyers, *Rediscovering Eve*.

7. The story of Naboth's vineyard is the classic biblical example of this system of land tenure (Habel, *The Land is Mine*).

is fundamentally about women "in a man's world." So she concludes, "They are women in culture, women against culture, and women transforming culture."[8] As she treats it, the "culture" around which the story revolves is composed entirely of people making decisions to affect their own destinies. But as I will suggest, the human characters in the story are consistently situated in a larger narrative scope that includes the landscape, and the fields themselves are of particular interest.[9] Here, "culture" is more broadly conceived—it includes, in particular, "agriculture."

RUTH THE MOABITE: THE PROBLEM OF IDENTITY

One way that the link between land and person is manifested in the book of Ruth is in the identity of the title character. While other characters are referred to simply by first name ("Naomi," "Boaz," etc.) Ruth's name rarely stands alone. Rather, the story repeatedly highlights her Moabite identity: she is consistently referred to as "Ruth the Moabite" or "the Moabite" (1:22; 2:2, 6, 21; 4:5, 10). The references to Moab might be taken as markers of ethnicity, religious difference, or cultural identity,[10] but they can also be taken as part of the story's larger interest in agriculture. This is apparent, for example, by the repeated use of the phrase "the fields of Moab" (*sde mo'ab*). When Elimelech and his family relocate due to famine, they seek refuge in "the fields of Moab," not merely in the polity of Moab, as the translation "country of Moab" (KJV, ASV, ESV, RSV, NRSV) perhaps implies. The phrase occurs with surprising concentration in chapter one—four times in seven verses— and will continue to appear later in the story (2:6; 4:3). "Fields of Moab" is not the standard appellative of the region: six of its ten occurrences are here in Ruth, and when the phrase occurs in other biblical texts, it emphasizes the agricultural potential of Moab (especially Gen 36:35 and Num 21:20, both of which have framing contexts emphasizing agricultural fertility). The phrase "fields of Moab" keeps the land itself in view, even as the women return to Bethlehem. When Ruth leaves home, she cannot shake her association with the fields of her home. As noted above, she is called "Ruth the Moabite" five times by either the narrator or other characters. But more than this, her identity is so closely knit with these other fields that other characters report, with an almost humorous redundancy, that she is "the Moabite who came back with Naomi *from the fields of Moab*" (2:6, emphasis added; also 1:22). This way of referring to Ruth suggests a close affiliation

8. Trible, *Rhetoric of Sexuality*, 196.
9. Sutskover, "Themes of Land and Fertility," 283–94.
10. Lau, *Identity and Ethics*; Brenner, *Ruth and Esther*.

between land and people. It is certainly the case that the references to "Ruth the Moabite" reveal an "ambivalence concerning . . . her Moabite ethnicity," because she is "ever a reminder that social, cultural, and ethnic boundaries are not altogether impermeable."[11] But this ambivalence also takes into account the landscape. Part of the tension around Ruth's identity seems to lie in the conviction that she belongs in some fundamental way to another set of *fields*. Underlying the tension of Ruth's entry into the Bethlehemite community is an assumed interconnectedness of people to their landscapes.

This interconnectedness helps explain why Ruth meets with such resistance when she decides to leave Moab with Naomi. Naomi had left Bethlehem only by necessity, as an agricultural refugee. But Ruth's motivations are less clear, and Naomi is so convinced that Ruth belongs in the fields of Moab that she resists volubly three times. Her admonitions hinge on the insistence that Ruth and Orpah "return each to her mother's house" to seek security and a husband (1:8–9, 11–13). Her third admonition comes after Orpah has returned to Moab: "See, your sister-in-law has gone back to her people and to her gods; return after your sister-in-law" (1:15). In these speeches, Naomi links the family ("mother's house," "sons," and "husbands") with the larger society ("her people") and the deity ("her gods"). She is evoking the land community, and the implication is that place, family, and gods are inseparable realities. The "mother's house" calls to mind the world of the domestic economy, including the literal house and the associated labor of food and textile production, as well as the communal and political structures of collaborative subsistence.[12] The choice for Orpah and Ruth is not merely between the mother and the mother-in-law; the choice is between a functional household (with access to land, filial and communal relationships of economic support, and integration into meaningful work) and an unconnected widow on a journey to a region recently ravaged by famine. The choice should be clear. Despite her obvious attachment to Naomi, Orpah weeps aloud, and kisses her, and returns to her community of origin (1:14). It is important to note that Orpah receives no judgment or censure in the text, either from characters within the story or from the narrator.[13] While Ruth chooses a relationship with a single individual, Orpah chooses a land community, returning to her place, her family, her people, and her gods (1:8; 15). Ruth's insistence, though, prevails. The oath she makes to Naomi evokes the land community in similar terms: "Where you go, I will go; where you lodge, I will lodge; your people will be my people, your God,

11. Lee, "Ruth the Moabite," 90–91.

12. Meyers, *Rediscovering Eve*.

13. Sakenfeld, *Ruth*.

my God" (1:16). Throughout, it is the *place* that is emphasized: the refrain of her oath is "where" (*'asher*) and it is finalized by the pointed culmination "there" (*sham*) she will be buried. These locative prepositions signal yet again the foundational interconnectedness that makes Ruth's decision to leave so radical, even problematic: Ruth forswears her own land community to seek the risk and difficulty of integrating into a new place.[14] Seeing that Ruth won't change her mind, Naomi ceases speaking to her (1:18). But the women enter Bethlehem just at the time of the barley harvest. The chapter is framed by reference to the status of the fields. Instead of famine, the women find a harvest, a signal of hope. Now the question is, how will Ruth's identity be resolved in a new land community?

WORKING AND EATING: RESOLVING IDENTITY

Agricultural labor, food production, and eating form the central parts of the story in chapters 2 and 3, and these land-based practices begin to resolve the question of Ruth's identity. The interconnection of these themes and their ability to provide this resolution should not be underestimated. Food literally binds the life of the eater to the earth, and in the rituals of eating, symbolically binds people together as well.[15] Norman Wirzba emphasizes the cruciality of food and its production for theological reasoning: "In the past, often because of scarcity, but also because of its inherent spiritual significance, food was central to a culture's attempt to define itself and what it held dear. It carried immense symbolic power since food consumption was the concrete act in terms of which social relations, work life, geographical identity, and religious ritual came together."[16] Chapters 2 and 3 both follow the same pattern—moving from agricultural practices to acts of eating to resolution with the feeding of Naomi.

In chapter 2, Ruth determines to go glean among the sheaves, which she hopes will have the benefit not only of securing food but also of connecting the two women with a social network (to "find favor in [someone's] eyes" 2:2). Boaz, in whose field she gleans, is a "prominent rich man," a property holder and a member of the clan of Elimelech (his *mishpahah*), and is therefore Naomi's kin. Kinship language here suggests that the future of these characters is not simply a matter of individual agency, but is dependent on the family network and its connection to land. Boaz is a promising character, whose relationship to the family and his possession of fruitful

14. Honig, "Ruth."
15. Douglas, *Active Voice*.
16. Wirzba, *Paradise of God*, 183.

land suggest that he may be in position to resolve the problem of hunger and alienation. And, indeed, Boaz advises Ruth on exactly these issues, instructing her to stay near his workers and to keep her "eyes on the field" (2:8–9). His plan is pragmatic: she must labor if she will eat. He goes on to acknowledge that Ruth is vulnerable, without economic security, having "abandoned [her] father, mother, native land" (2:11). Then he says:

> May the Lord compensate your work
> and may your wages be compensated
> from YHWH the God of Israel
> under whose wings you have come to seek refuge. (2:12)

This verse is typically taken to refer back to Ruth's actions in leaving Moab, and is usually translated to reflect this: "May the Lord reward you for your deeds!" (NRSV). But the words here have a more basic economic sense. The verb that I have translated "compensate" above conveys the sense of remuneration (*yeshallem*, e.g., Exod 22:13–14; 2 Kgs 4:7; Ps 37:21; Prov 22:27). "Work" (*po'alek*) denotes labor, especially labor in food production (esp. Job 24:5; Ps 104:23, cf. Jer 31:16; 2 Chr 15:7; Eccl 1:3; Lev 19:13; Ezek 29:20; Prov 10:16; 11:18), and "wages" (*maskurtek*) always refers to payment for work done (Gen 29:15; 31:7; 31:41).[17] YHWH is the guarantor of wages in the sense already established in chapter 1: it is YHWH who provides food from the fields of Bethlehem (1:6; 2:12). All of this makes sense in light of the economic context of the chapter, which includes descriptions of field work, harvesting practices, and workers of various statuses (2:5, 8, 9, 13, 15). Boaz gives Ruth the opportunity to formalize her relationship to this land community by working in the fields. She does so, and the work itself brings her into the community. Ruth goes from gleaning behind the reapers to eating beside them at Boaz's invitation: "'Come here. Eat from the bread, and dip your morsel in the sour wine.' She sat beside the reapers, and he heaped up for her parched grain" (2:14). The next lines succinctly report the fulfillment of her physical needs: "She ate. She was satisfied. She had some left over" (2:14). Boaz's strategy works: Ruth's labor in the fields provides for her needs. But it does so with more than food. Before this moment, the other workers speculate about her alterity: "She is the Moabite who came back with Naomi from the fields of Moab" (2:6), but after she sits with the reapers and shares their meal, the workers make no further comment about her identity as a Moabite. Eating with the workers "must certainly have implied acceptance in the 'familia.' Beyond receiving water promised her in

---

17. A noun with the same root, *skr*, occurs more commonly (Gen 30:32; 31:8; Ezek 29:18–19; Deut 15:18; Mal 3:5; Isa 19:10) and similarly refers to compensation for work.

verse 9, she is now to share in the communal meal."[18] At the end of the day, Ruth brings the parched grain home, along with the barley she has gleaned and beaten, and feeds her mother-in-law (2:18). While this is food enough perhaps for a few weeks, there is the promise of future work. The narrator ends this chapter commenting on the state of the fields, noting that Ruth will have work through the wheat harvest, which would take place in the following month (2:23). Wheat is a more vulnerable crop than barley, and the notice of its success marks again the attentive interest in the state of the fields.[19] The movement from agricultural labor to eating to providing for Naomi will be repeated in a different form in chapter 3. It must be repeated because the long-term security of the women is not yet established.

Chapter 3 is also structured around the centrality of agricultural acts and culminates in the provision of food for Naomi. It begins with an agricultural practice: threshing, the first step in processing the harvested grain for food production.[20] Naomi's plan is for Ruth to approach Boaz after he has finished his work at the threshing floor. The meal featured here is Boaz's eating and drinking (3:7). Ruth does not participate in this meal but waits until he is satiated (his "heart was glad," indicating that he has enjoyed himself, perhaps with alcohol; see 1 Sam 25:36; 2 Sam 13:28; Esth 1:10; Judg 19:22).[21] Once again, the bounty of the fields, evidenced in the fruitful results of the harvest at the threshing floor, points to the positive ecological environment that bodes well for its human participants. This link is pointed up by the subtle but clear undercurrent of eroticism at this scene. Ruth approaches Boaz "at night"; the verb "to lie down" is repeated no less than eight times; and Ruth uncovers Boaz's "foot-places" (*margelotayw*, 3:7), which recalls the biblical euphemism for genitalia ("feet," *regel*).[22] The eroticism connects the fecundity of the earth with the potential fecundity of Ruth. The enfolding of Ruth into the land community, first through her own labor and then through Boaz's acknowledgment at the threshing floor, results again in the feeding of Ruth and Naomi: the six measures of barley that Boaz gives Ruth to carry home to Naomi is more than a meal.[23] But it will remain to chapter

18. Sasson, *Ruth*, 55.

19. Barley has strong similarities to wheat, but has several advantages, including its higher tolerance for salination, its early maturation, and its lower demands on the spring rainfall, factors that make it more dependable in areas of marginal moisture supply (Clawson, Landsberg, and Alexander, *Agricultural Potential*).

20. Dalman, *Arbeit und Sitte*.

21. Linafelt, *Ruth and Esther*.

22. The erotic potential of this scene is discussed by Fewell and Gunn in *Compromising Redemption*, 84–89.

23. Campbell, *Ruth*.

four to finally provide the long-term "security" the two women so desperately need (1:9; 3:1).

FINDING OBED: A LONG-TERM SOLUTION

Now that Ruth and Naomi's immediate needs have been provided for, the question remains as to how they will find long-term stability in this land community. Against the backdrop of an intricately interwoven community of family, land, food production, and human labor comes the late-breaking news that Naomi is selling a "portion of a field" that was the inheritance (*nahalah*) of Elimelech (4:3, 5). Although the family had left the region, and although the proper inheritor had died, the family still had a functional relationship to this bit of arable field.[24] The theological rationale for this opaque situation is given in one of the most famous formulations of land tenure, found in the Holiness Code in Leviticus: "The land must not be sold permanently, because the land is mine and you are but aliens and my tenants" (25:23). As Ellen Davis describes it, this land as a permanent entitlement to a small family group is "to be held as a trust and transmitted from generation to generation. Although the rights to land use may temporarily be sold to pay off debts, the land reverts to the original family unit every fiftieth year."[25] Thus, there emerges a need for a redeemer who can intercede with the women on behalf of Naomi's land. The question of who will provide for the women is now circumscribed by the question of who will provide for the land. Care of people, it is revealed, is inextricably linked to care of land.

In chapter 4, in a scene that mirrors the decisions made in chapter 1, two people once again make decisions about how they will relate to a land community. In chapter 1, women weigh decisions about fidelity to the mother's household, while here in chapter 4, two men weigh decisions about fidelity to ancestral lands. It turns out there is a kinsman to Naomi (a nearer kinsman than Boaz) who is in a position to redeem her field for her. Initially, he decides affirmatively, "I will redeem it" (4:4), just as Orpah initially insists

---

24. Only a cluster of texts deal specifically with estate distribution case law in the Hebrew Bible (Deut 21:15–17; Num 27:1–11; 36:6–9; Ezek 46:16–18). In most cases, primogeniture is taken to be the norm (Deut 21), but there are several cases that deal with the problem of the absence of the firstborn. These include the case of the daughters of Zelophehad (Num 27), who seek an inheritance despite the absence of the male heir, and the case of Ruth and Naomi, who need to seek help to find a claim to Naomi's parcel of land (her husband's *nahalah*). Micah 2:2 condemns the practice of possessing a person's *nahalah* for the repayment of debt, emphatically underscoring the principle of inalienability.

25. Davis, *Scripture, Culture, and Agriculture*, 39.

on going with her mother-in-law to Judah (1:10). But for both characters, the possibility of choosing a new land is complicated by the social and ethical responsibilities that attend the land community. Acquiring this piece of land means acquiring a set of binding responsibilities: "The day you acquire the field from the hand of Naomi, you are also acquiring Ruth the Moabite, the widow of the dead man, to maintain the dead man's name on his inheritance (*naḥalah*)" (4:5). This is no mere property transaction. It involves the people who belong to the field and cannot be alienated from it. This man cannot take on these responsibilities without damaging his own ancestral inheritance (*naḥalah*), and so he changes his mind (4:6). Like Orpah, the nearer kinsman makes the sensible choice. These two characters make decisions that frame the whole arc of the story with questions about how people relate to their agricultural homes. Ruth makes the problematic decision to leave and must be brought into the community by a combination of her own agricultural labor and—finally—the hospitality of others. Boaz agrees to care for both the land and Ruth. The elders at the gate publically ratify the transferal of land to Boaz and solve the problem of permanency for Ruth and Naomi, connecting Elimelech's portion of land to the wellbeing of the larger land community. This includes both forebears (Elimelech, Mahlon, and Chilion, the dead, who are all evoked in 4:9) as well as descendants (Jesse and David; 4:17).

Some readers have noted that in a story otherwise centrally interested in women, the character of Ruth herself fades into the background in this final chapter.[26] This suggests not the erasure of women from the story but the nesting of their stories in a larger concern about care for land. (The reader will remember that is also where the story began, with the description of famine in 1:1.) The narrative returns at the end to the fate of the ancestral field (*naḥalah*, 4:10), dwelling with the details of the proceedings (4:7–10). This return of attention to the land is further confirmed by a final crucial detail of the story. After her marriage to Boaz, YHWH grants Ruth conception and she bears a son (4:13). In an unusual practice of communal naming, the women of the neighborhood name the child "Obed" (4:17). The symbolic significance of the name should not be overlooked.[27] While "Obed" is often connected to "servant" (*ebed*), the root word *'bd* means, more specifically, "tilling the land" (Gen 4:2 calls Cain a "tiller [*'obed*] of the ground"; cf. 1 Chr 27:26).[28] As Talia Sutskover notes, "By [Obed's] birth Ruth is inextricably

26. Bledstein, *A Feminist Companion to Ruth*. See also Wolde, *Ruth and Naomi*.

27. LaCocque, *Ruth: A Continental Commentary*.

28. "Tilling the land" is the principal meaning of the verb: see Gen 2:5; 3:23; 4:12; 2 Sam 9:10; Isa 30:24; Jer 27:11; Zec 13:5; Ps 104:14; Prov 12:11; 28:19, etc.

connected to the fertile land of Beit-lehem, and the child's name epitomizes this connection."[29] The human community recognizes that the proper bond between people and land is one of reciprocal provision. Not only will the fertility of the land provide for the people, the fertility of the people will provide a caretaker for the land. As Naomi's family is restored to its land, they will also return to the tasks of caring for it, fulfilling the vocation of stewardship in Gen 2:15, in which the role of humans with respect to the land is to "to till it [l'obedah] and to keep it."

The story of Ruth returns repeatedly to issues of land and community. While it centers on the human characters of Ruth and Naomi, their actions and fates are circumscribed by a larger vision of land community. Ruth the Moabite is able to enter into the Bethlehemite community by participating in agricultural life—through field work, eating, and providing for Naomi from the local food economy. When the narrative returns in chapter 4 to Naomi's field, the focus shifts from the land's provision for people to the people's provision for the land. Through the birth of Obed, fertility of land and people are imagined in a mutually sustaining relationship. In these ways, the story of Ruth highlights the ethical complexities of leaving home, entering a new community, and of caring properly for land.

BIBLIOGRAPHY

Berry, Wendell. "Conservation and Local Economy." In *Sex, Economy, Freedom and Community: Eight Essays*, 3–18. New York: Pantheon, 1992.

Bledstein, Adrian J. "Female Companionships: If the Book of Ruth were Written by a Woman . . ." In *A Feminist Companion to Ruth*, edited by Athalya Brenner, 116–33. Sheffield: Sheffield Academic, 1993.

Brenner, Athalya, ed. *Ruth and Esther*. A Feminist Companion to the Bible, 2nd Series 3. Sheffield: Sheffield Academic, 1999.

Campbell, Edward F. *Ruth*. Anchor Bible 7. Garden City, NY: Doubleday, 1975.

Clawson, Marion, Hans H. Landsberg, and Lyle T. Alexander. *Agricultural Potential of the Middle East*. New York: American Elsevier, 1971.

Dalman, Gustaf. *Arbeit und Sitte in Palästina* III. Gütersloh: C. Bertelsmann, 1933.

Davis, Ellen F. *Scripture, Culture, and Agriculture: An Agrarian Reading of the Bible*. New York: Cambridge University Press, 2009.

Douglas, Mary. *In the Active Voice*. New York: Routledge, 1982.

Dybdahl, Jon. "Israelite Village Land Tenure: Settlement to Exile." PhD diss., Fuller Theological Seminary, 1981.

Fewell, Danna Nolan, and David M. Gunn. *Compromising Redemption: Relating Characters in the Book of Ruth*. Louisville: Westminster John Knox, 1990.

Habel, Norman C. *The Land is Mine*. Minneapolis: Fortress, 1995.

---

29. Sutskover, "Themes of Land and Fertility," 293.

Habel, Norman C., ed. *Readings from the Perspective of Earth*. Sheffield, UK: Sheffield Academic, 2000.

Honig, Bonnie. "Ruth, the Model Emigrée: Mourning and the Symbolic Politics of Immigration." In *Ruth and Esther*, edited by Athalya Brenner, 50–74. Sheffield, UK: Sheffield Academic, 1999.

LaCocque, André. *Ruth: A Continental Commentary*. Minneapolis: Fortress, 2004.

Lau, Peter H. W. *Identity and Ethics in the Book of Ruth: A Social Identity Approach*. BZAW 416. Berlin: de Gruyter, 2011.

Lee, Eunny P. "Ruth the Moabite: Identity, Kinship, and Otherness." *Engaging the Bible in a Gendered World: An Introduction to Feminist Biblical Interpretation*, edited by Linda Day and Carolyn Pressler, 89–101. Louisville: Westminster John Knox, 2006.

Leopold, Aldo. *A Sand County Almanac and Sketches Here and There*. New York: Oxford University Press, 1968.

Linafelt, Tod. "Ruth." In *Berit Olam: Studies in Hebrew Narrative and Poetry; Ruth and Esther*, edited by David W. Cotter. Collegeville, MN: Liturgical, 1999.

Meyers, Carol L. *Rediscovering Eve: Ancient Israelite Women in Context*. New York: Oxford University, 2013.

Sakenfeld, Katharine Doob. *Ruth*. IBC. Louisville: Westminster John Knox, 1999.

Sasson, Jack M. *Ruth: A New Translation with a Philological Commentary and a Formalist-Folklorist Interpretation*. Sheffield, UK: Sheffield Academic, 1989.

Sutskover, Talia. "The Themes of Land and Fertility in the Book of Ruth." *JSOT* 34, no. 3 (2010) 283–94.

Trible, Phyllis. *God and the Rhetoric of Sexuality*. Philadelphia: Fortress, 1978.

Wolde, Ellen J. van. *Ruth and Naomi*. London: SCM, 1997.

Wirzba, Norman. *The Paradise of God: Renewing Religion in an Ecological Age*. Oxford: Oxford University Press, 2003.

5

Speaking from Ground Level

Vineyards, Fields, and Trees among Israel's Prophets

Patricia K. Tull

Some years ago, writing a commentary on the prophet Isaiah[1] at the same time that I was taking Master Gardener and Master Naturalist classes from Purdue Extension in Indiana, I found myself noticing new things hidden in plain sight. Reading Isaiah alongside what ancient theologians used to call God's other book, the book of nature, I was startled to see what a master naturalist the prophet himself was.

Isaiah's imaginative world vibrates with nature's buzzing. There are many animals in his book but even more plants.[2] They appear in three ways that frequently intertwine. First, fields, vineyards, and trees serve repeatedly as metaphors for humans. Israel and Judah are imagined as a vineyard that fails to produce edible fruit (Isa 5:1–7). Humans are a tree stump that is burned (6:13) or that regenerates (11:1). Judah is a field of grains and herbs that are being sown and harvested by a wise farmer (28:24–28). Such metaphors occur over and over, not just in the portions that scholars think go back to the prophet himself but also in the portions that came later. In Isaiah, the root metaphors for human beings arise from the world of botany.

1. Tull, *Isaiah 1–39*.
2. Tull, "Persistent Vegetative States," 21.

The same thing happens in reverse: plants, especially trees, are imagined as people. Trees are anthropomorphized as a taunting, clapping, rejoicing, or praising chorus, as when the cypresses and cedars exult over the fallen tyrant who was attempting to clear cut them for profit (14:8), and when forests and trees sing along with heaven, earth, and mountains (44:23). People show up as plants, and plants show up as people.

The third relationship between people and plants in Isaiah manifests over and over as humans' utter dependence on plants for survival. Unlike in the metaphors, this relationship is not reciprocal. The land may dry up in response to human misdeeds (24:4–5), but there is no place in Isaiah where plants need people for their survival. In fact, it is when civilization is destroyed that wild, humanly undesirable plants flourish: briers and thorns (5:6; 7:23–25; 32:13). In Isaiah's understanding, the wild earth may be disturbed by us, but it can get along without us. Yet when the fields fail to flourish, humans cannot survive.

These three ideas—plants as people, people as plants, and people dependent on plants—function singly and together in Isaiah to describe several movements in the divine/human relationship. They are used in accusations (e.g., 5:1–7, 8–10; 17:10–11). They describe divine judgments (e.g., 5:24; 6:13; 9:18–19; 10:16–19; 34:9–15). And they project hope for the future, hope that humans will flourish within a larger-than-human creation (e.g., 30:23–24; 32:15; 35:1–7). In other words, Isaiah sees kinship among creation's living elements, specifically between humans and plants—a kinship biologists now describe in terms of shared genetics and absolute dependencies.

Noticing this about Isaiah made me curious about botany's role in the related Book of the Twelve so-called minor prophets, and especially among Isaiah's near contemporaries—Amos, Hosea, and Micah. All four of Israel's earliest written prophets appear to have preached within a generation of one another in the eighth century BCE. Yet each of them—Isaiah, Hosea, Amos, and Micah—originates from a different geographical location. Isaiah spoke in Jerusalem during the time of Assyrian dominance. He saw the capital of the northern kingdom of Israel, Samaria, destroyed by Assyria in 722 BCE, and he also saw Jerusalem attacked by Assyria in 701. He was the only one of the four original eighth-century prophets who lived and spoke in Jerusalem.

Of the other three, the earliest was Amos, a resident of Tekoa, a small Judean town about sixteen kilometers to the south of Jerusalem. He traveled north to prophesy against the more powerful northern kingdom of Israel about a generation before Isaiah's time. Hosea was the only prophet who was Israelite rather than Judean. He spoke in the vicinity of Samaria before it was destroyed by Assyria. Micah was from the town of Moresheth near

Gath, in Judah's low country southwest of Jerusalem, outside the capital city's protective walls. Hosea was probably slightly earlier than Isaiah; Micah was around the same time.

These four prophets set the standard for all that follows them in the two most complicated books in the Hebrew Bible, Isaiah and the Twelve. Isaiah's book extends through Jerusalem's darkest times—to the Babylonian destruction in the sixth century and into (or perhaps even past) the Persian empire's domination, when Jerusalem was rebuilt. At least three hundred years, maybe five hundred, along with dramatic social upheavals, find their way into Isaiah's complicated book. Amos, Hosea, and Micah, on the other hand, became the first three of twelve prophets found in the Book of the Twelve, which came down through history as a single scroll, reflecting all the same centuries Isaiah does.

The violence of the eighth century, the internal and external upheavals through which most if not all of these prophets lived, inspire wonder: How did they, despite their circumstances, manage to envision a just and secure society? I find their company welcome now, when prosperity seems fragile and poorly distributed, and when every resource including agriculture is being exploited for profit at the expense of both people and land.[3]

The many parallels between then and now are gripping. But so are the differences. These prophets had a take on the world that they shared with other biblical writers and with every generation up to the recent past—an awareness of being part not just of human society but of a larger chain of being. For ancient writers, it was all of a piece: what happened in the human sphere affected not just society but also everything else. And what happened in the natural world shaped the human community's fortunes. This is an insight that has been largely missing from modern awareness, and this missing information influences our theological assumptions and biblical readings as much as our everyday practices.

If we compare Isaiah's discussions of the plant world with those of Amos, Micah, and Hosea, both the similarities and the distinctions between them are striking. The same usages—the metaphorical and the literal—and the same forms—accusation, judgment, and hope—show up in the Twelve as in Isaiah. The three botanical categories found in Isaiah—vines, trees, and field plants—are also found in the Twelve. But the other prophets' discussions differ from Isaiah's in striking ways.

Both Isaiah and the Twelve speak of grain, not only as grain itself but also as seed or simply as fields. Isaiah's usages range widely in breadth. In the parable of the farmer's sowing and threshing in chapter 28, for instance, in

3. Davis, *Scripture, Culture, and Agriculture*, 122.

addition to wheat, barley, and spelt, the prophet mentions two herbs found nowhere else in Scripture.[4]

Isaiah also takes advantage of linguistic opportunities such as those presented by the Hebrew word *zera'*, which denotes both plant seed and human seed, or semen.[5] Human descendants are spoken of as *zera'*, that is, "seed," in Isaiah sixteen times, beginning already in 1:4 and extending all the way to 66:22, as opposed to only twice, in very late texts, in the Twelve (Mal 2:3, 15). Humans are compared to grass frequently in Isaiah, both in their perishing (5:24) and in their flourishing (66:14) but seldom in the Twelve. Blossoms and blossoming (from the root *prh*) are a frequent metaphor in Isaiah (5:24; 17:11; 18:5; 27:6; 35:1, 2; 66:14), appearing only fleetingly in Hosea (14:5, 7). Uncultivated grass, reeds, and rushes frequent Isaiah (e.g., 19:6; 35:7) but not the Twelve. Even thorns and briers are less common in the Twelve than in Isaiah. In short, Isaiah speaks in a wide variety of ways about forbs and grains both wild and domestic. But such discussions in the Twelve are mostly limited to agricultural settings and issues involving field grain.

When it comes to vines, Isaiah and the Twelve seem to have comparable uses, speaking often of vines, vineyards, and grapes, both literally and metaphorically (Isa 5:2; 7:23; Hos 2:12; Mic 4:4). But the product of vineyards—wine—appears far more often in the Twelve than in Isaiah (e.g., Hos 4:11; 7:5, 14; Amos 2:8, 12; Mic 2:11; 6:15).

Differences between Isaiah and the Twelve are most striking of all when it comes to trees. In Isaiah many different trees appear. Some are fruit trees (figs, palms, and olives; e.g., 28:4; 9:14; 17:6). But nonagricultural trees dominate Isaiah's landscape: oaks and cedars, pines, planes, acacias, and cypresses (e.g., 1:30; 6:13; 37:24; 41:19). The generic term *'ets*, or "tree," appears frequently in Isaiah (e.g., 7:2; 10:15) but not so in the Twelve, where *'ets* describes wood or timber more than living trees (e.g., Hos 4:12; Hab 2:11; Zech 5:4). Forests are regular features of Isaiah's landscape (e.g., 7:2; 10:18–19; 29:17; 44:23; 56:9). But not so in the Twelve. Tree components—roots, branches, shoots, and leaves—likewise appear often in Isaiah (e.g., 11:10; 18:5; 33:9; 40:24; 53:2) but not in the Twelve. Like grains and vines, trees in the Twelve are primarily agricultural. Figs appear thirteen times in the Twelve (e.g., Hos 2:12; Amos 4:9; Mic 7:1), only four in Isaiah. Olives and olive oil appear twenty-three times in the Twelve (e.g., Hos 14:6; Amos 4:9; Mic 6:15), as opposed to three mentions of olives and five of oil in Isaiah.

---

4. The first of the two plants named in vv. 25 and 27, *ketsah*, has been variously translated as "dill," "black cumin," "caraway," "fitches," and "small black poppy." The second, *kamon*, is more clearly what we know today as cumin.

5. All Scripture translations in this essay are my own unless otherwise indicated.

In short, the book of Isaiah discusses agricultural as well as nonagricultural and wild plants of all classes. But throughout the Twelve, beginning with Amos, Hosea, and Micah, our primary encounters with plants are domestic and agricultural. Since both books stretch out over comparable generations, and intertextual cross-fertilization is evident between them from early to late, these differences are curious.

Prophets in the Book of the Twelve often mention the Mediterranean triad we know especially from Deuteronomy: "grain, wine, and oil" (see, e.g., Deut 7:13; 11:14; 12:17). The set phrase "grain, wine, and oil" figures into the drama of Hosea 2 as part of the abundance provided to God's wife, Israel, taken away when she proves untrue, and finally restored (vv. 8, 22).[6] It reappears in Joel: because of the locusts, "the grain is destroyed, the wine dries up, the oil fails" (1:10 NRSV). Then in Joel 2:19 and 24, God promises to restore the grain, wine, and oil, as in Hosea and Deuteronomy. In Hag 1:11, once again, a drought precipitated by the people's failure to build the temple leads to the loss of grain, wine, and oil.

The Hebrew words used in this set phrase are very particular, and unusual. For grain, rather than the more common *bar*, the word is *dagan*; for wine, rather than the common *yayin*, it is *tirosh*. And instead of *shemen* for oil, it is *yitshar*.[7] The significance of the use of these distinct words is not fully known, but the same triad also occurs in the literature of neighboring Ugarit.[8] The words do indeed seem to form a thought-set: in the Hebrew Bible, *dagan* and *tirosh* usually occur together, and *yitshar* almost never appears without the other two.

But "grain, wine, and oil" is not just a set phrase. It's also a set concept, showing up in other forms, in other words, but still in the same triad, and frequently in the same order. Amos 4:6–9 describes God's taking away *bread* and destroying *vineyards* and *olive trees*, in this order. Micah 6:15 warns,

---

6. Regarding this metaphor and its agricultural dimensions, see Davis, *Scripture, Culture, and Agriculture*, 130–35.

7. Allen, *Books of Joel, Obadiah, Jonah, and Micah*, 54n42, suggests that *dagan* is the general term for cereal from which bread is made; *tirosh* is probably the archaic Semitic word for wine, which the foreign loanword *yayin* generally replaced, and *yitshar* is a descriptive term for *shemen*, "oil," as shining.

8. Wolff, *Hosea*, 39, cites a Ugaritic use of the triad in A. Herdner, *Corpus des Tablettes en Cunéiformes Alphabetiques déecouvertes à Ras-Shamra-Ugarit de 1929 à 1939* 16.III–V (Gordon 126.III) (Paris, 1963), in which the "rain of Baal" is described as being "sweet for the earth," and the same three words as in Hos 2:8 occur: "spent is the bread (grain) from their jar, spent is the wine from their bottles, spent is the oil from their cruses." Watson and Vyatt, *Handbook of Ugaritic Studies*, 228, narrate a scene from the late Bronze Age Ugaritic "Legend of Keret" in which "the king's illness . . . has resulted in drought, and the stocks of grain, wine, and oil are depleted."

"You shall *sow*, but not reap; you shall tread *olives*, but not anoint your-selves with oil; you shall tread *grapes*, but not drink wine" (NRSV, emphasis added). The triad is the same but not the words. Hosea 14:6–7 predicts that Israel's beauty will be like the olive tree, that they will flourish like grain and blossom like the grapevine.[9] There are several other examples like this.

Here's what is striking: archaeologists have shown that in ancient Is-rael's subsistence farms, grain, wine, and oil were produced alongside fruits, legumes, vegetables, and livestock. The Gezer calendar, an agricultural cal-endar from two centuries before Isaiah, includes grain, wine, and oil along-side other foods. Such small-farm diversification spread the risk of crop failure throughout the year and allowed farmers to use diverse ecological niches on their land.[10] They could spread their labor over the year too, tend-ing each crop in its own time. Vegetables, though perishable, served well in their seasons. But threshed grain, wine from crushed grapes, and pressed olive oil could all be stored at home for long periods. These three products supplied the framework of food security in subsistence Israel.

And here is what seems to be at stake with these three foods: since they could be stored, transported, and sold, grain, wine, and oil made good taxes, good levies, good exports. As David C. Hopkins has noted, "The liter-ary, epigraphic, and artifactual evidence converges on oil, wine, and wheat as the commodities of choice in the monarchic economic network."[11] This demand, as Marvin Chaney adds, "ran counter to the village's objective of spreading risk and optimizing labor through a diversity of subsistence means."[12] Grain, wine, and oil could be made to serve people who had not labored to produce them, whether these were the king and his officials, for-eign neighbors, or Assyrian forces. In fact, at one time or another in Judah's history, all of these powerful beneficiaries of agricultural labor seem to be suggested.

Archaeological evidence and ancient inscriptions show that diversi-fied subsistence farming gave way to cash cropping of ever-larger fields and mountainsides for export to Phoenicia and beyond, so that the wealthy could import luxury items. Before the eighth century, a single family would engage in agriculture, horticulture, herding, fishing, weaving, and pottery, exchanging surpluses with other groups. But under the perceived threat from Assyria, a grand redistributive system was created, in which

9. The Hebrew phrase involving grain (*dagan*) is difficult to translate, leading the NRSV to emend it to "like a garden" (*kegan*). But the NIV and Tanakh both retain "grain."

10. Chaney, "Bitter Bounty," 22.

11. Hopkins, "Dynamics of Agriculture," 196.

12. Chaney, "Bitter Bounty," 23.

households were forced to limit their agricultural production to grain or oil, send in-kind payments to the governmental center, and buy grain for cash in the marketplace.[13] This benefited not the farmers but the urban elite, who could not only inflate the prices of basic necessities but also trade surplus goods internationally for various luxury items.[14] And because "exports competed directly with peasant sustenance,"[15] and agriculture itself was subject to capricious natural conditions, famines resulted. This happened progressively, with a sharp rise in the late eighth century, at the time when Hosea, Amos, and Micah spoke. Unethical methods of land acquisition, such as driving small landowners into debt and then bankruptcy, as well as cheating in the marketplace, have been suggested both by the prophets themselves (e.g., Amos 2:6; 8:5; Mic 6:11) and by comparisons with other cultures where agribusiness has disrupted farming.

First Kings mentions that Solomon exported wheat and fine oil to Tyre (5:11), and there is evidence that even in pre-Israelite times such trade went on.[16] But in the eighth century, such cash cropping multiplied dramatically. Notes jotted on ostraca indicate the trade of oil and wine and possibly grain in Israel. Large oil-processing installations have been found in several locations in Judah,[17] including large-scale state-controlled oil production presses at Tell Beit Mirsim and Beth-Shemesh.[18] More than a hundred presses found at Ekron may have produced a thousand tons of oil annually, mostly for export.[19] Other apparatuses of bureaucratic mass distribution began to appear around this time: standardized weights, mass-produced pottery, official jars and seal impressions.[20] By Isaiah's time, King Hezekiah was able to collect taxes in the form of grain, wine, and oil,[21] transforming Judah "from an isolated, formative tribal state into a developed state, fully incorporated into the Assyrian global economy."[22] Evidence of luxury imports enjoyed by the wealthy in both Samaria and Jerusalem suggest that cash cropping

---

13. Chaney, "Systemic Study," 73.

14. Chaney, "Bitter Bounty," 18.

15. Ibid., 19.

16. Richter, "Environmental Law," 361.

17. King and Stager, *Biblical Israel*, 96.

18. Finkelstein and Silberman, "Temple and Dynasty," 264.

19. Richter, "Environmental Law," 362n15.

20. Finkelstein and Silberman, "Temple and Dynasty," 264; Lipschitz et al., "Royal Judahite Jar Handles."

21. Boardman et al., *Cambridge Ancient History*, 353.

22. Finkelstein and Silberman, "Temple and Dynasty," 266.

replaced many subsistence farms. Grain, wine, and oil were exported from the land, and with them, of course, the soil's fertility.[23]

In light of all this, the story of the manna in the wilderness stands out. This manna, which Ps 78:24 calls *degan shamayim*, (grain of heaven) could not be stored for even one day (Exod 16:19–20), creating an absolutely equitable diet among the Israelites in the wilderness.[24] Deuteronomy correlates this manna with the eating habits commanded in the promised land. According to Deut 8:3, 6–7 (NRSV):

> [God] humbled you by letting you hunger, then by feeding you with manna . . . in order to make you understand that one does not live by bread alone . . . Therefore keep the commandments of the Lord your God, by walking in his ways and by fearing him. For the Lord your God is bringing you into a good land, a land with flowing streams.

As the passage continues, subsistence production of grain, wine, and oil comes into view:

> . . . a land of *wheat and barley*, of *vines* and fig trees and pomegranates, a land of *olive trees* and honey, a land where you may eat bread without scarcity, where you will lack nothing . . . Do not say to yourself, "My power and the might of my own hand have gotten me this wealth." (Deut 8:8–9, 17 NRSV; emphasis added)

Deuteronomy 24 clarifies that the harvest of grain (v. 19), oil (v. 20), and wine (v. 21) are not to be hoarded but shared. Deuteronomy 28 warns of the consequences that would result from failure to "serve . . . God joyfully and with gladness of heart for the abundance of everything" (v. 47 NRSV): a long and dreary series of curses. Israel would serve enemies in hunger, thirst, nakedness, and lack, and a grim-faced nation would destroy Israel, leaving no grain, wine, or oil (v. 51, see also vv. 38–40). These prescriptions are deeply related to discussions of these commodities in Hosea, Amos, and Micah, where they are surrounded by accusations of economic cheating and violence. According to Deuteronomy, a tithe every three years of grain, wine, and oil was to be taken for Levitical priests along with other landless people, including resident aliens, orphans, and widows (14:28–29;

23. Nam, *Economic Exchange*, 170–72, cites 2 Kgs 4:1–7, the story of the widow's sale of oil for debt payment, as evidence for a market economy operating in Elisha's time. Finkelstein and Silberman, "Temple and Dynasty," 265, note Judah's participation in "Assyrian-dominated Arabian trade . . . along routes that led from Arabia via Edom to the Mediterranean ports, which were turned into Assyrian emporia."

24. Davis, *Scripture, Culture, and Agriculture*, 75–77; Tull, *Inhabiting Eden*, 78.

26:12). But evidently the redistribution principle was turned on its head by monarchies in both the north and the south, to serve not poverty but urban wealth-seeking.

In the midst of that great social upheaval, so reminiscent of the redistribution of farming practices and commodities today, here is the thing I find most striking: for all the prevalence of grain, wine, and oil in the Book of the Twelve, and for all Isaiah's other similarities to Amos, Hosea, and Micah in social justice themes and in critique of legal policies, this triad appears in Isaiah not one single time—neither in the set phrase nor in the more variant forms, not even out of order. In fact, olives hardly appear at all in Isaiah. Even grain and wine without oil appear together relatively infrequently. And Second Isaiah, which often invokes verses and ideas surrounding Jeremiah's one and only mention of grain, wine, and oil in 31:12—and which envisions verdancy in many other ways—never mentions the grain, the wine, or the oil.

Perhaps location contributes to this difference. Amos doesn't hide his farming roots, Micah comes from a small town, and while we don't know where exactly Hosea was from, some posit Levitical, countryside connections for him. Isaiah's discussions range more widely among forms of vegetation that are cultivated and those that are simply found, among those that are edible and those that are simply verdant. It's tempting to speculate that this peculiarity could be traced to a more urban angle of vision. Perhaps as a city boy—or as close to a city boy as one could be in those days—Isaiah had more bent toward aestheticizing nature, and a less clear eye on the economics of agriculture than the other three prophets. Perhaps he was too implicated in the system, too close to Hezekiah's government to be completely frank. These are only speculations. Still, the absence in Isaiah of this agricultural triad seems especially striking, given Hezekiah's involvement in collecting and redistributing these farm commodities. Both Hosea and Isaiah criticize exports to Egypt, for instance, but only Hosea specifies the export of oil (Isa 30:6; Hos 12:1).

Whatever the causes of these differences, what the prophets share is understanding of the centrality of the natural world to human life and health, and a common stake in gauging societal health along with the fortunes of field and vegetation. Isaiah and the Twelve present two sides of the conversation that we increasingly know we need to have now: on the one hand, with Isaiah, appreciation for and affinity with the living world, both wild and domestic, as valuable in and of itself; and on the other hand, with the Twelve especially, willingness to challenge systems that misuse agriculture and waste its gifts, that pollute the land and hoard its abundance, and that exploit the poor to increase personal and corporate wealth.

Biblical scholars have been compelled in recent generations to interrogate some aspects of Scripture, particularly its patriarchy and violence. It is refreshing when Scripture offers its own critique of our present economic and ecological practices. Learning to live well with the earth's other species is, in part, an act of reclaiming what the human race once knew.

BIBLIOGRAPHY

Allen, Leslie C. *The Books of Joel, Obadiah, Jonah, and Micah*. NICOT. Grand Rapids: Eerdmans, 1994.

Boardman, John, et al., eds. *The Cambridge Ancient History*. Vol. 3, part 2. Cambridge: Cambridge University Press, 1992.

Chaney, Marvin. "Bitter Bounty: The Dynamics of Political Critiqued by the Eighth-Century Prophets." In *Reformed Faith and Economics*, edited by Robert L. Stivers, 15–30. Lanham, MD: University Press of America, 1989.

———. "Systemic Study of the Israelite Monarchy." *Semeia* 37 (1986) 53–76.

Davis, Ellen F. *Scripture, Culture, and Agriculture: An Agrarian Reading of the Bible*. Cambridge: Cambridge University Press, 2009.

Finkelstein, Israel, and Neil Asher Silberman. "Temple and Dynasty: Hezekiah, the Remaking of Judah, and the Rise of Pan-Israelite Theology." *JSOT* 30 (2006) 259–85.

Hopkins, David C. "Dynamics of Agriculture in Monarchical Israel." *SBLSP* 22 (1983) 177–202.

King, Philip, and Lawrence Stager. *Life in Biblical Israel*. Louisville: Westminster John Knox, 2001.

Lipschitz, Oded, et al. "Royal Judahite Jar Handles: Reconsidering the Chronology of the *lmlk* Stamp Impressions." *Tel Aviv* 37 (2010) 3–32.

Nam, Roger S. *Portrayals of Economic Exchange in the Book of Kings*. Leiden: Brill, 2012.

Richter, Sandra. "Environmental Law in Deuteronomy: One Lens on a Biblical Theology of Creation Care." *BBR* 20, no. 3 (2010) 355–76.

Tull, Patricia K. *Inhabiting Eden: Christians, the Bible, and the Ecological Crisis*. Louisville: Westminster John Knox, 2013.

———. *Isaiah 1–39*. Smyth and Helwys Bible Commentary 14A. Macon, GA: Smyth and Helwys, 2010.

———. "Persistent Vegetative States: People as Plants and Plants as People in Isaiah." In *The Desert Will Bloom: Poetic Visions in Isaiah*, edited by A. Joseph Everson and Hyun Chul Paul Kim, 17–34. Atlanta: SBL, 2009.

Watson, Wilfred G. E., and Nicolas Vyatt. *Handbook of Ugaritic Studies*. Leiden: Brill, 1999.

Wolff, Hans Walter. *Hosea: A Commentary on the Book of the Prophet Hosea*. Hermeneia. Philadelphia: Fortress, 1973.

6

Enduring Hope, Patient Toil[1]

Psalm 37 and YHWH's Agrarian Vision

Ryan D. Harker

In a 1993 article, Walter Brueggemann describes two different ways of reading Ps 37: (1) as the voice of a "self-assured, property-owning class";[2] that is, as an establishment psalm interested in preserving the status quo; and (2) as an expression of hope for a "utopian" future—a "profound act of determined hope" in YHWH.[3] Somewhat surprisingly, Brueggemann prefers the former of these two readings, and with just a few exceptions, scholars have tended to agree with him. Every interpreter of the book of Psalms has agreed, though, that Ps 37 is an example of wisdom literature. For those who worship YHWH —says at least part of the wisdom tradition—life happens according to reliable rules. God has promised this, and it need only be trusted and obeyed. These rules usually set before us two paths, two options for life: the way of the righteous and the way of the wicked. Along these lines,

1. I would like to thank Brenna Harker, Janeen Bertsche Johnson, Safwat Marzouk, and Ben Ollenburger of Anabaptist Mennonite Biblical Seminary for their helpful suggestions in editing this article. Any remaining errors or ill-founded conclusions are my own.

2. Brueggemann, "Psalm 37," 239. (Note: Brueggemann's article originally appeared in *Of Prophets' Visions and the Wisdom of Sages: Essays in Honour of R. Norman Whybray on His Seventieth Birthday*, edited by Heather A. McKay and David J. A. Clines, 229–56 [Sheffield, UK: JSOT Press, 1993]).

3. Ibid., 249–50.

interpreters such as Brueggemann, Artur Weiser, and Sigmund Mowinckel have read Ps 37 as a naïve text written by a member of the "intelligentsia,"[4] for whom the world simply works by reliable rules and expectations.

I argue, however, that strong support for something like the second of Brueggemann's interpretative options can be found in Ps 37's early reception, its parallels with significant canonical motifs, and key contemporary scholars who read it as such. Psalm 37, I believe, can be read as a sage's agrarian apology for a patient, resolute faithfulness in the face of communal temptation to acquiesce to the way of the "wicked," as the psalm puts it[5]—the way of dominance, violence, and destruction of the land. And for this reason, as I will outline, Ps 37 also has clear parallels with the work of the contemporary agrarian farmer and practitioner Wendell Berry.

Contrary to Brueggemann's interpretation, I propose that Ps 37 is an encouragement toward faithfulness to a traditional agrarian way of life—one of hope, patience, and trust in YHWH —in the midst of a situation in which unfaithfulness, the abandonment of hope, and the impatient acquiescence to the way of dominance would have made good sense. Counterintuitively, the psalmist is presenting a vision for a future in which the faithful poor possess the land in place of the wealthy—a future in which the oppressed will be liberated and the wicked will dwell in the land no longer. In other words, the psalmist is reminding the community of YHWH's vision for the land, which is evident throughout the Old Testament, especially the Pentateuch and the Prophets. To put it in contemporary terms, in encouraging enduring hope and patient agricultural toil as a response to violent oppression, Ps 37 presents the vision for a kind of agrarian pacifism—a rooted and embodied shalom grounded in unwavering hope in the fidelity of YHWH. As Ellen Davis has noted, Ps 37 calls to mind not comfort with the status quo but "the elements of a traditional world that is threatened or eclipsed, namely, the world of the Israelite village."[6]

In reading Ps 37 as an agrarian call to abstain from the ways of the wicked, I will first examine past proposals for the form and provenance of Ps 37, making my own proposal regarding the social location and function of the psalm. I will then consider the social location and function of Ps 37. Finally, I will suggest how Ps 37 might be instructive for our ecological crisis, which has set before us the same two ways that confronted the psalmist and the psalmist's community: the way of the righteous and the way of the wicked—the way of shalom and the way of violent destruction of the land.

4. Mowinckel, *Psalms in Israel's Worship*, 2:104.

5. All Scripture translations in this essay are my own unless otherwise indicated.

6. Davis, *Scripture, Culture, and Agriculture*, 115.

In reading Ps 37 in this way, I hope I am modeling how the biblical text, interpreted faithfully in its historical and literary contexts, can be a valuable tool for the church in an age of ecological destruction.

FORM AND PROVENANCE OF PSALM 37

Psalm 37 is highly structured and poetically attuned. It is an acrostic, which is to say that every other line of the poem begins with each succeeding letter of the Hebrew alphabet. This pattern would have aided memorization or recitation in liturgical or synagogal settings, which would have been important since the psalm "is dominated . . . by didactic imperatives."[7] So, it has appropriately been labeled a "didactic psalm," a specific class within the more general "wisdom" category. Formally, parallels can be drawn between this psalm and Proverbs,[8] a fact made much clearer by the acrostic nature of the psalm.

Though these parallels should not lead us to read Ps 37 as some interpreters read Proverbs—as a disjointed collection of sayings of various provenances—such an interpretive path, unfortunately, is commonly traveled. R. N. Whybray claims, for instance, that "Ps. 37 consists of a series of short independent sayings . . . strongly reminiscent of sayings in the book of Proverbs."[9] Attempting to denigrate the psalm further, he goes on to claim that Ps 37 is "reminiscent . . . of the speeches of the friends of Job."[10] Brueggemann agrees: "This is the most obviously sapiential of all the psalms. Indeed it is a collection of sayings that might easily be found in the book of Proverbs. It appears to be a rather random collection of sayings without any order or development."[11] Still, even though he finds a certain randomness in the psalm, Brueggemann is careful to point to the acrostic as evidence of some intentional structuring by the psalmist/redactor. In the end, Brueggemann is right to conclude that the psalm has thematic intentionality in that it is concerned chiefly with *how to keep land and how to lose it*,[12] though one might disagree with him on who exactly is doing the teaching in the psalm and who is keeping the land.

---

7. Gerstenberger, *Psalms*, 157.

8. See Schaefer, *Psalms*, 91.

9. Whybray, "The Social World," 245.

10. Ibid.

11. Brueggemann, *The Message*, 42. See also Schaefer, *Psalms*, 91, who writes that Ps 37 is "a collection of diverse elements, somewhat disjointed and repetitive."

12. Brueggemann, *The Message*, 43.

The question of the compositional setting (*Sitz im Leben*) of Ps 37 is anything but simple to answer. Because the Psalter has such a long and perplexing redactional history, it's difficult to arrive with certainty at any compositional setting, let alone a setting of rural oppression by the urban elite.[13] Why not read the psalm as simply a "private" instruction written by a wealthy, property-owning, wise old Israelite to those not quite as far along on the journey of life, as Brueggemann and others would have us read? Why not as the work of a priest attached to the Jerusalem Temple, as others have read it?

Erhard Gerstenberger locates the origin of the early "wisdom psalms" in "worshipping communities far away from Jerusalem," who rely "on the Word of God, on prayer and obedience," on the "solidarity of the faithful" community, and on "hope" in YHWH's vindication.[14] As such, wisdom psalms like Ps 37 "were read and prayed in local assemblies and, at least primarily, not in the temple community of Jerusalem."[15] Though the Psalter was obviously redacted over time and arranged in its current, richly theological ordering, Gerstenberger and others have shown that these psalms clearly had particular local, almost certainly rural, worshipping communities as their place of origin. And in these particular local, rural places of origin were also local, particular social impetuses that brought about the composition of the various psalms. As Gerstenberger again notes, "Religious rituals . . . never occur in isolation from social life."[16]

Furthermore, because "the didactic psalms . . . were composed for and were used in early Jewish worship services, very probably on the local level, outside Jerusalem," Gerstenberger argues that this more refined classification, along with clear clues in the psalm itself, gives reason to more accurately situate Ps 37 in a social background that might have exhibited something of a "class struggle" between the wealthy—or the wicked (*rasha*)—and "the

---

13. The degree to which interpreters distance this psalm from a context of oppression varies. For a small sampling, see Dahood, *Psalms*, 1:225–32, for a reading that makes no mention at all of the psalm's context; cf. Gerstenberger, *Psalms*, 159; and Miller, "The Land,"189–92, for quite different perspectives from that of Dahood.

14. Gerstenberger, *Psalms*, 28. This is contra Sigmund Mowinckel, who locates the *Sitz im Leben* of the book of Psalms in the temple worship in Jerusalem. See Mowinckel, *Psalms*, 2. Of course, this is not to deny that the psalms were eventually used in temple worship, only that the temple is not necessarily the origin of every individual psalm. See also Robert Davidson, who writes that Ps 37 "is the work of a wisdom teacher" and that "the content of the psalm has many similarities with the wisdom tradition found in Proverbs." Davidson, *Vitality of Worship*, 124.

15. Gerstenberger, *Psalms*, 28.

16. Ibid., 30.

'righteous,' who are 'faithful' . . . and 'poor' . . . and 'waiting for the Lord,'" as the psalm calls them.[17]

Brueggemann, on the other hand, is more comfortable following the traditional pattern, labeling Ps 37 as a particular kind of "wisdom psalm" concerned with a reliable and trustworthy world.[18] What is more, Brueggemann labels Ps 37 a "psalm of orientation" in his three-part typology of the Psalter.[19] In claiming that the wisdom tradition denies the way the world actually works, Brueggemann writes that "such denial consists in an inability or refusal to notice the failure of the system.[20] Psalm 37 is a clear example of a perception of the world that is skewed by supreme and uncritical confidence in the system (vv. 25, 28b–29)."[21]

But I follow Gerstenberger and argue that Ps 37 can and very likely should be read with a class struggle as a sociological backdrop—an agrarian, land-based poor oppressed at the hands of a wealthy, probably urban, elite. This could have occurred during any number of military, political, or economic upheavals in the history of early Canaan/Israel/Palestine, but the fact that it was an established part of the Psalter by the second century BCE indicates that it was written at least well before then. In addition, the author was not some austere senior citizen looking to hold onto his/her upper-class, landed interests,[22] but rather a wise, older community member who had lived a long life of faithfulness to YHWH's agrarian vision and call. To summarize, then, Ps 37 has as its setting local, synagogal worship in the midst of a situation of sociological upheaval. In the end, John Eaton's evaluation is appropriate:

17. Ibid., 159.

18. Brueggemann, *The Message*, 42. See also Anderson, *Out of the Depths*, 217. This reading has sometimes given interpreters an excuse to "spiritualize" the meaning of the psalm, as in Mays, *Psalms*, 158–61.

19. Brueggemann divides the book of Psalms into three types of psalms: orientation, disorientation/dislocation, and reorientation. According to Brueggemann, psalms of orientation "are not the most interesting, for there is in them no great movement, no tension to resolve. Indeed, what mainly characterizes them is the absence of tension." See Brueggemann, "Psalms and the Life of Faith," 6.

20. For a treatment of the wisdom tradition and its literature that is contrary to Brueggemann's view expressed here, see Perdue, *Sword and the Stylus*, in which Perdue argues that wisdom tradition does not, in fact, refuse to notice the failure of the system but is written in response to and in critique of the domination of various Ancient Near Eastern empires.

21. Brueggemann, *Israel's Praise*, 115.

22. For the most overt treatment of the author of Ps 37 in this way, see Weiser, *The Psalms*, 315. See also Davis, *Scripture, Culture, and Agriculture*.

The psalm is from one of those times when holding to what is good and true seems to bring disadvantage, and even suffering or death. The rising generations look eagerly for models, and many are impressed by worldly success, rather than by quiet virtues that seem unrewarded. The psalmist earnestly engages with this situation, and would have the young recognize the transience and vanity of the evil course, and the true satisfaction and delight of humble trust in the Lord . . . to find peace and to dwell on his land amid the harvest of his faithfulness.[23]

A LOOK AT THE TEXT

Given the sociological backdrop (*Sitz im Leben*) of Ps 37 that I've suggested in this article, the *tsadiqim*, (righteous) to whom this psalm is written may have been addressing YHWH with a complaint much like Ps 88, a profound lament that calls into question YHWH's very *hesed*, (steadfast love, faithfulness). The message of the psalm comes sharply into focus when understood with this backdrop. In the midst of acute oppression, the psalmist encourages trust in YHWH[24] and strict distance from the way of life of the wicked.[25] Konrad Schaefer does a good job of capturing the psalmist's encouragement toward enduring hope, patient toil, and faithfulness when he speaks of the psalmist's message to fellow community members. He writes that the community

> is urged to ward off the temptation to defect to the ranks of the wicked. Abandoning God wins only illusory delights. The poet reassures the virtuous and asserts that God will save them from the wicked (v. 40). The resounding theme of the possession of the land or earth is held out for all who banish evil from their lives and cooperate with God for a better world.[26]

23. Eaton, *The Psalms*, 166.

24. Of course, this is not to imply that lament is not itself an act of trust. A community could not reasonably express lament to a God in whom it does not trust; rather, confident hope (encouraged in Ps 37) and lament should equally be understood as acts of trust in God. For a more detailed treatment of this issue, see Brueggemann, *Life of Faith*, chap. 5, "The Costly Loss of Lament."

25. The encouragement to avoid the way of the wicked should be read in light of Ps 1 and the "two ways" presented there. Indeed, given the fivefold division of the Psalter in the mold of the Torah, the entirety of the Psalter could be considered a commentary on the "two ways": the way of life and the way of death. For a fuller treatment, see McCann Jr., *A Theological Introduction*, esp. 25–40.

26. Schaefer, *Psalms*, 93.

Along with the psalm's focus on faithfulness to YHWH in the midst of oppression is the theme of "inheritance of the land (*yirshu-'arets*)." In fact, Ps 37, as Schaefer argues above, intends to situate faithfulness to YHWH and rejection of the ways of the wicked as the means by which the righteous will again come to possess the land. One must be careful, however, not to read this association of faithfulness and land possession as a naïve understanding of the world, as Brueggemann does; rather, the psalm is a radical reframing of the world, of the mindset of the people in the face of their oppression. This reframing comes out of the psalmist's conviction that YHWH is a faithful God despite present appearances to the contrary. Assimilation to the ways of the wicked would thus constitute a disastrous rejection of the very God who promises deliverance. *But*, the psalm argues, YHWH promises deliverance *on YHWH's terms*; redemption, the psalmist says, is living in step with YHWH's agrarian vision, "tending faithfulness," as verse 3 exhorts.

This contrast between the ways of the wicked and the ways of the faithful, who will inherit the land, becomes obvious in a close look at the text where the terms *tsadiq* (righteous) and *rasha'* (wicked) are placed in opposition seven times (vv. 12, 16, 17, 21, 28–29, 32, 38–40), with *tsadiq* used as a parallel term for *anavim* (meek/poor).

Anavim is a technical term, the use of which would have denoted a specific group of people for the hearers/performers of the psalm—namely, themselves as "the people of the Land" who are in an experience of oppression.[27] The *anavim* are those who are "trapped in a killing system that still appears to be strong, though it has already far outreached itself."[28] Or, as Miller puts it, "The term ענו encompasses the poor and the faithful who are afflicted by the deeds of the wicked."[29]

As for the identity of the "wicked," Schaefer thinks they, too, are Israelites: "The wicked are members, but they are agents of division and destruction (v. 12)."[30] Thus, if one follows Schaefer, "cut off" (v. 28) has the sense of being excommunicated. Regardless, though, we can surely affirm William Brown's claim that "the one who abides by [Torah] is destined to flourish and remain secure and efficacious in all matter of conduct. The wicked, by contrast, are mere 'chaff' blown hither and yon."[31]

---

27. See Davis, *Scripture, Culture, and Agriculture*, 115–19, esp. 117, and Miller, "The Land," 190.

28. Davis, *Scripture, Culture, and Agriculture*, 117.

29. Miller, "The Land," 191.

30. Schaefer, *Psalms*, 92.

31. Brown, *Psalms*, 148.

As much as Brueggemann and other scholars find a certain random-ness with respect to the theme of the land in Ps 37, I find the theme of the inheritance of the land by the righteous to be centrally located in a chiasm of five verses that each contain the phrase *yirshu-'arets* (they will inherit the land).[32] The chiasm is girded by two injunctions from the psalmist to the addressee to "wait for YHWH":

A   "those who wait for YHWH will inherit the land" (v. 9)

  B   "meek will inherit the land" (v. 10–11)

    C   "blessed by him [YHWH] will inherit the land" (v. 22)

  B'   "righteous will inherit the land" (v. 29)

A'   "those who wait for YHWH will inherit the land" (v. 34)

It is reasonable to believe that the psalmist/redactor intended the com-munity to which this psalm was addressed to notice this chiastic arrange-ment that is bookended by the imperative to "wait for YHWH." In other words, to "be patient." This is an important injunction if this psalm has agrarian undertones. There are a few more things to be said concerning this chiasm: First, it is a matter of patient confidence and hope in the Lord's in-volvement to "make your vindication shine like the light, and the justice of your cause like the noonday (v. 6 NRSV)."[33] Second, this conceptualization of the five "land verses" is made more credible by the important place given to line C in the psalm's acrostic pattern: "The third mention of 'possess the land' is in letter *lamed*, 'l' (v. 22), a privileged position in alphabetic arrange-ment since it marks the beginning of the second half" of the poem.[34] And third, we see that the "meek/poor" (*anavim*) and the "righteous" (*tsadiqim*) are equated.

So, the word picture painted by this chiasm is clear: it is those who "wait on YHWH" in the midst of oppression—the meek—who are ultimate-ly the righteous and will thus be vindicated by YHWH. The path to true life, says the psalmist, is not to defect to the ranks of the wicked but literally to dig in with the community of the landed righteous ones. Therefore, though Brueggemann appears not to notice a chiasm here, precisely on the basis of this chiastic arrangement we can affirm with him that "if we seek to find a

---

32. On the supposed randomness of the psalm, see again Brueggemann, *The Mes-sage*, 43, in which he writes that "the five statements that dominate the psalm are in fact synonymous. There is no development in the sayings, but each reiterates the main point."

33. See Miller, "The Land," 190.

34. Schaefer, *Psalms*, 92.

more substantive concern in this psalm, we may find it in a series of reflections on *how to keep land and how to lose it*."[35]

CONCLUSION

Though Ps 37 itself gives plenty of clues as to how it should be read, there are others who can also help us. Davis offers a reading not unlike my own. According to her, "Psalm 37 is generally undervalued by theological interpreters, because it is taken to be the worst kind of 'wisdom literature': a somewhat random collection of truisms that may not be so true after all."[36] While Davis agrees with Brueggemann that "land possession is the poem's recurrent theme," she critiques Brueggemann's reading, saying that it "fails to take account of the note of keen expectation that runs throughout; the tone of the psalm is encouragement for the dispirited, not contentment with the *status quo*."[37] Davis's brief treatment is convincing.

While other scholars have read Ps 37 along the same lines as Brueggemann's second reading, none that I know of have noticed the agrarian undertones in the poem except Davis. Historically, though, Davis might not be alone. It would be fruitful to consider two readings that perhaps back up her reading: the commentary on Ps 37 from the secluded, rural Qumran community and the use of Ps 37 in Matthew's Sermon on the Mount. Both of these ancient sources self-identify with "the righteous," and the Qumran *pesher* (commentary) identifies the community's enemies with "the wicked" of the psalm. Both of these sources read the psalm much like Brueggemann's second reading, and both can be instructive for us as we interpret the poem. These two early readings could be fruitful areas for future study.

Indeed, much like the Beatitudes, Ps 37 promises that, despite appearances, it *is* the meek who will inherit the land. Psalm 37 is a liturgical document that seeks to call to mind YHWH's faithful promise to enact an agrarian justice on behalf of the covenant people (i.e., "the people of the land") in the midst of their oppression. It is a call to an embodied patience, a call issued also by Berry. Like Ps 37, Berry draws out in his writings the tension between embodied patience (agrarian resistance to violence and oppression) and the way of impatience (violence, dominance, war, agricultural destruction). This is especially the case in his poetry, such as "To My Children, Fearing for Them," "Mad Farmer Liberation Front," and "The Want of Peace." What both Ps 37 and Berry encourage is a resolute refusal to divorce

---

35. Brueggemann, *The Message*, 43.

36. Davis, *Scripture, Culture, and Agriculture*, 115.

37. Ibid.

means from ends, to abstract peace and well-being (*shalom*) from one's life on the land. Both call us to embody the agrarian vision, though all around us the way of impatience reigns.

What we have in Ps 37 seems to be a sage who understands this tension. The psalmist understands the importance (and the difficulty!) of a resolute, embodied life of shalom. But the psalmist, like Berry, also understands the draw toward the way of dominance, the way of the wicked. The former is not only the long way of patience, suffering, pain, and labor but also of family, community, joy, and endurance. The latter is the impatient way of force, war, and dominance. Ultimately, this latter way severs our relationship with the land to which the wise teacher of Ps 37 and the wise sage from Kentucky both guide us. In our age and clearly in the age in which Ps 37 was composed, the draw toward the way of dominance, the quick and easy way, is incredibly strong and acquiescence seems inevitable. But there is hope in the shared vision of the wise psalmist and Berry.

Berry's guidance toward this resolute, embodied wholeness is perhaps best summed up in his 2004 novel, *Hannah Coulter*, when Hannah is describing her life at her place with her husband, which Michael Stevens speaks of as "a lived benediction within a circle of damnable fire."[38] I hope the commonalities with Ps 37 in that sentence are by now clear—"A lived benediction within a circle of damnable fire." I end with Hannah recalling life together with her husband on their land, a life that I see as the embodiment of the vision of both Ps 37 and Berry's agrarianism—a refusal to acquiesce to the way of impatience, though it seems to have won the day:

> And so I came to know, as I had not known before, what this place of ours had been and meant to him. I knew, as I had not known before, what I had meant to him. Our life in our place had been a benediction to him, but he had seen it always within a circle of fire that might have closed upon it.[39]

BIBLIOGRAPHY

Anderson, Bernhard W. *Out of the Depths: The Psalms Speak for Us Today*. Rev. ed. Philadelphia: Westminster, 1983.
Berry, Wendell. *Hannah Coulter: A Novel*. Berkeley, CA: Shoemaker & Hoard, 2004.
Brown, William P. *Psalms*. Interpreting Biblical Texts. Nashville: Abingdon, 2010.
Brueggemann, Walter. "The Costly Loss of Lament." In *The Psalms and the Life of Faith*, edited by Patrick D. Miller, 98–111. Minneapolis: Fortress, 1995.

38. Stevens, "Living Peace," 123.
39. Berry, *Hannah Coulter*, 173.

————. *Israel's Praise: Doxology against Idolatry and Ideology*. Philadelphia: Fortress, 1988.

————. *The Message of the Psalms: A Theological Commentary*. Minneapolis: Augsburg, 1984.

————. "Psalm 37: Conflict of Interpretation." In *The Psalms and the Life of Faith*, edited by Patrick D. Miller, 235–57. Minneapolis: Fortress, 1995.

————. "Psalms and the Life of Faith: A Suggested Typology of Function." *JSOT* 17 (1980) 3–32.

————. "The Psalms in Theological Use: On Incommensurability and Mutuality." In *The Book of Psalms: Composition and Reception*, edited by Peter W. Flint and Patrick D. Miller, 581–602. Leiden: Brill, 2005.

Dahood, Mitchell J. *Psalms*. 3 vols. Anchor Bible 16–17A. Garden City, NY: Doubleday, 1966.

Davis, Ellen F. *Scripture, Culture, and Agriculture: An Agrarian Reading of the Bible*. Cambridge: Cambridge University Press, 2009.

Davidson, Robert. *The Vitality of Worship: A Commentary on the Book of Psalms*. Grand Rapids: Eerdmans, 1998.

Eaton, John H. *The Psalms: A Historical and Spiritual Commentary with an Introduction and New Translation*. Edinburgh: T. & T. Clark, 2003.

Gerstenberger, Erhard S. *Psalms: Part 1; With an Introduction to Cultic Poetry*. Forms of the Old Testament Literature 14. Grand Rapids: Eerdmans, 1988.

Mays, James Luther. *Psalms*. IBC. Louisville: John Knox, 1994.

McCann, J. Clinton, Jr. *A Theological Introduction to the Book of Psalms: The Psalms as Torah*. Nashville: Abingdon, 1993.

Miller, Patrick D. "The Land in the Psalms." In *Land of Israel in Bible, History, and Theology: Studies in Honor of Ed Noort*, edited by Jacques van Ruiten and J. Cornelius de Vos, 183–96. Leiden: Brill, 2009.

Mowinckel, Sigmund. *The Psalms in Israel's Worship*. Rev. ed. 2 vols. Translated by D. R. ap-Thomas. Biblical Resource Series. Grand Rapids: Eerdmans, 2004.

Perdue, Leo G. *The Sword and the Stylus: An Introduction to Wisdom in the Age of Empires*. Grand Rapids: Eerdmans, 2008.

Schaefer, Konrad. *Psalms*. Berit Olam: Studies in Hebrew Narrative and Poetry. Collegeville, MN: Liturgical, 1996.

Stevens, Michael. "Living Peace in the Shadow of War: Wendell Berry's Dogged Pacifism." In *The Humane Vision of Wendell Berry*, edited by Mark T. Mitchell and Nathan Schlueter, 106–23. Wilmington, DE: ISI, 2011.

Weiser, Artur. *The Psalms: A Commentary*. Translated by Herbert Hartwell. OTL. Philadelphia: Westminster, 1962.

Whybray, R. N. "The Social World of the Wisdom Writers." In *The World of Ancient Israel: Sociological, Anthropological, and Political Perspectives; Essays by Members of the Society for Old Testament Study*, edited by R. E. Clements, 227–50. New York: Cambridge, 1989.

7

Healing, Kairos, and Land in the New Testament[1]

Eschatology and the End of Empire

Barbara Rossing

In this essay, I will address "rooted and grounded" through an overarching New Testament lens of healing. I also will frame our time in history—our moment—as a kairos moment, a turning of the ages, a moment in need of healing, and a moment of profound hope. In short, a moment perhaps not unlike what the earliest followers of Jesus faced.

KAIROS

We are living today in what Greek Orthodox Patriarch Archbishop Bartholomew calls a "kairos" moment in terms of the health of the planet and

---

1. As a Lutheran, I consider it a privilege to contribute an essay to this book birthed out of the 2014 AMBS Rooted and Grounded conference. I was serving on the executive committee of the Lutheran World Federation in 2010 when we apologized to the Mennonites for persecution of Anabaptists by Lutherans in the sixteenth century and asked for forgiveness, both for that persecution and for theological justifications of it. A wonderful document titled "Healing Memories: Reconciling in Christ" was adopted by Mennonite World Conference and Lutheran World Federation in 2009–2010, in which we agreed to jointly tell our history differently.

its climate.[2] A kairos moment is a moment when one's whole life comes to a focus—an "urgent moment" in time.

The apostle Paul uses this Greek word *kairos* in Rom 8:18: "I consider the sufferings of this present time (*kairos*) are not worth comparing with the glory that is to be revealed."[3] And he uses this same word in Rom 13:11: "Besides this you know what time it is (what *kairos* it is), how it is now the moment to wake from sleep." The book of Revelation uses this term in chapter 11, declaring that the time—*kairos*—has come to "destroy the destroyers of earth" (v. 18). Jesus used the term *kairos*, too, when he counseled people to read the signs of the times.

At the time of this writing (fall 2014), communities of faith are preparing for the largest climate march in history in New York and in other cities around the world, calling on world leaders to take steps toward ratifying a binding climate agreement before the 2015 United Nations Climate Change Conference in Paris.[4] General Secretary Ban Ki-Moon invited religious leaders to be part of a climate summit with world leaders during this conference. How do we speak to this moment? How do we frame crisis?

Different biblical models could be used for framing this crisis. We could talk about climate change in terms of sin and forgiveness. Or we could talk about it as idolatry, the dangerous ways humans are "playing God" by altering the climate. But what best reaches people today is to frame the issues of climate as a sickness—we are ill. The world is ill; we are making ourselves sick. We need healing.

This framework can connect us to all the healing stories in the Gospels. *Sōzō*, the Greek word for "save," also means "heal." Salvation is more about healing than we have traditionally preached. In Mark 10, for instance, disciples of Jesus who see a rich man become disheartened by Jesus's instructions about how to receive eternal life, ask, "Who then can be saved?" (v. 26). Their question can just as well be translated, "Who then can be healed?"

We are ill, our planet is ill, and God wants to heal us. Vergel Lattimore, a pastoral care professor, says that what we need is healing for our souls and healing for the biosphere.[5] The core image that I take to heart from this call to healing is the tree of life from Rev 22:2, the most ecological vision of the New Testament: "The leaves of the tree are for the healing of the nations." Oh how we need those healing leaves. The message of the Bible is not that

2. Bartholomew, "Arctic," September 7, 2012.

3. All Scripture translations in this essay are my own.

4. The People's Climate March was held September 21, 2014.

5. Lattimore, "Pastoral Care Perspective," September 12, 2014.

God wants to destroy our world in some end-times fire but that God wants to heal our world and each one of us.

I find the framework of illness helpful for describing the crisis of creation we are facing, perhaps most of all because the Bible provides so many wonderful stories of healing—stories of Jesus who reaches out to sick people and heals them, and stories of a God who wants to heal Israel's wounds. "I am the Lord your healer" (Exod 15:26) is a promise that permeates the entire Bible.

WE ARE ILL

We are like a diabetic who has to make big changes in diet and lifestyle; we need to go on a carbon diet. As diabetics must do with blood sugar numbers, we have to get the carbon dioxide emission numbers down for the sake of the poor, for the sake of future generations, for the sake of all creation.[6]

It really is a health issue. Dr. Matthew Sleeth, founder of Seminary Stewardship Alliance, former emergency room physician and an evangelical Christian, says he was "converted" to the urgency of global warming through seeing rising rates of asthma, cancer, and other health problems in his urban Boston hospital.[7] A report from the American Academy of Pediatrics warns about the potential impact of climate change on our children's health in this country.[8] This is even more noticeable around the world. The climate crisis is a public health crisis.

HOPE

We are ill, our world is ill, but this crisis of land, food, agriculture, climate, theology—of everything we have studied at this Rooted and Grounded conference—does not have to be a sickness unto death. That is what Jesus told Mary and Martha in the Gospel of John about their brother Lazarus's illness (11:4). And that's what he says to us. Jesus loves us, just as he loved Lazarus and Martha and Mary. He loves us and wants to heal us.

Indeed, I believe the church has an amazing opportunity for *mission*, to claim this moment for good, for healing. This is a moment for re-vitalizing

6. When my colleague Larry Rasmussen speaks, he puts three chairs up in the front of the room representing those who have no voice: the poor, future generations, and all other creatures—those in the hymn "God of the Sparrow" (Vajda) who are trying to cry "woe" about what is happening to our world.

7. Sleeth, *Serve God*.

8. Shea, "Global Climate Change."

our local communities, for helping people discover the true meaning of abundant life—not as "More,"[9] not as a hoarder, not as bigger barns like those of the man in Luke's Gospel. We need to offer a vision of abundance as something deeper—as community, as relationships, as the sense of meaning and purpose, as a renewed vision for life together in community, in the church, rooted and grounded as Jesus teaches us: abundant "life does not consist in the abundance of possessions" (Luke 12:15).

The church is called to open up the space between denial on the one hand and despair on the other hand. The temptation will be to despair, to say it's too late to avoid dangerous global warming. But the church has to open up that wedge between denial and despair and be a model of *hope*. How do we give people pictures of hope? What does it look like to live differently? How do we read the Bible that way? More specifically, how do we read the New Testament, and how do we read it ecologically?

Ellen Davis reminds us that all of the Jewish writers of the New Testament are rooted and grounded in the Hebrew Scriptures, especially the eighth-century agrarian prophets. They are rooted and grounded in the land, in a way of life that is fundamentally agrarian.[10]

There are also some key differences between the Old Testament and New Testament settings. I will note three of them here.

1. *Urban context.* The apostle Paul's work, especially, took place in an urban context. This doesn't mean we give up the agrarian perspective. To the contrary, Richard Horsley and Neil Asher Silberman say that early Christians recreated a village amid the city. They propose that for displaced Jewish peasants and urban dwellers in Jerusalem, the *koinōnia* described in Acts 2 and Acts 4 constituted a "conscious attempt to create a 'village' in the streets and slums of the city."[11] Similarly, the model of a village within the city became the pattern also for Pauline Christian communities in cities of Asia Minor and Greece.[12]

   This urban New Testament perspective can be helpful, because as most of us now live in cities, so did many of the early Christians. Cities in themselves are not bad; in fact, the per capita carbon footprint is much

---

9. McKibben, *Comforting Whirlwind*.

10. Davis, *Scripture, Culture and Agriculture*.

11. Horsley and Silberman, *Message and the Kingdom*, 103.

12. "The principle of creative economic cooperation and sharing between neighbors—as a practical technique of survival, not simply as an ethical virtue—was one of the cornerstones of Jesus's teachings about the way that the Kingdom of God might be gained" (ibid.).

lower in cities than in most rural and suburban areas.[13] So for us today, the question of how to be a village in the midst of the city is crucial.

2. *Imperial occupation*. Empire was not yet the situation of the eighth-century prophets, although imperial conquests and exile came in the Hebrew Bible. Certainly much of the Hebrew Bible reflects that reality. But the imperial occupation of Rome clearly shaped the New Testament writers.

3. *Eschatology*. The New Testament carried with it a strong sense of eschatology. Jesus, Paul, John of Patmos, and all the authors of books in the New Testament believed that they and the world were at a *turning of the ages* and that the turning of the ages had already been inaugurated in Jesus Christ. What was this turning of the ages?

DUELING ESCHATOLOGIES

It's all about eschatology. "Eschatology" is the name given to the study of the last things—what is ultimate versus what comes to an end. When I was in seminary at Yale Divinity School in the 1970s, we paid scant attention to eschatology except for the humorous student magazine called "Eschatology Today." Its motto was "All's well that ends." But I shall never forget the New Testament class in my doctoral program at Harvard in the 1980s that opened my eyes to the relevance of eschatology. The assignment was an article by Dieter Georgi about how the Roman Empire of Jesus's time had an eschatology of its own—a credo of empire without end. [14] Roman eschatology of the eternal empire was engraved on monuments and arches for everyone to see. Official court poets Virgil and Horace proclaimed this credo in their epics and odes. Rome's theology was that the empire itself was eternal and would last forever. Emperor Augustus (27 BCE to 14 CE) was heralded as the "savior" (*sotēr*)—born of a human mother and divine father—whose birth ushered a new "golden age." "World without end" for Rome meant "empire without end," in both the spatial sense of conquering the "ends of the earth" geographically and the temporal sense of lasting forever.

Roman propaganda, imperial coins, and monuments bore slogans like *Roma Aeterna*—"eternal Rome"—all promoting the idea that Rome was a divinely ordained way of life, eternally victorious, an empire that was

13. Vaughn, "Smaller Carbon Footprints."
14. Georgi, "Who Is the True Prophet?," 100–126.

destined to last forever.[15] Hymns such as Horace's *Carmen Saeculare*[16] included the claim that Rome had already brought about a golden age of peace and prosperity.

One of the most potent illustrations of Roman imperial eschatology is the Gemma Augustea—an exquisitely carved cameo from the middle of the first century CE, on display in Vienna. This carving gives an amazingly candid picture of the Roman Empire as a two-tiered system. The upper tier shows Emperor Augustus and the goddess Roma sharing a throne, their feet resting upon weapons. The next emperor, Tiberius, steps out of a chariot driven by Nike, the winged goddess of military victory. Personified figures of Earth and Ocean, holding a cornucopia and symbols of sea-trade respectively, gaze adoringly at Augustus. Earth and Ocean give their blessing to the Roman system. The lovely figure of *Oikoumenē* (the "Inhabited World" or "Imperial World") even places a crown on Augustus's head. Underneath, however, the lower register shows the violent military conquest that fuels the whole system. In Abu-Graib-like poses, captive figures representing conquered nations sit naked and humiliated, hands bound behind their backs. They await execution by the Roman soldiers who raise a victory trophy.

Together, the two tiers of this disturbingly beautiful cameo give an unforgettable window into the Roman imperial system and its eschatology. Rome was eternal and blessed, extending its reach to the ends of the earth, the ends of the entire *oikoumenē*. The only proper response to such a system of benefaction is adoration, similar to the adoring postures of Earth and Ocean.

The Great Cameo of France continues Augustus's trajectory of eschatological claims after his death into the reign of his adopted successor, Tiberius.[17] This three-tiered cameo portrays Augustus and Aeneas up in heaven holding the orb of the globe as a symbol of Rome's divinely sanctioned domination over the entire *oikoumenē*. The deceased emperor gives his blessing to Emperor Tiberius, who now reigns on earth, the middle tier. As in the Gemma Augustea, the lowest register of the Great Cameo of France portrays conquered barbarians with hands bound. What the lower tier's portrayal of enslaved captives underscores is why resistance to such a system would be futile.

Georgi argued, however, that it is precisely against the official Roman eschatological credo of eternity and omnipotence that Jesus and the early Christian communities say a firm "No." Only God is eternal—not Rome.

15. Pratt, "Rome As Eternal," 25–44; Dowling, "A Time to Regender," 170–83.

16. *Carmen Saeculare.*

17. See discussion in Ando, *Imperial Ideology*, 287–89.

Whereas Roman propaganda claims that the whole earth gazes on adoringly at Roman imperial power, biblical authors make the daring claim that Rome's dominance over the earth—including creation itself—is coming under God's judgment and will, in fact, soon end. To Roman claims of eternity and omnipotence, Jesus and the Gospels and Revelation all say "No."[18]

This anti-imperial perspective is clearest in Revelation, but it is evident in other New Testament texts as well. The apostle Paul is much more anti-empire than we have realized—including in the Epistle to the Romans—as Robert Jewett and Jeremiah Punt have shown in their work on Rom 8.[19] With his apocalyptic perspective, Paul was creating new communities, new identities, challenging the empire's theology and its eschatology.

"What time is it?" Paul asks, using the word *kairos*. It is time to wake up (Rom 13:11). Paul declares the time in which he is living to be the "end of the age" (1 Cor 10:11). Such pronouncements about the "end of the age" are not just vague end-of-the-world talk that many of us grew up learning in Sunday school. Nor are they about going to heaven after you die. Paul is making daring anti-imperial pronouncements, undercutting the empire's propaganda of the "golden age" and "world without end." Phrases such as "the rulers of this age who are doomed to perish" (1 Cor 2:6) refer to the Roman political powers, as seen two verses later by Paul's reference to the rulers' having crucified Jesus. Christ delivers us from "this evil age" (Gal 1:4)—a not-so-veiled criticism of the Roman imperial order.

UNDERSTANDING "END OF AGE" AS TRANSFORMATION

The New Testament has multiple eschatologies. Earliest writings tend to focus on "not yet," while some later texts say we "already" experience resurrection life (Colossians). The Gospel of John, like Colossians, has a more "realized eschatology." Second- and third-generation followers of Jesus, aware that Jesus had not yet come back, started to think that they are already living in abundant life. The Gospel of John says, "To know Jesus is to have eternal life" (John 17:3). Other New Testament texts have a more future-oriented eschatology. There is a whole range of eschatologies, sometimes even within a single text. What you never see in the New Testament, however, is the idea that the purpose of life is to go to heaven after you die. That is a Platonist eschatology, as the New Testament scholar N. T. Wright has pointed out.[20]

18. Georgi, "True Prophet," 123–26.

19. Jewett, "Reading Rom 8:18–23"; Punt, "Imperial Times."

20. Wright, *Surprised by Hope*, 18. See also Wright, "Jesus Is Coming," 1–72.

An escapist eschatology, in which "the earth is not my home" and going up to heaven is the goal, is not good New Testament theology. Even the term we translate as "eternal life" (*zoē aionion*) means "life for the ages" or "life that can last." That has important implications today for how we talk about issues of sustainability and the world. What is the ecological risk of an escapist eschatology as we face a kind of impending end? In the most recent report from the Intergovernmental Panel on Climate Change, scientists for the first time use the word "irreversible" with regard to some of the changes happening in the world.[21] This is eschatological language. "Irreversible" refers to a kind of an end to which we need to speak, drawing on the New Testament and its eschatologies.

Our culture, too, has eschatologies. Our culture teaches us what Brian McLaren calls "a framing story."[22] What are our eschatologies today? One of them is the notion of the "Rapture." This escapist eschatology, embodied most recently in the *Left Behind* novels, came to us from premillennial dispensationalism, which was developed in the nineteenth century. It is not biblical teaching, and it is very problematic.[23]

Another American eschatology is what environmentalist Bill McKibben calls "More," with a capital "M."[24] This refers to the American way of life that arises out of the idea of no limits. The eschatology of "More" says that unlimited economic growth and expansion is the lifeblood of the economy. It is proclaimed in our advertising slogans and the cultural assumptions we share.

Our consumer culture, our American society, operates with an eschatology and religion that may be unspoken and assumed but is no less powerful than the eschatology of the Roman imperial world. We are seeing the cracks in its eschatological credo: disease, cancers, obesity, diabetes, the growing gap between rich and poor, the financial collapse of 2008. Why is this important? Because *we are living in a moment when our American cultural eschatology isn't working anymore.* Indeed, although we try to deny it, most people realize in their bones that something is wrong, that we are probably facing a kind of "end" to our way of life. People are seeking a different path. They are beginning to realize that our extreme consumption-driven American way of life that we've carved out these past fifty years is not sustainable. McLaren calls the path our culture is on a "suicide machine," a

21. Warrick and Mooney, "Climate Change," November 2, 2014.

22. McLaren, *Everything Must Change*, 5.

23. See Johns, "Apocalypse of John," chap. 8 [77–94] in this book for a critique on the theology of the *Left Behind* series. See also Rossing, *Rapture Exposed*.

24. McKibben, *Comforting Whirlwind*.

system going out of control.[25] I believe this realization of an "end" that we are at can be a very important moment for the people of God.

As we face this "end," a key conceptual distinction we must draw is between the end of a way of life and the end of the world. In biblical terms, it's comparable to the distinction between end of "empire" and end of the "created world" itself. Colin Campbell of the Association for the Study of Peak Oil makes a distinction between the human species in general and our current way of life that he calls "Petroleum Man." "Petroleum Man will be virtually extinct this Century," he says. While "Homo sapiens faces a major challenge in adapting to [this] loss," the important point is that the end of fossil fuels does not equal the end of humanity.[26]

A strong sense of an impending "end" pervades much of the New Testament. But if we look more closely, the "end" that these texts envision seems to be not so much the destruction of the earth or the end of the created world. Rather, the texts envision an end to the Roman imperial order of oppression and injustice, an end to what Luke's Gospel and the book of Revelation call the *oikoumenē*.

The Greek word *oikoumenē* that we have mistakenly translated as "world" has given the sense that the New Testament fixates on the end of the world. But a better translation for *oikoumenē* is "empire." Roman imperial propagandists use the word to mean the "civilized world"—that is, the world to which Rome laid claim for itself. One Roman orator declared that the "whole *oikoumenē* prays that Rome's rule will last forever."[27] Over against such pro-empire propaganda, it is striking that the New Testament refrains from referring to the *oikoumenē* in any positive sense. In my view, this is because the *oikoumenē* had come to represent the Roman Empire—an empire that must come to an end. Declarations such as the "hour of trial that is coming upon the whole *oikoumenē*" (Rev 3:10) should then be read not so much as a general end-times tribulation that God will inflict upon the planet earth, as fundamentalists claim, but more pointedly as the trial or judgment that God will bring upon the entire Roman Empire and on all those who benefit from Rome's injustice.[28]

Words such as "creation," "earth," and "kosmos" are used more positively. Jesus uses the word "earth," or *gē*, much like the Old Testament *adamah*. This crucial New Testament distinction between "world" and "empire" can help us today.

25. McLaren, *Everything Must Change*, 52–53.
26. Campbell, "Understanding Peak Oil."
27. Behr, "Aelius Aristides," Roman Oration 29.
28. See Richard, *Apocalypse*. See also Rossing, "(Re)Claiming *Oikoumenē*?", 74–87.

LEARNING FROM THE EARLY FOLLOWERS OF JESUS

Facing a sense of "end," what did early followers of Jesus do? What can we learn from communities of the Gospels, Paul's letters, Revelation? They created new communities, counter-imperial communities, a new Exodus. Right in the heart of the Roman empire, right in the middle of its cities, they created joyful, abundant communities of people who lived differently. They couldn't leave the empire, so they undertook an exodus in their cities. They shared, they practiced *koinōnia*, and they proclaimed the kingdom of God.

One of the ways the disciples lived differently was by eating differently! Food was a core element of Jesus's vision of the kingdom of God. Food, hunger, food security, water, and justice for farmers are absolutely central in the whole Bible, the New Testament as well as the Old Testament. Jesus rooted his message in the Hebrew Scriptures, drawing on Israelite traditions about food justice and farming that can speak to us now about sustainability issues. The Lord's Prayer is profoundly ecological: "on earth as in heaven" (Matt 6:10). And "Give us today our daily bread" (Matt 6:11, Luke 11:3), the prayer for manna. Jesus taught people how to eat!

Indeed, recent work of New Testament scholars such as Hall Taussig in his book *In the Begininng Was the Meal*,[29] suggests that *meals* were the central settings in early gatherings of Jesus's followers in the city, where much of what became early Christian identity, theology, and, indeed, the New Testament Scriptures, got worked out. Using a model of Greco-Roman banquets or guild meals, in somewhat the same way as other Greco-Roman "symposium" meals or dining clubs in their city, the followers of Jesus ate together, talked together, shared stories and testimonies—subversive, countercultural, boundary-crossing stories of contrasting banquets such as Herod's banquet versus Jesus's banquet (Mark 6:17–44).

They sang songs about Jesus, their Lord (undercutting claims of the lordship of the Roman emperor); they heard an oral performance or recitation of a letter from Paul delivered by a member of another community; they heard a recitation of Israelite Scripture stories about Moses, Elijah, or the prophets; and they took turns sharing visions of kingdom-of-God memories of Jesus—his teachings, his parables about the kingdom, his healings. It was out of these meals that Scripture itself developed, that Eucharist developed. In the beginning was the meal!

Sometimes people at these meal-sharing gatherings had to confront issues of who could eat how much when others were hungry (1 Cor 11:17–34); whether everyone should get the same amount, even those who

---

29. Taussig, *In the Beginning*.

brought nothing; and how Jews and Gentiles could eat together. Could they eat meat if some of that meat was not kosher or—worse—had been sacrificed to imperial divinities (we see this issue in 1 Corinthians, Romans, and Revelation)?

If Taussig and others are right that meals are one of the major settings in which the New Testament came together, where early Christians did theology together, that's significant for us: if early Christians could not do theology without food, then neither can we!

And certainly we see the focus on food in the Hebrew Scriptures as well. My Mennonite colleague Ted Hiebert makes the case in his book *The Yahwist's Landscape* that we cannot understand the Old Testament without understanding farming.[30] Davis says that "from the eighth century BCE on . . . the economics of food production was a matter contested between the crown and its agents, on the one hand, and the bulk of the population, on the other. The biblical writers were located at the heart of the contest, held there by a conviction and a calling . . . Their theological understanding led them directly into confrontation with the economic and political systems dominant in their society."[31]

Daily bread was central to early Christian understandings of who Jesus was. It was central to their worship as it is central to our worship today—the bread of God's word from which we have been fed and the bread of Holy Communion. And daily bread is central to our life as God's people in the world. Breaking bread together leads to recognition of Christ (see the Emmaus story, Luke 24:13–35).

All four Gospels have the core story of feeding the crowds—Mark and Matthew even twice,[32] where Jesus refuses to send the people away and instead teaches his disciples to feed the hungry. He says to them, "You give them something to eat" (Mark 6:37, Matt 14:16). And the baskets of leftovers are said to be "abounding" (*perisseuō*)—the same Greek adjective used to modify *zoē* (life) in the phrase "abundant life." Jesus wants to give us abundant life (John 10:10), and we see in these core stories that abundant life has something to do with food-sharing, the opposite of hoarding or craving.

Jesus loved to eat, he loved to break bread with people, and he loved to teach them about breaking bread together. Whereas John the Baptist fasted and taught his disciples to fast, Jesus was apparently known as a "glutton and

30. Hiebert, *Yahwist's Landscape*.

31. Davis, *Scripture, Culture, and Agriculture*, 3.

32. In Mark 6:30–44 and Matt 14:13–21, Jesus feeds the 5,000, and in Mark 8:1–10 and Matt 15:29–39, he feeds the 4,000.

a drunkard" (Matt 11:19, Luke 7:34). Jesus not only liked to eat, he also told stories about God's kingdom in terms of food—a banquet to which all are invited from the highways and byways (Luke 14:15–24), a banquet where we'll "recline" at a feast with Abraham and the prophets (Matt 8:11). He told stories about God's reign in terms of farming, planting seeds, tending trees, tending a vineyard, bearing fruit.

Most of us also have very deep connections with the land, with food. In a world of displacement and hunger, many Christians are thinking about themes of land and food and the kingdom of God, about how to live differently as a village in the midst of the city.[33]

HEALING FOR THE WORLD

The world is ill. We are ill. What Jesus does is help us diagnose the world's ills and then to bring a message of healing to these crises. In writing the apocalyptic book of Revelation, John of Patmos, similarly, functions like a doctor. He diagnoses the entire Roman imperial system as monstrous, even Satanic, devouring peoples and the whole creation with its predatory economy. And then he gives people the medicine—a different vision of hope.

The book of Revelation offers two alternative future scenarios, two trajectories—Babylon versus new Jerusalem. The Babylon vision (Rev 17–18) is the future trajectory of the Roman empire, which is very bad for the world. John the visionary uses apocalyptic imagery like plagues, bowls, and seals to show the logical consequences of the rapacious way of life of the Roman Empire and its conquest of the nations. But John also gives us the alternative vision of the new Jerusalem (Rev 21–22). This is the vision that can heal our world, the vision into which we are all invited as participants. It is a vision of a city whose gates are open to all nations, through whose midst flows the river of life, and on either side is the tree of life with food for all. Its leaves are for the healing of the nations. Everything in the new Jerusalem is given as a gift (*dorean*), free of charge. It is priceless. That is how God's gifts are given.

---

33. There are many great food books that help us connect our lives with the earth, with the source of our food: Kingsolver, Hopp, and Kingsolver, *Animal, Vegetable, Miracle*; Goodwin, *Year of Plenty*; Bittman, *Food Matters*; Pollan, *Omnivore's Dilemma*; Ayres, *Good Food: Grounded Practical Theology*; Bahnson, *Soil and Sacrament*; Bahnson and Wirzba, *Making Peace with the Land*; Wirzba, *Food and Faith*.

My colleague David Rhoads has authored the eco-justice article "Who Will Speak for the Sparrow?," with insights from the early church and from which I quote in conclusion:

> Most early Christians believed that the end of the world as they knew it was imminent and that soon Christ would return for final judgment and salvation . . . We too are facing a possible end of the world as we humans know. . . .
>
> So, how did the early Christians act in the face of their expectation of the possible end of the world? What can we learn from them? Here are several characteristic behaviors of some early Christians who were shaped by their expectation of the end of the world.
>
> - There was a deep *sense of mission* . . . The early Christians had a tremendous urgency to spread the message from village to village, from city to city—to call people and cities and nations to repentance and change of behavior.
>
> - Like Jesus, the early Christians were *truth-tellers*. They made penetrating analyses of the human condition . . . They identified many of the destructive dynamics of their culture . . .
>
> - They *created alternative communities*, quite different from the culture around them . . . They had a vision of the future and sought to live it now, in the present. In so far as they lived that vision in the present, the kingdom had come! . . .
>
> - Like Jesus, they did *prophetic acts*. In a sense, their lives were prophetic symbols, for every act is a prophetic act when done out of a vision of the future. So healing the sick, feeding the hungry, eating with outcasts, forgiving sinners-- these were all prophetic symbols of a new age impinging on the present.
>
> - In all of this, they were willing to *act unilaterally*, as far as they were able, to create a new world without waiting for the leaders of the nation or the rest of the populace to lead the way or even to agree with them.[34]

WE SAVE WHAT WE LOVE

"People will only save what they love," environmentalists are realizing. Where does your congregation live? What is its watershed? Go canoeing in your watershed. What is the beauty there? What do people *love* there? For

34. Rhoads,"Who Will Speak for the Sparrow?," 83–85.

it's *love*, urgent love, God's love for the world, our love for this home that is our planet, our love for the ocean, the brown hills, our particular watershed, our own grandchildren—it is this *love* that will empower us to be part of a vision for communities to face the public health reality of climate change, to have the courage and imagination to work for a change in public policy, in energy policy . . . for the sake of the healing of the world.

Today, as in the first century, we are called to live according to that compelling, joy-filled, counter-imperial vision, as communities deeply rooted and grounded in Jesus's vision of abundant life, gathered around the tree of life whose leaves are for healing the world.

BIBLIOGRAPHY

Ando, Clifford. *Imperial Ideology and Provincial Loyalty in the Roman Empire.* Berkeley: University of California Press, 1990.

Ayres, Jennifer R. *Good Food: Grounded Practical Theology.* Waco: Baylor University Press, 2013.

Bahnson, Fred. *Soil and Sacrament: A Spiritual Memoir of Food and Faith.* New York: Simon & Schuster, 2013.

Bahnson, Fred, and Norman Wirzba. *Making Peace with the Land: God's Call to Reconcile with Creation.* Downer's Grove, IL: InterVarsity, 2012.

Bartholomew, Ecumenical Patriarch. "Closing Address of Ecumenical Patriarch Bartholomew at the Environmental Symposium 'Arctic: The Mirror of Life' in Greenland." September 7, 2012. https://www.patriarchate.org/addresses1/-/asset_publisher/66W3SwqyvI2z/content/closing-address-of-ecumenical-patriarch-bartholomew-at-the-environmental-symposium-arctic-the-mirror-of-life-in-greenland?redirect=https%3A%2F%2Fwww.patriarchate.org%2Faddresses1%3Fp_p_id%3D101_INSTANCE_66W3SwqyvI2z%26p_p_lifecycle%3D0%26p_p_state%3Dnormal%26p_p_mode%3Dview%26p_p_col_id%3Dcolumn-1%26p_p_col_pos%3D1%26p_p_col_count%3D2%26_101_INSTANCE_66W3SwqyvI2z_advancedSearch%3Dfalse%26_101_INSTANCE_66W3SwqyvI2z_keywords%3D%26_101_INSTANCE_66W3SwqyvI2z_delta%3D15%26p_r_p_564233524_resetCur%3Dfalse%26_101_INSTANCE_66W3SwqyvI2z_cur%3D3%26_101_INSTANCE_66W3SwqyvI2z_andOperator%3Dtrue (accessed June 25, 2015).

Behr, Charles A., trans. *P. Aelius Aristides: The Complete Works.* 2 vols. Leiden: Brill, 1981.

Bittman, Mark. *Food Matters: A Guide to Conscious Eating with More Than 75 Recipes.* New York: Simon & Schuster, 2009.

Campbell, Colin J. "Understanding Peak Oil." In the website section "About Peak Oil," *Association for the Study of Peak Oil & Gas.* http://www.peakoil.net/about-peak-oil (accessed June 2, 2015).

Davis, Ellen F. *Scripture, Culture, and Agriculture: An Agrarian Reading of the Bible.* Cambridge: Cambridge University Press, 2009.

Dowling, Melissa Barden. "A Time to Regender: The Transformation of Roman Time." *KronoScope* 3, no. 2 (2003) 170–83.

Georgi, Dieter. "Who Is The True Prophet?" *Harvard Theological Review* 79 (1986) 100–126.

Goodwin, Craig. *Year of Plenty: One Suburban Family, Four Rules, and 365 Days of Homegrown Adventure in Pursuit of Christian Living.* Minneapolis: Sparkhouse, 2011.

Hiebert, Theodore. *The Yahwist's Landscape: Nature and Religion in Early Israel.* New York: Oxford University Press, 1996.

"Horace: The Epodes and Carmen Saeculare." Translated by A. S. Kline. 2005. http://www.poetryintranslation.com/PITBR/Latin/HoraceEpodesAndCarmenSaeculare.htm#anchor_Toc98670048 (accessed June 26, 2015).

Horsley, Richard, and Neil Asher Silberman. *The Message and the Kingdom: How Jesus and Paul Ignited a Revolution and Transformed the Ancient World.* Minneapolis: Fortress, 2002.

Jewett, Robert, "The Corruption and Redemption of Creation: Reading Rom 8:18–23 within the Imperial Context." In *Paul and the Roman Imperial Order*, edited by Richard A. Horsley, 25–46. Harrisburg, PA: Trinity, 2003.

Kingsolver, Barbara, Steven L. Hopp, and Camille Kingsolver. *Animal, Vegetable, Miracle: A Year of Food Life.* New York: HarperCollins, 2007.

Lattimore, Vergel. "A Pastoral Care Perspective on Creation and Sabbath: Affirming the Biosphere and the Self." Presentation to the Seminary Stewardship Alliance Conference, September 12, 2014.

McClaren, Brian D. *Everything Must Change: When the World's Biggest Problems and Jesus' Good News Collide.* Nashville: Nelson, 2007.

McKibben, Bill. *The Comforting Whirlwind: God, Job, and the Scale of Creation.* Grand Rapids: Eerdmans, 1994.

Pollan, Michael. *The Omnivore's Dilemma: A Natural History of Four Meals.* New York: Penguin, 2006.

Pratt, Kenneth J. "Rome As Eternal." *Journal of the History of Ideas* 26 (1965) 25–44.

Punt, Jeremy. "Negotiating Creation in Imperial Times (Rm 8:18–30)." *HTS Teologiese Studies* 69, no. 1 (2013). http://www.hts.org.za/index.php/HTS/article/view/1276 (accessed September 22, 2015).

Report of the Lutheran-Mennonite International Study Commission. *Healing Memories: Reconciling in Christ.* Lutheran World Federation and Mennonite World Conference, 2010.

Rhoads, David M. "Who Will Speak for the Sparrow? Eco-Justice Criticism of the New Testament." In *Literary Encounters with the Reign of God*, edited by Sharon H. Ringe and H. C. Paul Kim, 83–85. New York: T. & T. Clark, 2004.

Richard, Pablo. *Apocalypse: A People's Commentary on the Book of Revelation.* Maryknoll, NY: Orbis, 1995.

Rossing, Barbara. *The Rapture Exposed: The Message of Hope in the Book of Revelation.* Boulder, CO: Westview, 2004.

———. "(Re)Claiming *Oikoumenē*? Empire, Ecumenism, and the Discipleship of Equals." In *Walk in the Ways of Wisdom: Essays in Honor of Elisabeth Schussler Fiorenza*, edited by Shelly Matthews, Cynthia Briggs Kittredge, and Melanie Johnson-De Baufre, 74–87. Harrisburg, PA: Trinity, 2003.

Shea, Katherine M. "Global Climate Change and Children's Health." *Pediatrics*. 130 (2): e467. http://pediatrics.aappublications.org/content/120/5/e1359.full (accessed June 17, 2015).

Sleeth, Matthew. *Serve God, Save the Planet*. Grand Rapids: Zondervan, 2006.

Taussig, Hall. *In the Beginning Was the Meal: Social Experimentation and Early Christian Identity*. Minneapolis: Fortress, 2009.

Vajda, Jaroslav J., composer. "God of the Sparrow." St. Louis: Concordia, 1983.

Vaughn, Adam. "City Dwellers Have Smaller Carbon Footprints, Study Finds." *Guardian*, March 23, 2009. http://www.theguardian.com/environment/2009/mar/23/city-dwellers-smaller-carbon-footprints (accessed September 22, 2015).

Warrick, Joby, and Chris Mooney. "Effects of Climate Change 'Irreversible,' U. N. Panel Warns in Report." *Washington Post*, November 2, 2014. http://www.washingtonpost.com/national/health-science/effects-of-climate-change-irreversible-un-panel-warns-in-report/2014/11/01/2d49aeec-6142-11e4-8b9e-2ccdac31a031_story.html (accessed September 22, 2015).

Wright, N. T. "Jesus Is Coming—Plant a Tree!" In *The Green Bible: New Revised Standard Version; Understand the Bible's Powerful Message for the Earth*, edited by Michael G. Maudlin and Marlene Baer, I-72-I-85. San Francisco: HarperOne, 2008.

———. *Surprised by Hope: Rethinking Heaven, the Resurrection, and the Mission of the Church*. New York: HarperOne, 2008.

Wirzba, Norman. *Food and Faith: A Theology of Eating*. New York: Cambridge University Press, 2011.

8

The Apocalypse of John and Theological Ecosystems of Destruction and Escape

Loren L. Johns

Environmental neglect that excuses its posture because of prophetic schedules falls prey to an odd modern phenomenon—eschatological idolatry. Those who 'conceive of history as a blueprint instead of a story' perpetuate a stewardship of neglect. But this is God's world, and [God] expects [God's] children to exercise responsible stewardship here and now.[1]

Until evangelicals purge from their vision of the Christian faith the wine of pessimistic dispensationalist premillennialism, the Judeo-Christian doctrine of creation and the biblical image of stewardship will be orphans in their midst.[2]

---

1. Clouse, *New Millennium Manual*, 287. The quotation within the quotation comes from Lapham, *History*, 287.
2. Truesdale, "Last Things First," 118.

THE RECORD OF PREMILLENNIAL DISPENSATIONALISM WITH REGARD TO CREATION CARE

The record of premillennial dispensationalists with regard to creation care has not been a good one. Nevertheless, it is important to separate fact from fiction here, especially when ideological commitments tempt one to blame another's theology on their politics, or their politics on their theology.

Perhaps the most famous illustration of the negative correlation between dispensational theology and creation care is that of James G. Watt, the first Secretary of the Interior under President Ronald Reagan,[3] though Watt's most famous statement may be apocryphal. According to Austin Miles in the book *Setting the Captives Free*, James Watt once said, "God gave us these things to use. After the last tree is felled, Christ will come back."[4] After Miles's book was published in 1990, various speakers, authors, and publishers—including Bill Moyers; Glenn Scherer, writing for *Grist* magazine; the *Washington Post*; *Time* magazine; and several books—repeated this quotation, occasionally adding that this was part of Watt's 1981 public testimony and/or that he said this before Congress. However, there is apparently no evidence that Watt ever gave such testimony publicly.

Watt himself denied ever having made the statement. In his own article in the *Washington Post*, Watt said,

> I never said it. Never believed it. Never even thought it. I know no Christian who believes or preaches such error. The Bible commands conservation—that we as Christians be careful stewards of the land and resources entrusted to us by the Creator.[5]

We cannot sort through Watt's public statements here. However, there appears to be a substantial gap between his actual record as Secretary of the Interior and his public statements. Watt consistently supported the reduction of funds for environmental programs while repeatedly supporting expanded mining, drilling, and the cutting of timber. Watt was impressed that the vast energy resources in the United States were not being developed or taken advantage of, and he was determined to rectify that deficiency. One

3. Watt was Secretary of the Interior from January 1981 to November 1983.

4. Miles, *Setting the Captives Free*, in chap. 12, the last chapter of the book; location 2549 of 2679 in the Kindle edition.

5. Watt, "The Religious Left's Lies." In the same article, Watt also challenges statements made about him by Barbara Rossing. Rossing apparently quoted Watt as saying, "I do not know how many future generations we can count on before the Lord returns," but failed to include what followed: "I do not know how many future generations we can count on before the Lord returns; whatever it is we have to manage with a skill to leave the resources needed for future generations."

important key to the development of public lands was to put them in private hands. In 1983 Watt formally approved strip mining in national parks. According to the *Washington Post*, Watt said, "My responsibility is to follow the Scriptures which call upon us to occupy the land until Jesus returns."[6] Thus, while consistently advocating a posture of creation care and protection, in his actual policies and work Watt "clearly had little interest in preserving the environment."[7] If Watt himself thought his actions cohered with his theology, most observers thought otherwise.

Harder to pin down are actual quotations or other indications of a direct correlation between Watt's dispensational theology and his views on the environment. In her article on "The Ecotheology of James Watt," Susan Power Bratton denies any link between Watt's religious views and his views on the environment.[8] As Laura Hartman puts it, "It is nearly impossible to find credible Christian voices who admit to supporting the eschatologically justified devastation of natural resources."[9] Gregory E. Hitzhusen, Land Stewardship Specialist for the National Council of Churches, goes a step further. He says, "Simply put, the spectre of biblical anti-environmentalism is largely a myth."[10] Hitzhusen is not talking about the role of the Bible itself. Rather, his point is that "the claim that Christians [hold anti-environmental views] in significant numbers and primarily *because* of their religious beliefs is baseless."[11] Hitzhusen's argument is perhaps understandable, since he hopes to show that "Judeo-Christian theology, like other religious perspectives, offers welcome resources for environmental education."[12] What may occasionally be worth distinguishing in these contexts is the theoretical difference between what a biblical text may be saying and what the history of its effects may have been over the centuries. This potential difference lies at the heart of the invitation to read it and read it again, looking for what new readings each new day makes possible.

6. McCarthy, "James Watt and the Puritan Ethic," L5.

7. Drelles, "James Watt," 5.

8. Bratton wrote her article in 1983, near the time when Watt resigned as Secretary of the Interior. Her contribution is weakened by her focus on whether "charismatic" theology influenced Watt. A question about whether premillennial or dispensational theology influenced him would have been more to the point. Bratton's thesis is that conservative political priorities, not theological beliefs, drove his environmental politics. See Bratton, "Ecotheology of James Watt."

9. Hartman, *Christian Consumer*, 129. See esp. chap. 5, "To Envision the Future," 128–68.

10. Hitzhusen, "Judeo-Christian Theology and the Environment," 62.

11. Ibid.

12. Ibid., 66.

In his fascinating analysis of American Evangelicals, environmentalism, and the book of Revelation, Harry O. Maier argues on the one hand
that "Revelation is patient of widely differing versions of the end of history
and hence of a present way to make sense of the meantime," and that "the
Book of Revelation as well as other eschatological texts and themes from the
Bible have had a profound influence on the way Americans, and especially
Evangelicals, have viewed the environment and how the faithful are to relate
to creation."[13]

Lest theologians concerned about creation care too quickly blame
dispensationalism for an eschatology of torching, burning, and escaping,
Maier reminds us that many of the nineteenth- and early twentieth-century
preachers of dispensationalism "taught that the New Heaven and Earth of
Rev. 21.1–2 will be a restored and revived present earth. Scofield envisioned
a creation healed from the marring effects of human 'avarice, . . . ruthless
use of [nature's] power, [and] unequal distribution of her benefits.'"[14]

However, as time passed, dispensationalists became more and more
dismissive of creation itself and began to adopt an escapist eschatology. The
optimism of postmillennialism was seriously weakened by two world wars.
At the same time, premillennial dispensationalism underwent a similar shift
from a more positive world- and peace-affirming theology to a more pessimistic view of the earth and the created order.[15] With a more pessimistic
eschatology came a greater readiness to read the breaking of the seven seals,
the sounding of the seven trumpets, and the pouring of the seven bowls as
a narration of "the ultimate ecological catastrophe."[16] In the same vein, this

13. Maier, "Green Millennialism," 247. Maier's article is one of the better analyses
of theological environmentalism among American Evangelicals. See especially his useful bibliography. See also Moo, "Environmental Ethics."

14. Maier, "Green Millennialism," 251–52. Kraus agrees: the "modern version of
premillennialism, which insists on a millennial dispensation dominated by Zionism,
is an apocalyptic version quite different from the 'peaceable kingdom' of traditional
[historic] premillennialism." Kraus, "Believers Church Hermeneutic," 258.

15. When to date the observable shift to a more pessimistic eschatology is debated.
Gribben dates it rather late, in the 1970s, claiming that "the modern roots of this pessimism can be traced through the reformulation of dispensationalism in the 1970s, when
Hal Lindsey, with all his lurid end-time calculus, popularized a fundamental rethinking
of the 'any-moment' rapture." Gribben, "After *Left Behind*," 114. In contrast, Truesdale
dates it too early, in my opinion—by the end of the Civil War. See Truesdale, "Last
Things First," 118.

16. Boyer, *When Time Shall Be No More*, 331. Boyer traces the theme of eschatological destruction and escapism in the theologies of dispensationalists in the latter half of
the twentieth century (ibid., 331–39). He admits that dispensationalist popularizers
"insisted that they were not *advocating* nuclear war. But in finding atomic war proph-
esied in scripture, they encouraged passivity toward the threat." Boyer, "666 and All

pessimistic eschatology made it easy to wed Old Testament theophanies in which the mountains shake and the earth trembles with Revelation's scenes of doom and destruction and with futurism. That is, all of these texts, when pieced together by determined dispensationalists, predict what the end of the world will look like.

One of the most popular and widely read dispensationalists in the latter half of the twentieth century was Hal Lindsey. His 1973 book, *There's a New World Coming: A Prophetic Odyssey*, sold over 1,500,000 copies. His more popular book, *Late Great Planet Earth*, sold more than 28,000,000 copies. As the title itself indicates, Lindsey's best-selling book takes a most-pessimistic view of the earth's future. "All the cities of the nations will be destroyed . . . Entire islands and mountains [will be] blown off the map" by way of an all-out attack of ballistic missiles. A nuclear exchange will end in worldwide destruction.[17] The seven trumpets predict "enormous ecological catastrophes," with God's judgment coming on vegetation in the form of "soil erosion, floods, and mudslides"[18] and God's judgment of the ocean coming in the form of a massive nuclear bomb that will destroy a "large percentage of marine life."[19] Lindsey goes so far as to say that Revelation predicts "the death of world ecology."[20]

The later Left Behind series of novels by Tim LaHaye and Jerry Jenkins was an even greater success in the marketplace. According to a Tyndale House web page, the series can now boast over 63,000,000 in sales, "making it the bestselling Christian fiction series in history."[21] But despite the label Christian, some readers have wondered what makes it so. In his January 2000 review of the series in the *Atlantic*, Michael Joseph Gross says that "'Left Behind' offers no strong alternative to the world's definition of what matters; it merely appropriates and baptizes worldly standards."[22] For instance, the series blesses both materialism and consumerism. The Tribulation Force has all the latest technology. Chloe Steele Williams develops a global black market network so that the inability of Christians to buy or sell without the mark of the beast won't crimp their consumerist lifestyle. All of

---

That," 245.

17. Lindsey, *Late Great Planet Earth*, 166.

18. Lindsey, *New World Coming*, 130.

19. Ibid., 131.

20. Ibid., 126–35.

21. According to http://www.leftbehind.com/06_help_and_info/faq_general.asp, accessed September 14, 2014.

22. Gross, "Trials of the Tribulation," 127.

the major characters have a ready supply of cash and can travel as much and as freely as they want.

Although the Left Behind series is fiction, its publisher claims that "the framework for the entire series is based on the theology found primarily in the book of Revelation."[23] It is doubtful, however, that its characterization of the antichrist comes from Revelation, since there is no antichrist in Revelation. Nevertheless, LaHaye and Jenkins portray the antichrist in most-interesting terms. He is a pacifist who inexplicably wages war and kills millions of innocent people.[24] He is an intellectual, a polyglot polymath.[25] He advocates love, peace, understanding, and brotherhood.[26] He accepts diversity and brings people together.[27] He is tolerant, peaceful, and understanding. He advocates ecumenical dialogue, and he is the only person in the series who supports organ donation.[28] Moreover, only the antichrist advocates gun control[29] and disarmament[30] in this series, while the Tribulation Force—God's special "Green Berets"[31]—carry Berettas, Glocks, Lugers, 50-millimeter shoulder guns, Uzi machine guns, and designer handguns—and they use them.

Christians witness for Christ in this series by hiding that they are Christians,[32] by lying,[33] by threatening to publicly expose lesbians,[34] and by killing enemies with their bare fists.[35] For just a moment I would like to argue that creation care includes how we treat the *human* animal world. The Christians in this series kill human enemies with guns and with other

---

23. According to http://www.leftbehind.com/06_help_and_info/faq_general.asp, accessed September 14, 2014.

24. LaHaye and Jenkins, *Left Behind*, 70, 413. See also LaHaye and Jenkins, *Tribulation Force*, 443–44.

25. See the helpful comments about the anti-intellectualism of the Left Behind series in Jones, "Liberal Antichrist," esp. 111–12.

26. LaHaye and Jenkins, *Left Behind*, 256.

27. LaHaye and Jenkins, *Apollyon*, 104.

28. LaHaye and Jenkins, *Tribulation Force*, 187.

29. Ibid., 163.

30. LaHaye and Jenkins, *Left Behind*, 70, 137, 273.

31. Ibid., 420.

32. LaHaye and Jenkins, *Tribulation Force*, 428. See also LaHaye and Jenkins, *Assassins*, 188.

33. LaHaye and Jenkins, *Tribulation Force*, 263–64, 361, 406.

34. Ibid., 348.

35. LaHaye and Jenkins, *Soul Harvest*, 347.

means.[36] They seethe with anger.[37] There is a subtle spiritual contest among the Tribulation Force about who seethes with anger more: Chloe or Rayford or Hattie,[38] as if seething with anger were the most reliable fruit of the Spirit in the Tribulation. Rayford hopes that God will let him pull the trigger and murder the antichrist,[39] as does Mac.[40] Rayford wants to be "God's hit man."[41] According to dispensationalist thought, none of this is problematic from a biblical point of view, since the ethical teachings of Jesus do not apply to this age but to the kingdom era following the second coming.[42]

In volume 11 of the series, *Armageddon*, messianic Jew Tsion Ben-Judah preaches a warning message. In this message he says that "the last judgment will be an earthquake that levels the entire globe. This judgment will bring hail so huge it will kill millions."[43] "Remember this [he says]: If you do not turn to Christ and are not saved from the coming judgment, *this awful earth* you endure right now is as good as your life will ever get."[44] "Some have legitimately questioned how a loving and merciful God could shower the earth with such horrible plagues and judgments . . . [but] think of how merciful he has been. He removed his church before the Tribulation began."[45]

In dispensationalist theology as articulated by recent proponents, God's future for the earth and its inhabitants is bleak. It cannot come without ecological disaster, pollution, and other forms of environmental degradation.

> In traditional Dispensationalist preaching there is no way to stave off sin's disastrous consequences either for humans or planet earth. To attempt to do so is to stand in the way of a divinely appointed end and God's plan for a new heaven and

36. LaHaye and Jenkins, *Assassins*, 46, 63. See also LaHaye and Jenkins, *The Indwelling*, 90, 166; LaHaye and Jenkins, *Desecration*, 223; LaHaye and Jenkins, *Glorious Appearing*, 27.

37. LaHaye and Jenkins, *Soul Harvest*, 90, 166. See also LaHaye and Jenkins, *Apollyon*, 100, 300; LaHaye and Jenkins, *Assassins*, 150, 282, 317, 351, 387, 400; LaHaye and Jenkins, *The Indwelling*, 50; LaHaye and Jenkins, *Glorious Appearing*, 51.

38. LaHaye and Jenkins, *Apollyon*, 256. See also Jenkins, Fabry, and LaHaye, *Uplink from the Underground*, 7.

39. LaHaye and Jenkins, *Soul Harvest*, 416.

40. LaHaye and Jenkins, *Glorious Appearing*, 51.

41. LaHaye and Jenkins, *Apollyon*, 100.

42. See Brenneman, "Making Prophecy Come True," esp. 25.

43. LaHaye and Jenkins, *Armageddon*, 277.

44. Ibid., 278; emphasis mine.

45. Ibid., 280.

earth. Christians should [therefore] distrust environmentalism as a distraction . . . Christians should not worry about the environment since the end is so imminent.[46]

The Left Behind series is premillennial dispensationalism infused with the spirit of American survivalism. In this story, Christians can't wait for Jesus to return and kick some butt! Rayford, the leading Christian character in the series, longs to "quit playing and get to war."[47] This story is the ultimate feel-good narrative of retributive justice. God's people can feel especially good about helping God out with the final eschatological battle because this, after all, is a holy war—God's war—a war with a guaranteed win! And in holy war, anything goes![48] In the period of the seven-year Tribulation, peace is *not* the will of God. Rather, God is pro-war. Without war, God's future cannot come. War is not only the *gateway* to God's future; *war is the will of God* in this period of history. Thus, anyone who works for peace and understanding is by definition opposed to the will of God and thus in league with the Deceiver.

As with Lindsey, LaHaye and Jenkins turn the Christology of Revelation on its head: Jesus came as a lamb the first time, but he will come as a lion the next time! So watch out! Out the window for LaHaye and Jenkins is any consideration that Jesus could be the same yesterday, today, and forever.[49] As Mark Davis has put it,

> Instead of letting the "Lion King" Jesus of Left Behind Theology imagination shape the way we read the Gospels, . . . [instead of treating] the Lamb Jesus as if he were a thirty-three year experiment with niceness that failed, . . . we should accept that the life, death, teachings, and resurrection of Jesus are indeed who Jesus is, and anything we might say about Jesus' second coming must be understood as this Jesus—the Jesus of the Gospels—and no other.[50]

The Left Behind series gives no consideration to the possibility that the final judgment of God may be more restorative than retributive.[51] LaHaye and Jenkins explain that the sword coming from Jesus's mouth is not to be taken literally; it is symbolic. It means that when Jesus *speaks*, unbeliev-

---

46. Maier, "Green Millenialism," 253.

47. LaHaye and Jenkins, *Apollyon*, 20.

48. LaHaye and Jenkins, *Indwelling*, 166. See also LaHaye and Jenkins, *Assassins*, 46.

49. Heb 13:8.

50. Davis, *Left Behind and Loving It*, 104.

51. For a hopeful reimagining of the theme of God's eschatological judgment in terms of restoration rather than retribution, see Neville, *Peaceable Hope*.

ers will die all over the place.[52] Flesh will melt off their bones. In *Glorious Appearing*, "tens of thousands . . . fell dead, simply dropping where they stood, their bodies ripped open, blood pooling in great masses."[53] And with every word from the mouth of Jesus, "more and more enemies of God dropped dead, torn to pieces . . . The living screamed in terror and ran about like madmen."[54] "For miles lay the carcasses."[55]

Jesus's word "continued to slice through the air, reaping the wrath of God's final judgment."[56] "Splayed and filleted bodies of men and women and horses" lay everywhere in front of Jesus, who "appeared . . . shining, magnificent, powerful, victorious."[57] "Rayford watched . . . as men and women soldiers and horses seemed to explode where they stood. It was as if the very words of the Lord had superheated their blood, causing it to burst through their veins and skin."[58] "And Jesus had killed them all, with mere words."[59]

Like the unbelievers and history itself, the earth seems to be going to hell, too. Thus, the implied ethic for Christians living in the period of Tribulation is an escapist ethic: their role is "getting more drowning people onto the life raft," an image embraced by one of the heroes in the Left Behind series.[60]

While it may be tempting to dismiss America's dispensationalists, that would be a mistake. As Paul Boyer has aptly put it, "to fail to understand the enduring appeal of dispensationalism is to fail to understand contemporary America."[61] The influence of dispensationalism on the history of American Christianity has indeed been substantial. But is its influence waning? The answer to this is a firm yes, . . . and no. On the one hand, dispensationalism has lost much of its influence among academics. Even at Dallas Theological Seminary, long seen as *the* bastion of dispensational theology, and rightly so, most of the current faculty have repudiated dispensationalism in its classic forms. In its stead, they are articulating what they call "progressive

52. For a similar rehearsal of the celebration of divine violence in the Left Behind series, see Johns, "Conceiving Violence."

53. LaHaye and Jenkins, *Glorious Appearing*, 204.

54. Ibid., 205.

55. Ibid.

56. Ibid., 208.

57. Ibid.

58. Ibid., 225.

59. Ibid., 258.

60. Ibid., 33.

61. Boyer, "666 and All That," 256.

dispensationalism," which is arguably a different beast.[62] One of the more significant differences is that the advocates of progressive dispensationalism no longer think that the promises of God to Israel in the Old Testament must be fulfilled in Israel, rather than in the church. That makes quite a difference and has the effect of weakening, if not cutting entirely, the century-old tie between Zionism and dispensationalism.

However, Boyer wrote his masterful *When Time Shall Be No More* several years before the first novel, *Left Behind*, appeared, and nearly twenty years before Harold Camping's highly publicized prediction of the end of the world on May 21, 2011. Before Camping died in December 2013, he admitted publicly that he had made a mistake and that it was wrong to set dates. While one might be tempted to think that Camping's ultimate effects on the American religious scene will be a kind of inoculation against alarmist apocalypticism in the United States, millenarian thinking has demonstrated a remarkable capacity to ignore its one hundred percent failure rate, morphing and surviving like the best—or is it the worst?—of viruses. So even if dispensationalism has lost footing among America's Evangelical scholars, its influence among rank and file Evangelicalism remains strong. As Crawford Gribben says, "The popular idea that early modern millennial beliefs disappeared 'into a world of cranks' must be revised in light of the remarkable mainstreaming of prophetic expectation at the end of the twentieth century."[63]

THE BOOK OF REVELATION

As an understanding of Scripture, dispensationalism was developed by John Nelson Darby, a Plymouth Brethren preacher, often called the founder of modern dispensationalism. In the United States, the charts and writings of Clarence Larkin, an American Baptist preacher, illustrated how the world would end. Larkin had an enormous influence on many millennial-minded preachers in the first half of the twentieth century.[64] One of the key features

62. For resources on "progressive dispensationalism," see Pate, *Book of Revelation*; Blaising and Bock, *Dispensationalism, Israel and the Church*; Blaising and Bock, *Progressive Dispensationalism*; Gerstner and Kistler, *Critique of Dispensationalism*; and Saucy, *Progressive Dispensationalism*.

63. Gribben, "After *Left Behind*," 113.

64. Clarence Larkin influenced generations with his explanations of Darby's dispensationalism and especially his illustrations of it through charts and diagrams. In his first chart in *Dispensational Truth* (between pages 2 and 3), he presents pictorially four different views on "The Ages." The first is how the Jews saw [*sic*] them; the second, how postmillennialists see them; the third, how premillennialists see them; and the fourth,

of premillennial dispensationalism was the practice of stitching "prophe-cies" together from disparate parts of Scripture. This practice could be quite fun and intellectually stimulating, which accounts in part for its popularity.

But this patchwork-quilt practice of biblical interpretation was based on two fundamental mistakes in biblical interpretation: first, not taking seri-ously the historical contexts out of which and for which different Scriptures were written and thus the kinds of rhetorical functions of the writing that cohere with those contexts. The second closely related mistake was under-standing "biblical prophecy" essentially as prediction about the future. The biblical prophets were much more interested in providing God's perspective on the challenges and issues facing God's people in their own time than they were in predicting something that would happen in the future. John clearly wants his readers/hearers to understand his book as "prophecy" (e.g., 1:3; 10:11; 22:6–7, 9–10, 18–19) though not in the sense of prediction but rather in the sense of traditional biblical prophecy—a word from God for God's people in the present. Any modern interpretation of biblical prophecy that is not rooted and grounded in its historical context is in danger of misread-ing it. The same is true of reading Revelation.

Revelation represents a wonderful resource for the Christian church today—if and when the book is read in light of its first-century context. While Revelation clearly has a lot to say about the future, we need to remem-ber that we are reading someone else's mail when we are reading Revelation. That is not to say that it doesn't have an important message for today. But just as we read Paul's first letter to the Corinthians, responsible interpreta-tion requires that we take seriously its historical context.

Revelation was likely written near the end of Domitian's reign as em-peror, as Irenaeus claimed,[65] around 95 ce. Steven Friesen has shown that a major temple was built in Ephesus in honor of the Sebastoi, or the Flavian family of emperors, during Domitian's reign. It was dedicated sometime between September of 89 and August of 90.[66] Revelation 1:9 says, "I, John, your brother, who share with you in Jesus the persecution and the king-dom and the consistent nonviolent witness, was on the island called Patmos because of the word of God and the testimony of Jesus."[67] Although this is admittedly somewhat speculative, I think there is a good chance that it

---

how God sees them. Being able to speak for God gave him a rhetorical advantage.

65. Irenaeus of Lyons, *Against Heresies* 5.30.3. See also the discussion in Mangina, *Revelation*, 33–34.

66. See Friesen, "Myth and Symbolic Resistance in Revelation 13," 300, among other writings by Friesen.

67. My translation. On using "consistent nonviolent resistance" to translate *hypomenē*, see 90fn78 below.

was John's protest against this temple and Asia's leading families' promotion of the imperial cult that got him banished to Patmos. Much of Revelation makes sense when read against the background of John's anti-imperial critique, and Revelation is clearly "the most politically critical of Rome of all New Testament books."[68]

When we read again and again in Revelation about the one who sits on the throne, we should be hearing the powerful and dangerous anti-imperial message that God is the one who sits on the throne, not Domitian. And even though Revelation has much to say about the future, what it has to say was intended primarily for seven cities in the Roman province of Asia. When it critiques at length the unchecked consumerism and worldwide trade in the first century in Rev 18, we should be hearing this critique as an appeal for creation care. As Barbara Rossing has put it, "Revelation's primary polemic is not against the earth as such, but rather against the exploitation of the earth and its peoples."[69]

When we read about God's judgment on "those who destroy the earth" (11:18),[70] we should be hearing in that judgment God's love and care for the earth. In Rev 12:15–16, the earth even becomes a character in the story—a character that saves God's people from destruction.[71] When we read that the holy city, the new Jerusalem, comes down out of heaven to earth, we should realize that the *earth* is the ultimate destination of this story and the *renewal* of the earth is also the story's goal. As Rossing has put it, "Revelation 21–22 is a wonderfully earth-centered vision of our future."[72] When God says, "Behold, I make all things new" (21:5), God is not saying, "Behold, I make all new things."[73] Yes, heaven is important as the spiritual referent in Revelation *for the earth*, but it is neither the goal nor the ultimate destination. Heaven's job is to care for the earth and to show the earth what is important.

Despite the importance of Revelation's Lamb Christology, Revelation is thoroughly theocentric. God is at the center, though the Lamb somehow seems to share God's seat (3:21). The earth is the creation of God, and God is the creator of the earth. Thus, one's relationship is best apprehended by recognizing the proper relationship of Creator and created. The message of

---

68. Bredin, *Ecology of the New Testament*, 169.

69. Rossing, "God Laments with Us," 123.

70. All quotations from Revelation are from the New Revised Standard Version unless otherwise indicated.

71. Bredin, *Ecology of the New Testament*, 177–78.

72. Rossing, *The Rapture Exposed*, 148.

73. See Waddell, "Green Apocalypse," 148.

Revelation is this: the seven churches of Asia are being invited to recognize and accept the sovereignty of God over against the sovereignty of the emperor. This recognition may be costly, and apparently at least one person has already died because of his faithful testimony (2:13). But Revelation was not written to Christians suffering some systematic persecution from Domitian. Domitian clearly didn't know much or even care much about Christians. He did care about his own sovereignty and more than one Roman historian reports that he demanded to be addressed as *dominus et deus noster* (our lord and our god) when people came into his presence.[74] So when the twenty-four elders address God in Rev 4:11 as "our Lord and our God," the political danger represented by this resistance literature should raise the hair on our necks!

There is a great deal of emphasis in Revelation on the "creatureliness" of God's creation. There are four "living creatures" who constantly worship God. There are descriptions of "every creature in heaven and on earth and under the earth and in the sea, and all that is in them" praising God and the Lamb (see 5:13). This is what it's all about—God's creatures properly worshiping and praising their Creator.

Chapters 2 and 3 of Revelation are interesting for what they reveal about the implied social and spiritual context of the seven churches. Some readers of Revelation read it as a message of comfort to those who are undergoing persecution. Leonard Thompson reads it as a message designed to alarm Christians who were overly acculturated. Why such different understandings? The answer is that in Revelation, chapters 2 and 3 in particular seem to allow both.[75] Some of the churches understand and embrace their countercultural calling, while others don't have a clue. Most of the churches have good things going for them, as well as some serious challenges. Smyrna and Philadelphia seem to be doing well; Jesus has no words of condemnation for these churches. But he has no words of commendation for Laodicea, just condemnation. Some of the Christians were making compromises with regard to the emperor cult so that they could participate in the trade guilds.[76] Some were becoming acculturated, while others were resisting

74. Although Leonard Thompson challenges the historicity of this charge against Domitian, I do not find the charge against Domitian inherently unlikely; see Aune, *Revelation 1–5*, 311–12.

75. See Stevenson, *Slaughtered Lamb*, for a particularly cogent argument about how and why one should not decide whether the historical background reflected in the text is persecution and duress, or comfort and accommodation. Both situations may be true and, in the case of Revelation, are. Apocalyptic literature is uniquely capable of addressing both issues in one writing. Although Revelation does not address theodicy philosophically, it does address it at the situational and practical level.

76. See Kraybill, *John's Apocalypse*.

that acculturation in the name of their faith, and were paying the price. In other words, their situation was not so different from the condition of the churches today.

So what were the Christians in the seven churches supposed to resist and how were they to do so? The clearest answer to the *what* question is that they were to resist idolatry. Idolatry can take many forms, but one of the more important forms in the first-century context was the form of emperor worship in the imperial cult. According to Steven Friesen, emperor worship was reaching its height near the end of the first century, especially in the province of Asia. The locus of the impetus to worship the emperor sometimes came from Rome, and sometimes from local communities. In general, the West frowned on the whole idea of emperor worship. Nevertheless, Caligula, Nero, and Domitian all enjoyed being worshiped so much that they were willing to demand that worship and even to demand the building of temples in their honor whether the locals wanted it or not. However, there was a clear, if unwritten, etiquette about such things in the Roman Senate. If an emperor crossed the line, his memory was officially damned when he died, which meant that his name needed to be literally chiseled out of all stones around the empire—a large public works project in its own right. However, if an emperor was sufficiently humble, if he publicly deflected attempts to worship him as an emperor, he was officially deified, or declared a god, at his death.

So how were they to resist this idolatry? First, by worshiping God and only God—and the Lamb.[77] Second, by maintaining a "faithful witness." Jesus is the paradigmatic faithful witness (see 1:5; 3:14) who was martyred as a result of it. Jesus's own martyrdom proved to be a model for the believers, who were encouraged to bear a similar faithful resistance, even if it eventuated in their own martyrdom as it did with Antipas, who is called "my witness, my faithful one" in 2:13. To bear faithful witness is to maintain a consistent nonviolent resistance[78] to the point of death. Although John does not call his readers specifically to die the death of martyrdom, he does certainly call them to bear faithful witness, and he also clearly expects that

77. Although one may be tempted to ask how one can worship *only* God . . . *and* the Lamb, the inclusion of the Lamb as an object of worship seems not to have challenged in any way the author's commitment to monotheism. See Stuckenbruck, *Angel Veneration and Christology*.

78. Schüssler Fiorenza translates *hypomenē* as "consistent resistance," in contrast to its typical translation, "endurance," or "faithful endurance." She does so because it is more consistent with the rhetorical message and program of the book. I add the word *nonviolent* because John sees nonviolence as essential to the readers' means of standing their ground. See Schüssler Fiorenza, *Book of Revelation*, 4, 8, 24–25; cf. also Schüssler Fiorenza, *Revelation*, 51.

witness to be sealed at martyrdom. Yes, John was pessimistic but not about the earth. He was pessimistic because he understood how thoroughly the human will to power challenges God's sovereignty!

The evidence shows that the primary impetus for emperor worship in the province of Asia did not come from Rome or from Domitian but from the leading families of Ephesus, as well as those in Sardis and elsewhere. Why? Because temples dedicated to the emperor brought *honor* to the city and the province, to say nothing of the visitors that a major temple would bring to a city and the revenue they would bring with them.

Revelation contains many scenes of destruction and earthly devastation. How do these scenes fit with a view of Revelation as earth-affirming? God's restoration of the earth comes *through* destruction and violence, and it survives that destruction and violence, but it does not necessarily come *by means of* it. And there is still time to repent.[79] In fact, there are numerous hints in Revelation that God and God's angels are busy *restraining* both violence and destruction (see esp. 6:6; 7:3; 9:4; 11:5).

Finally, the goal toward which this revelation reaches is renewal and healing. The river of the water of life flows from the throne of God and of the Lamb. The tree of life lines the river "and the leaves of the tree are for the healing of the nations" (22:2). This vision is a vision of life, with God and God's creation in their proper place with respect to each other. Revelation ends in a remarkably open-ended way. There is no actual "end" in Revelation, just an invitation to experience life on earth (see esp. 22:17).

CONCLUSION

Although the charge that Christian eschatology necessarily undercuts concerted attention to the needs of this world is an old one, as Douglas Moo complains, I agree with him that the charge is largely unfounded from a biblical perspective. Clearly Moo embraces a more futurist interpretation of Revelation than I think is warranted, but even a futurist eschatology need not be environmentally dismissive. Indeed, it was not environmentally dismissive until sometime in the twentieth century, when a deep pessimism about both the human condition and the value of the created order in God's future distorted its sense of human responsibility for God's creation. So there is reason to embrace what Maier calls "green millennialism."[80]

Whatever else it does, biblical eschatology, especially that reflected in the book of Revelation, is designed to evoke in God's people an "alternative

---

79. See Rossing, "God Laments with Us," 126–30.
80. Maier, "Green Millenialism."

consciousness." It is designed in part to wake up God's people so that they can see what is really going on in the world. Perhaps the role of God's people today is similar. As Ron Guengerich has put it, "Our task is the ministry of nurturing, nourishing, and evoking a consciousness and perception that can serve as an alternative to those of the dominant culture around us."[81] With such a consciousness, the earth has a good chance of making it.

BIBLIOGRAPHY

Aune, David E. *Revelation 1–5*. WBC. Dallas: Word, 1997.

Blaising, Craig A., and Darrell L. Bock, eds. *Dispensationalism, Israel and the Church: The Search for Definition*. Grand Rapids: Zondervan, 1992.

———. *Progressive Dispensationalism*. Grand Rapids: Baker, 1993.

Boyer, Paul S. "666 and All That." In *Apocalypticism and Millennialism: Shaping a Believers Church Theology for the Twenty-First Century*, edited by Loren L. Johns, 236–56. Kitchener, ON: Pandora, 2000.

———. *When Time Shall Be No More: Prophecy Belief in Modern American Culture*. Studies in Cultural History. Cambridge: Belknap, 1992.

Bratton, Susan Power. "The Ecotheology of James Watt." *Environmental Ethics* 5 (1983) 225–36.

Bredin, Mark. *The Ecology of the New Testament: Creation, Re-Creation, and the Environment*. Colorado Springs: Biblica, 2010.

Brenneman, James E. "Making Prophecy Come True: Human Responsibility for the End of the World." In *Apocalypticism and Millennialism: Shaping a Believers Church Theology for the Twenty-First Century*, edited by Loren L. Johns, 21–34. Studies in the Believers Church Tradition 2. Kitchener, ON: Pandora, 1999.

Clouse, Robert G., Robert N. Hosack, and Richard V. Pierard. *The New Millennium Manual: A Once and Future Guide*. Grand Rapids: Baker, 1999.

Davis, D. Mark. *Left Behind and Loving It: A Cheeky Look at the End Times*. Eugene, OR: Cascade, 2011.

Drelles, Annie. "James Watt, the Environment, and Public Opinion: How Stubborn is Too Stubborn?" Honors thesis, Rutgers, The State University of New Jersey, 2010.

Friesen, Steven J. "Myth and Symbolic Resistance in Revelation 13." *JBL* 123, no. 2 (2004) 281–313.

Gerstner, John H., and Don Kistler, eds. *Wrongly Dividing the Word of Truth: A Critique of Dispensationalism*. 2nd ed. Orlando: Soli Deo Gloria Ministries, 2000.

Gribben, Crawford. "After *Left Behind*—The Paradox of Evangelical Pessimism." In *Expecting the End: Millennialism in Social and Historical Context*, edited byKenneth G. C. Newport and Crawford Gribben, 113–30. Waco: Baylor University Press, 2006.

Gross, Michael Joseph. "The Trials of the Tribulation." *Atlantic Monthly* (2000) 122–28.

Guengerich, Ron. "Evoking an Alternative Consciousness: A Response to Johns." In *Apocalypticism and Millennialism: Shaping a Believers Church Eschatology for the Twenty-First Century. Apocalypticism and Millennialism: Shaping a Believers*

---

81. Guengerich, "Alternative Consciousness," 381. Guengerich draws from Brueggemann's *Prophetic Imagination* in calling us to this task.

Church Eschatology for the Twenty-First Century, edited by Loren L. Johns, 380–85. Kitchener, ON: Pandora, 2000.

Hartman, Laura M. *The Christian Consumer: Living Faithfully in a Fragile World.* Oxford: Oxford University Press, 2011.

Hitzhusen, Gregory E. "Judeo-Christian Theology and the Environment: Moving Beyond Scepticism to New Sources for Environmental Education in the United States." *Environmental Education Research* 13 (2007) 55–74.

Irenaeus of Lyons. "Against Heresies." In *The Apostolic Fathers with Justin Martyr and Irenaeus*, edited by Alexander Roberts, James Donaldson, and A. Cleveland Coxe, 1:559–60. Buffalo: Christian Literature, 1885.

Jenkins, Jerry B., Chris Fabry, and Tim F. LaHaye. *Uplink from the Underground.* Wheaton, IL: Tyndale House, 2002.

Johns, Loren L. "Conceiving Violence: The Apocalypse of John and the Left Behind Series." *Direction: A Mennonite Brethren Forum* 34 (2005) 194–214.

Jones, Darryl. "The Liberal Antichrist—*Left Behind* in America." In *Expecting the End: Millennialism in Social and Historical Context*, edited by Kenneth G. C. Newport and Crawford Gribben, 97–112. Waco: Baylor University Press, 2006.

Kraus, C. Norman. "Defining a More Adequate Believers Church Hermeneutic: A Response to Boyer." In *Apocalypticism and Millennialism: Shaping a Believers Church Theology for the Twenty-First Century*, edited by Loren L. Johns, 257–63. Kitchener, ON: Pandora, 2000.

Kraybill, J. Nelson. *Imperial Cult and Commerce in John's Apocalypse.* JSNTSupp 132. Sheffield, UK: Sheffield Academic, 1996.

LaHaye, Tim F., and Jerry B. Jenkins. *Apollyon: The Destroyer is Unleashed.* Left Behind. Wheaton, IL: Tyndale House, 1999.

———. *Armageddon: The Cosmic Battle of the Ages.* Left Behind. Wheaton, IL: Tyndale House, 2003.

———. *Assassins: Assignment: Jerusalem, Target: Antichrist.* Left Behind. Wheaton, IL: Tyndale House, 1999.

———. *Desecration: Antichrist Takes the Throne.* Left Behind. Wheaton, IL: Tyndale House, 2001.

———. *Glorious Appearing: The End of Days.* Left Behind. Wheaton, IL: Tyndale House, 2004.

———. *The Indwelling: The Beast Takes Possession.* Left Behind. Wheaton, IL: Tyndale House, 2000.

———. *Left Behind: A Novel of the Earth's Last Days.* Left Behind. Wheaton, IL: Tyndale House, 1995.

———. *Soul Harvest: The World Takes Sides.* Left Behind. Wheaton, IL: Tyndale House, 1998.

———. *Tribulation Force: The Continuing Drama of Those Left Behind.* Left Behind. Wheaton, IL: Tyndale House, 1995.

Lapham, Lewis H., ed. *History: The End of the World.* History Book Club. New York: History Book Club, 1997.

Larkin, Clarence. *Dispensational Truth; or, God's Plan and Purpose in the Ages.* 3rd ed. Philadelphia: Larkin, 1920.

Left Behind. "General FAQ." Left Behind, http://www.leftbehind.com/06_help_and_info/faq_general.asp (accessed September 14, 2014).

Lindsey, Hal. *The Late Great Planet Earth.* Grand Rapids: Zondervan, 1970.

————. *There's a New World Coming: A Prophetic Odyssey*. Santa Ana, CA: Vision House, 1973.

Maier, Harry O. "Green Millennialism: American Evangelicals, Environmentalism and the Book of Revelation." In *Ecological Hermeneutics: Biblical, Historical and Theological Perspectives*, edited by David G. Horrell et al., 246–65. London: T. & T. Clark, 2010.

Mangina, Joseph L. *Revelation*. Brazos Theological Commentary on the Bible. Grand Rapids: Brazos, 2010.

McCarthy, Colman, "James Watt and the Puritan Ethic." *Washington Post*, May 24, 1981.

Miles, Austin. *Setting the Captives Free: Victims of the Church Tell Their Stories*. Buffalo: Prometheus, 1990. Kindle edition.

Moo, Douglas J. "Eschatology and Environmental Ethics: On the Importance of Biblical Theology to Creation Care." In *Keeping God's Good Earth: The Global Environment in Biblical Perspective*, edited by Noah J. Toly and Daniel I. Block, 23–43. Downers Grove, IL: IVP Academic, 2010.

Neville, David J. *A Peaceable Hope: Contesting Violent Eschatology in New Testament Narratives*. Grand Rapids: Baker Academic, 2013.

Pate, C. Marvin. *Four Views on the Book of Revelation*. Grand Rapids: Zondervan, 1998.

Rossing, Barbara R. "God Laments with Us: Climate Change, Apocalypse and the Urgent *Kairos* Moment." *Ecumenical Review* 62 (2010) 119–30.

————. *The Rapture Exposed: The Message of Hope in the Book of Revelation*. Boulder, CO: Westview, 2004.

Saucy, Robert L. *The Case for Progressive Dispensationalism: The Interface between Dispensational and Non-Dispensational Theology*. Grand Rapids: Zondervan, 1993.

Schüssler Fiorenza, Elisabeth. *The Book of Revelation: Justice and Judgment*. Philadelphia: Fortress, 1985.

————. *Revelation: Vision of a Just World*. Proclamation Commentaries. Minneapolis: Fortress, 1991.

Stevenson, Gregory. *A Slaughtered Lamb: Revelation and the Apocalyptic Response to Evil and Suffering*. Abilene, TX: Abilene Christian University Press, 2013.

Stuckenbruck, Loren T. *Angel Veneration and Christology: A Study in Early Judaism and in the Christology of the Apocalypse of John*. WUNT 2 (70). Tübingen: Mohr/Siebeck, 1995.

Truesdale, Al. "Last Things First: The Impact of Eschatology on Ecology." *Perspectives on Science and Christian Faith* 46 (1994) 116–20.

Waddell, Robby. "A Green Apocalypse: Comparing Secular and Religious Eschatological Visions of Earth." In *Blood Cries Out: Pentecostals, Ecology, and the Groans of Creation*, edited by A. J. Swoboda, 133–51. Eugene, OR: Pickwick, 2014.

Watt, James G. "The Religious Left's Lies." *Washington Post*, May 21, 2005.

Excerpts from Isaiah 34 (NRSV) and a Contemporary Interpretation

Hannah E. Johnson

¹Draw near, O nations, to hear; O peoples, give heed!
Let the earth hear, and all that fills it; the world, and all that comes from it.
² For the Lord is enraged against all the nations, and furious against all
    their hordes; he has doomed them, has given them over for slaughter.

*All the nations, come together and listen! Let the earth hear, and all that is
    within it.*
God is furious about the ways the nations have polluted creation;
God is letting them destroy themselves along with the earth.

⁸ For the Lord has a day of vengeance, a year of vindication by Zion's cause.
⁹ And the streams of Edom shall be turned into pitch, and her soil into
    sulphur; her land shall become burning pitch.
¹⁰ Night and day it shall not be quenched; its smoke shall go up for ever.
From generation to generation it shall lie waste; no one shall pass through
    it for ever and ever.

The day of judgment is coming, and signs are already visible!
Rivers are polluted with toxic metals and e coli bacteria.
The soil is poisoned with pesticides, and blown away by erosion.
They are destroying my mountains for cheap coal,
    clear-cutting the rainforests to graze fast-food cattle,
    and devastating my oceans with their oil spills.

As fossil fuels burn night and day, acid rains fall, icebergs melt, deserts
spread, and species disappear.

[11] But the hawk and the hedgehog shall possess [the land]; the owl and the
raven shall live in it.

[13] Thorns shall grow over its strongholds, nettles and thistles in its
fortresses.

It shall be the haunt of jackals, an abode for ostriches.

[14] Wildcats shall meet with hyenas, goat-demons shall call to each other;

[15] There shall the owl nest and lay and hatch and brood in its shadow;
there too the buzzards shall gather, each one with its mate.

For the mouth of the Lord has commanded, and his spirit has gathered
them.

[17] He has cast the lot for them, his hand has portioned it out to them with
the line; they shall possess it for ever, from generation to generation
they shall live in it.

In future generations, the ruins of creation will stand in judgment against our
greed.
The wastelands will lie polluted, and will not support human life.
The former grasslands will be choked with autumn olive and Asian
honeysuckle,and the remnants of lakes will be filled with algae blooms,
purple loosestrife, canary grass, and zebra mussels.
Only the Asian long-horned beetles, Canada geese, coyotes, and vultures will
flourish.
The earth will be emptied of the richness of biodiversity and will return to
chaos.

Isaiah 35 (NRSV) and a Contemporary Interpretation

[1] The wilderness and the dry land shall be glad, the desert shall rejoice and
blossom; like the crocus [2] it shall blossom abundantly, and rejoice with
joy and singing.
The glory of Lebanon shall be given to it, the majesty of Carmel and
Sharon.
They shall see the glory of the Lord, the majesty of our God.

*The wastelands of earth will rejoice; the toxic dumps will bloom with
trillium!*
The Gulf of Mexico will sing with regenerated life;
the Appalachian mountains will rise up again with a shout!
*The wastelands will be as green as the hills of Ireland, as glorious as Sequoia
National Park.*
They will see the wonderful restoration of God the Creator.

[3] Strengthen the weak hands, and make firm the feeble knees.
[4] Say to those who are of a fearful heart, "Be strong, do not fear! Here is
your God.
He will come with vengeance, with terrible recompense. He will come and
save you."
[5] Then the eyes of the blind shall be opened, and the ears of the deaf un-
stopped; [6] then the lame shall leap like a deer, and the tongue of the
speechless sing for joy.

*Strengthen the hands of the organic farmers, and make firm the knees of the
bicyclers.*
Say to everyone who lives with dread of climate change and extinction,
*"Don't give up! Don't be afraid! God is coming to save you, to save
creation."*
*Then the people who have been blind to global warming will see evidence,
and the people who have been deaf to the cries of the environmentalists
will finally understand.*
*Those who have been victims of cancers due to toxins in the air and water
will dance, and those who have been silenced by polluting corporations
will sing and shout.*

For waters shall break forth in the wilderness, and streams in the desert;
> 7 the burning sand shall become a pool, and the thirsty ground springs
> of water; the haunt of jackals shall become a swamp, the grass shall
> become reeds and rushes.

For crystal-clear waters will spring up out of the brownfields and flow
through the sluiceways.
The landfills will become swimming holes, and eroded fields will become
lush wetlands.

8 A highway shall be there, and it shall be called the Holy Way;
> the unclean shall not travel on it, but it shall be for God's people;
> no traveler, not even fools, shall go astray.
9 No lion shall be there, nor shall any ravenous beast come up on it;
> they shall not be found there, but the redeemed shall walk there.
10 And the ransomed of the Lord shall return, and come to Zion with
> singing; everlasting joy shall be upon their heads; they shall obtain joy
> and gladness, and sorrow and sighing shall flee away.

A pervious pavement road will stretch across the land
and will lead people to the places where God is restoring creation.
Everyone will live in sustainable ways, and no one will stray from God's way.
No oil wells, or strip mines, or military bases, or belching factories will be
there, but people will share the road with the endangered species God is
saving.
All of creation will be restored, all reasons for discouragement will disappear,
and people will live in joyous harmony with each other and with the
earth.

PART TWO

Theological Reflections

9

A More Excellent Way

The Promise of Integrating Theological Education and Agrarianism

Nathan T. Stucky

Theological education faces a contradiction. On the one hand, consider the scriptural account of the formation of the first humans at the dawn of time: in both versions of the creation story in Gen 1–3, God forms humans in the context of the broader created order; human formation takes place as a result of God's action, and God charges humankind with direct responsibility toward the created order. The Christian tradition affirms that the purpose of God's creation is love. Creation provides the context for humankind to receive and learn the love of God and subsequently share that love with God, neighbor, and—if we follow an agrarian reading of the text—the whole created order. The formation that takes place here binds God, humankind, and the sum of creation together in love.

On the other hand, consider Suzie: after more than a decade of service as a church youth director, Suzie felt called to pursue formal theological education. Full of ambition and hope, Suzie started a Masters of Divinity program at a top-tier school, yet before the end of her first year, she felt gripped by imposter syndrome—fear that she simply did not belong in theological education. This imposter syndrome left Suzie feeling as though she could never be or do enough: she could not read enough, write well enough, work hard enough, or accomplish enough to fit in, and she felt divided from friends, family, classmates, creation, and the God who called her to pursue a theological degree in the first place.

The images of formation in Genesis and in Suzie could not contrast more starkly. If Genesis offers a vision of formation tightly woven to God, neighbor, and creation all for love's sake, Suzie's experience looks more like formation held captive by industrial and consumerist ideals.

The contradiction that theological education faces is that too much—from congregation to university to seminary—it continues to assume an industrial or consumer anthropology by way of its methods, curriculum, and understanding of teacher and student. It looks too often to efficiency, productivity, profitability, and ceaselessness as ideals, and too little to educational practices rooted in our best theological anthropology. Theological education will always be flawed. However, contemporary growing interest in agrarian thought and practice coupled with renewed recognition of agrarianism within the Judeo-Christian tradition suggest that an integration of theological education with agrarianism can help theological education redress the divisive influence of industrialism and consumerism, and thereby renew our love of God, neighbor, and the whole created order.[1]

What if students in theological education studied Jesus's parables of sheep, sower, or harvest and then spent time tending a garden or caring for livestock? What if students of the doctrine of creation actually spent time in creation? What if those learning about the ethical issues of food justice and food deserts learned how to grow food? What if students of the history of monasticism learned *ora et labora* in a way that truly echoed monastic rhythms of physical labor and prayer? Would not these pairings yield new insight, knowledge, and love? All of these possibilities point to a broad overlap between agrarian and ministerial proficiencies. Both the skilled agrarian and the skilled church leader know how to tend life, watch the seasons, and hold the interrelatedness of life and death in reverence and wonder.[2]

Gardens at churches, universities, and seminaries across the country point to the fact that entrées into agrarian practice are already taking place,

---

1. My work here joins the growing momentum of those who are resisting industrial and consumer ideals in theological education by integrating theological education and agrarianism. See, for example, Seminary Hill Farm at the Methodist Theological School in Ohio, http://www.mtso.edu/academics/seminary-hill-farm/; the Food, Faith, and Religious Leadership Initiative at Wake Forest, http://divinity.wfu.edu/food-and-faith/; and the Farminary at Princeton Theological Seminary, http://farminary.ptsem.edu.

2. Indeed, the English language conveys the depth of the connection between the agrarian and the minister: in a word, the skills of minister and agrarian are both *pastoral.*

yet if these efforts are to avoid the pitfalls of industrialism or thought-lessness they will require great intentionality. They will require resources both educational and theological, and they will invite us into courageous practices. The moves from educational resources to theological resources to courageous practice roughly outline the moves in this essay. Education-ally, L. S. Vygotsky provides a framework for aligning pedagogical practice with a robust understanding of what it means to be human. Theologically, the Sabbath calls for the death of industrial and consumer identities so that the life and grace of God may take root. Finally, this essay closes with brief reflection on practical implications.

VYGOTSKY, ANTHROPOLOGY, AND METHOD

L. S. Vygotsky came into the field of psychology in its infancy when it wrestled with questions basic to human anthropology: "What are the relationships between animal and human behavior? Environmental and mental events? Physiological and psychological processes? Various schools of psychology attacked one or another of these questions, providing partial answers within theoretically limited perspectives."[3] Vygotsky insisted on the expansion of these theoretical perspectives. He sought description and explanation of specifically and uniquely human psychology and therefore proclaimed the fundamental insufficiency of both botanical and zoological models for understanding specifically human behavior. While botanical schools of thought led to kindergartens, and those in the zoological school studied apes, Vygotsky sought a more complex account of human psychology and a subsequent revolution in the methods of psychological experimentation. In other words, Vygotsky insisted that the outcomes of psychological research were being held captive by their methods.[4] The question Vygotsky might pose to theological education is this: Do the methods of theological educa-tion reflect best understandings of what it means to be human, or do they miss something critical and thereby limit outcomes?

Much contemporary theological education—whether in church, uni-versity, or seminary— continues in a way that is overwhelmingly text-based. Methods depend predominantly on words—written, spoken, and occasion-ally invented. Words, as Vygotsky points out, are part of what makes hu-mans uniquely human. From a Christian perspective, the problem emerges when our fixation with words and text obscures the fact not only that we as teachers and students are more than mere intellects but also that *the* Word

3. Cole and Scribner, "Introduction," 3.
4. See Vygotsky, "Child Development," 19–30; and "Problems of Method," 58–75.

did not merely come as letters on a page. The Word became flesh and dwelt among us. If we confine theological education to mere verbiage, we fall short of our best account of who we are and who God is, and we thereby limit the outcomes of theological education. On the other hand, to plant seeds and tend them, to water and nourish, to harvest and consume the flesh of fruits and vegetables is to enact a fuller, richer account of who we are. These practices—when engaged in light of the Word that brought forth all life in the beginning—form in us an awareness of and a reverence for our existence as embodied creatures, created both in the image of God and from the soil of the earth. To educate in this way is to know and love ourselves, our students, our Creator, and the land more fully.[5]

DYNAMISM OF CONTEXT

In mentioning the potentially formative impact of agrarian practice, we turn to a critical second tenet of Vygotsky's theory—his understanding of the interrelatedness of learning and context.[6] For Vygotsky, mutual formation and transformation mark the relationship between learner and context; both context and learner act in the learning process. The context may provide the tools for solving a problem—sticks and moss, for example—but the learner uses the tools and thus transforms them. Instead of mere sticks and moss, the learner transforms the tools into a shelter. Yet the transformation of the tools also transforms the learner. The learner can no longer see sticks and moss in the same way. New transformative knowledge has been gleaned. The relationship between learner and context is thus dynamic and dialectic, for better and for worse. Though Vygotsky does not account for a potentially degenerative dialectic, the interrelated transformation of humans and environment within industrialism surely illustrates the point. Industrialism at its worst showcases the degeneration that can take place when humans relate to nature in short-sighted and unsustainable ways. We have, in fact, acted in these ways, and we have been transformed in the process.

Theological education faces a similar situation. Much theological education takes place in rooms that reflect the influence of the industrial revolution on education. Students sit in uniform rows of desks and face a single lectern in a seminary classroom, or they are divided by age and

5. The integration of theological education and agrarianism in this fashion reunites humans, plants, and animals in a way that preserves both the interrelatedness and the distinctions of the created order.

6. To be clear, context here refers to the physical setting in which learning takes place. See Vygotsky, "Problems of Method."

placed in separate rooms in rather industrial-looking education wings in congregations. Vygotsky would argue that these settings, in and of themselves, actively form students, teachers, and the relationships between the two. Used thoughtlessly, these learning spaces can reinforce the industrial ideals of uniformity, efficiency, productivity, and control. They can ignore the influence of the learning context on the learning process, or they can imply that such settings are normative for the act of theological education.[7]

The hope of an integration of theological education and agrarianism is not that traditional classrooms cease to exist but that we (both teachers and students) would undergo the formation and transformation that uniquely take place in other contexts, particularly the aforementioned planting, tending, watering, nourishing, and harvesting. The hope is that we would work toward generative rather than degenerative transformation, and that in so doing our knowledge and love would grow.

To summarize, Vygotsky provides us with a framework for understanding the importance of aligning our educational practices with our richest and fullest accounts of what it means to be human. In so doing, he has helped us highlight some of the limitations of industrial education and some of the promise of agrarianism. We come now to some of Vygotsky's own limits. If we seek an integration of agrarianism and theological education, then our anthropology must be truly theological. It must account for and count on the ongoing dynamic life and activity of the God revealed to us as Creator, Redeemer, and Sustainer of life. Therefore, we turn now to the Sabbath as one such theological basis.

SABBATH

At its core, the Sabbath invites God's people to regularly cease their labor and rest; the roots of the word Sabbath mean simply to cease or to stop. Industrialism and consumerism, on the other hand, invite people into lives of ceaseless production and consumption. Too frequently the lives of theological educators, students, and the institutions of theological education reflect more the ceaselessness of industrialism and consumerism than the rhythmic rest of the Sabbath. Without this basic shift from an industrial mentality rooted in ceaselessness to a Sabbath mentality that seeks fullness of life and freedom by way of limits, the integration of theological education

---

7. The point here is not to unnecessarily castigate industrialism or to suggest that industrialism holds the sole influence on contemporary theological education and formation. Rather, the point is to recognize influence and encourage intentionality in theological education.

and agrarianism risks a ceaselessness even more feverish than we have already known, and the struggle to know and love ourselves, our students, the land, and the Creator will continue. Thus, in this section I make three suggestions regarding Sabbath theology and the integration of theological education with agrarianism:[8]

1. Sabbath partially constitutes the created order. Our full humanity as well as the health and vitality of the whole creation depends in part on Sabbath.

2. Sabbath directs us overwhelmingly to the life, grace, and provision of God.

3. Sabbath—like agrarianism—clarifies that our fullness of life comes only through death.

SABBATH PARTIALLY CONSTITUTES CREATION

When Gen 2 tells the story of the seventh day of creation, it does so confusingly. Note the use of the term "finished" in the NRSV:

> Thus the heavens and the earth were finished, and all their multitude. And on the seventh day God finished the work that he had done, and he rested on the seventh day from all the work that he had done. (Gen 2:1–2)[9]

The text suggests that on the seventh day, creation is both finished and unfinished. The peculiarity of the NRSV's translation points to a more general interpretive question: What does God uniquely do on the seventh day, and how does it relate to the first six days? Karl Barth argues that God's creative work is done at the close of day six. To impose more modern categories, we might think of the entire material world being in order. Even so, creation remains incomplete or unfinished. God finishes creation on the seventh day,

---

8. I am by no means the first to suggest congruence between the Judeo-Christian doctrine of the Sabbath and agrarian thought and life. Wendell Berry, Ellen Davis, and Norman Wirzba—among others—have made significant contributions in this regard. I hope to build here on their work in a way that is focused more explicitly on theological education and that takes Vygotsky's educational insight seriously. See, for example, Wirzba, *Food and Faith*; Davis, *Scripture, Culture, and Agriculture*; and Berry, foreword to *Living the Sabbath*.

9. All Scripture quotations in this essay are from the NRSV Bible unless otherwise indicated.

not by way of further creative activity but by way of God's own rest and the implied invitation to all creation to participate in God's rest. [10]

God's provision of a Sabbath rhythm for the Israelites in the wilderness at the Exodus, the Sabbath commandments in the Decalogue, and the Sabbatical and Jubilee years all suggest the same point. God's people—God's whole creation—remains incomplete apart from Sabbath rest. In other words, our best account of what it means to be human and part of the broader created order includes Sabbath rest. This insistence resists categorically the ceaselessness of industrialism, and it challenges contemporary theological education to the core. By this account, to refuse Sabbath rest is to deny ourselves and our students our full humanity. It is also to abuse the land, for as Wendell Berry reminds us, we cannot love ourselves or others differently than we love the land. [11] This raises a basic question: If we are to practice Sabbath on the journey of integrating theological education and agrarianism, on what basis may we do so?

SABBATH: SHEER GRACE

When Barth exegetes the seventh day of creation, he emphasizes the fact that on the seventh day—the first day of rest, the first full day of existence for the first humans—these first humans have no work of their own on which to reflect. The only work they have to reflect on is God's—the "very good" creation. At this point in the story, humankind cannot possibly conceive that Sabbath rest comes as a reward for good work or a prize for accomplishment. At this point in the story, Sabbath rest is a gift of sheer grace. Sabbath depends utterly on the action, provision, and grace of a loving God. [12]

The Sabbath commandments in Exodus and Deuteronomy similarly point the people of God to the life and activity of God as the basis for Sabbath rest. In Exod 20, the Sabbath commandment points to God's rest at creation; in Deut 5, the Sabbath commandment points to God's deliverance of the Israelites from Egypt. In every case, the Sabbath rest that God gives to God's people depends not on human productivity or accomplishment but rather on the grace and salvation of a loving God. As we pursue the integration of theological education and agrarianism, this fills out something essential in our understanding of what it means to be human. It clarifies that life from the dawn of creation utterly depends on God's grace, action,

---

10. Barth, *Church Dogmatics*, 3/1:213–28.
11. Berry, "The Body and the Earth," 93–134.
12. Barth, *Church Dogmatics*, 3/1:213–28.

and provision. In theological perspective, it is as true of human life as it is of plant and animal life. Practiced in the light of this theological perspective, planting seeds, tending plants or animals, or caring for a congregation all point to the life-giving grace of God. As Paul noted two thousand years ago, one plants, one waters, but only God brings growth (1 Cor 3:6).

Receiving God's gift of Sabbath rest on the journey of this integration thus plants a stake in the ground in a particular place. It is the place that radically trusts that God still grants growth and that our lives depend ultimately on God's life and provision, not on our productivity or accomplishment. As we lead students into gardens, forests, and fields, we will do well to point them to God's growth-granting life, and we can marvel that the invitation to tend and keep—and rest—still stands. This shift from human productivity and accomplishment to God's grace and provision transforms our work. It moves us away from the fear and anxiety that inevitably accompany our fixations on what we can accomplish and toward the joy, satisfaction, and humility that come in realizing that we do not work alone and that our lives and the life of all creation ultimately rest in the hands of a good and gracious God.

LIFE THROUGH DEATH

Even as the Sabbath overwhelmingly points to God's grace and love, it also clarifies the particularity of the identity that God seeks to shape within and among God's people. Through the Sabbath, God challenges God's people to be a people who trust radically in God's grace and provision. Any lesser identity must pass away. When God delivers the Israelites out of Egypt and into the wilderness, God provides for the Israelites by way of manna, quail, and a Sabbath rhythm all-in-one. Why? Why would God provide manna with such peculiar instructions? Why not just give manna every day and keep the whole sequence simple? The broad movement of the narrative from captivity in Egypt to wilderness wandering to promised land suggests that God gives the manna and Sabbath combination to the Israelites to begin the long process of reforming the identity of the Israelite people. They are coming out of a context where their identity was bound inextricably to what they could produce. Each person was only as valuable as the number of bricks he or she could make.

With the manna and the Sabbath rhythm, God calls for the death of an identity held captive by either productivity and achievement or consumption, and thus challenges the Israelites to instead be known as those who trust radically in God's grace and provision. The anxiety we experience at the thought and practice of Sabbath rest surely echoes the anxiety of the Israelites who tried to hoard manna on the first five days or went in search of manna on the seventh.

Barbara Brown Taylor says it succinctly, "Sabbath . . . it's a little death."[13] God shapes us through the Sabbath by calling for the death of all lesser identities and calling us to lives dependent on God's grace and provision, to both rest and work in the identity-altering light of God's provision and grace. This notion within the Sabbath, that our fullness of life cannot be separated from death, finds a close parallel in agrarianism—indeed in the life of Christ whose body lay lifeless in the tomb on a Sabbath. We live—whether we acknowledge it with gratitude and reverence or not—in, by, and through death, not for the sake of death but for the sake of health, vitality, true knowledge, and love.

Thus, the Sabbath clarifies theologically what agrarianism echoes practically. Sabbath proclaims that freedom comes by way of limits, not in their absence. Agrarianism insists on economies of scale even as it resists the ceaselessness of industrialism. Sabbath comes to us as a gift of sheer grace; agrarianism holds us captive in the mystery of growth and the wonder of creation. Sabbath calls for the death of our lesser identities that we may be known and know ourselves as people who trust in God; agrarianism reminds us that we have no way to live but by way of death.

WHAT MIGHT THIS LOOK LIKE?

Like Suzie, Garrett attended a top-tier theological school in order to earn a Masters of Divinity degree.[14] Upon graduation, Garrett and his wife, Kaitlyn—who also earned an MDiv—longed for a way to get theological education "out of their heads" and into their bodies, and this led them to a year-long internship at a small farm in Pennsylvania. Garrett's first week on the farm brought him to the intersection of life and death. He was asked to help butcher chickens. Garrett is a vegetarian and had never killed anything in his life, yet he reflected on the act of killing chickens with reverence and even gratitude. "I don't know yet what it all means, but I know it was very important. I learned more in one month on the farm than I did in years of higher theological education." Garrett noted that agrarian practice brought Scripture to life in new ways; it created new spaces for theological conversation; and it nurtured rich and loving bonds between Garrett and the others on the farm.

13. Taylor, "Sabbath."
14. To be clear, Garrett and Suzie attended different top-tier schools.

The farm where Garrett works is unique. It is owned and operated by a part-time, seminary-trained pastor and her husband. As farm owners, Krista and Tim engage agrarian work as an expression of their Christian faith and as a means of ongoing theological education and formation. This reality creates the context where theological education and formation can happen for all who work on their farm. All farmhands gather for prayer and Scripture before the day begins; they eat together; they weed carrots together; and in so doing, their love and knowledge grow. All of this points again to the tremendous potential for integrating theological education and agrarianism. All of this reflects a robust theological anthropology—a conviction that to be human is to be an embodied creature, made both in the image of God and from the soil of the earth. The ceasing of work to share meals reflects a Sabbath sensibility and deep gratitude for the growth that God graciously grants.

Garrett, Kaitlyn, Krista, and Tim point the way for the integration of theological education and agrarianism. What might happen if such rich formation became a regular part of formal theological education? Surely such an integration would create tremendous challenges, yet it would also provide the possibility that love, knowledge, and a great variety of produce may grow and bear fruit for God's kingdom throughout the world. To form and be formed in this way—through Sabbath rest in the context of God's very good creation, in full awareness and reverence for the death that brings us life—is to come into awareness of who we have always been: created, redeemed, sustained, known, and loved by God, and called to love, know, and care for God's people and all of God's good creation.

BIBLIOGRAPHY

Barth, Karl. *Church Dogmatics*. Vol. 3/1. Edited by G. W. Bromiley and T. F. Torrance. Edinburgh: T. & T. Clark, 1958.

Berry, Wendell. "The Body and the Earth." In *The Art of the Commonplace: The Agrarian Essays of Wendell Berry*, edited by Norman Wirzba, 93–134. Berkeley, CA: Counterpoint, 2002.

———. Foreword to *Living the Sabbath: Discovering the Rhythms of Rest and Delight*, by Norman Wirzba. Grand Rapids: Brazos, 2006.

Cole, Michael, and Sylvia Scribner. "Introduction." In *Mind in Society: The Development of Higher Psychological Processes*, edited by Michael Cole et al., 1–14. Cambridge, MA: Harvard University Press, 1978.

Davis, Ellen F. *Scripture, Culture, and Agriculture: An Agrarian Reading of the Bible*. New York: Cambridge University Press, 2009.

Taylor, Barbara Brown. "Sabbath: A Practice in Death." Work of the People, http://www.theworkofthepeople.com/sabbath-a-practice-in-death (accessed September 22, 2015).

Vygotsky, L. S. "Problems of Method." In *Mind in Society: The Development of Higher Psychological Processes*, edited by Michael Cole et al., 58–75. Cambridge, MA: Harvard University Press, 1978.

———. "Tool and Symbol in Child Development." In *Mind in Society: The Development of Higher Psychological Processes*, edited by Michael Cole et al., 19–30. Cambridge, MA: Harvard University Press, 1978.

Wirzba, Norman. *Food and Faith: A Theology of Eating*. New York: Cambridge University Press, 2011.

10

Lived Theology in the Little Campbell Watershed

A Primer on Bioregional Discipleship

Matthew Humphrey

Tell me the landscape in which you live and I will tell you who you are.[1]

Alan Durning, founder of the Seattle-based Sightline Institute, recounts the story of a trip he took to the Philippines. After interviewing several elders as part of the trip, he was introduced to a frail, elderly priestess who, through a translator, turned one of his questions back on him. "What is your homeland like?" she asked. Durning was thrown off by the question. He silently pondered his conflicted feelings toward his home neighborhood in Washington, DC. Undeterred, she asked again, "Tell me about your place." He then realized how little connection he had to his home and place. "'In America,' [he] finally admitted, 'we have careers, not places.' Looking up, [he] recognized pity in her eyes."[2]

This story would be surprising were it not so familiar. Most North Americans live (and read our Bibles) as though issues of land and place

1. Spanish philosopher José Ortega y Gasset is quoted in Lane, *Landscapes*, 20.

2. Durning, *This Place*, 3–4. I thank Loren Wilkinson for first introducing me to Durning's work.

matter very little. Attempts to explain this "loss of a sense of place" abound, yet seldom have they taken seriously the biblical story as it relates to these themes.[3]

A cursory reading of the biblical story reveals that issues of place and land are central to its overall structure and content. The triangular covenant narrated between YHWH, Israel, and the promised land furnishes the historic people of faith with a unique ecological and social ethic intended to ground their life in care for people and place alike. With memories of slavery in Egypt and wandering in the desert both representing a kind of placelessness, Israel is given the Torah and commanded to keep it to ensure their tenure in the promised land. When they violate this way of life, they face exile. This is an ancient tale and one that the New Testament does not dispense with but reorients according to the way of Jesus, whose lordship now extends over all peoples in all places. Inhabiting the way of Jesus thus becomes the authoritative mark of the discipleship community as they go about their lives in their various places now spread about all over the world.

Yet life in the modern world has now freed us from the particularity of place, rendering Durning's quip, "we have careers, not places," true and leaving us to suffer the consequences. In light of the ecological crisis that now confronts us, it is ever more urgent that the church recover a sense of place. If we are to respond faithfully to our present circumstances, we can begin by carefully rereading the biblical story, which furnishes us with a new set of practices that can anchor our life together in a place. We should also learn a different language with which to speak about our place, one that avoids the abstraction and romanticism latent within much of the environmental discourse. To that end, we may draw on an important stream within environmental philosophy known as *bioregionalism*. Reading these two stories together—the biblical and the bioregional—may teach us to reinhabit our own places, to honor memberships to which we belong, and in so doing, to recover a long-neglected matter for our life of faith. This is the work of bioregional discipleship.

Bioregionalism emerged within the environmental movement of the late 1970s and was popularized by writers such as Peter Berg, Gary Snyder, and Kirkpatrick Sale. Sale offers a definition of bioregionalism in his 1985 text *Dwellers in the Land*:

> *Bio* is from the Greek word for forms of life ... and *region* is from the Latin *regere*, territory to be ruled ... They convey together: a life-territory, a place defined by its life forms, its topography

---

3. One recent and notable exception is Bartholomew, *Where Mortals Dwell.*

and its biota, rather than by human dictates; a region governed
by nature, not legislature.[4]

Another way of explaining the concept of a bioregion is to quote the poet-
ecologist Gary Snyder, who wrote simply, "The world is places."[5] For Snyder, abstract entities such as *world* or *planet*, or popular sayings like the
adage "Think global, act local," are not helpful. The problem, Snyder argues,
is that intangible references fail to ground meaningful action locally. As
the Kentucky farmer and writer Wendell Berry writes, "In order to make
ecological good sense for the planet, you must make ecological good sense
locally. You *can't* act locally by thinking globally."[6] This insight forms the
backbone to bioregional thinking—if you get the scale right, everything else
follows. As Sale contends, "At the right scale human potential is unleashed,
human comprehension magnified, human accomplishment multiplied. I
would argue that the optimum scale is the bioregional, not so small as to be
powerless and impoverished, not so large as to be ponderous and impervi-
ous, a scale at which at last human potential can match ecological reality."[7]

A related insight of bioregionalism is that we cannot solve these issues
from the top down. Rather, we must begin in some particular place, prefer-
ably our own place: the ground upon which we stand, the water we drink,
and the soil from which we derive our food. This requires that we confront
the detachment and alienation we may harbor toward our place and ask
again the basic question, "Where am I?"

As Michael McGinnis, editor of the seminal text *Bioregionalism*,
writes, "To get bioregional, humanity needs to cultivate an ecological
consciousness and communal identity, and develop relationships with the
neighborhood."[8] The neighborhood includes both human and nonhuman
neighbors. These nonhuman neighbors have long been overlooked or ma-
ligned by the faith community, whereas the Hebrew Bible is unequivocal
about humanity's em*place*ment within a vast network of other creatures, all
given life and breath by God. The bravado with which humanity has inap-
propriately asserted dominion over the rest of creation now threatens the
future health of creation itself. We therefore need more than ever to recover
the deep sense of our membership within, and dependence upon, creation.
Bioregionalism offers a compelling narration of human identity as thoroughly situated in ecological place—an insight that readers of the Hebrew

4. Sale, *Dwellers*, 43.

5. Snyder, *Practice*, 25.

6. Berry, "Out of Your Car," 23.

7. Sale, *Dwellers*, 55.

8. McGinnis, "Rehearsal," 8.

Bible should find deep resonance with in the text. Rather than taking cues from modern political boundaries, bioregionalism looks to the landscape itself as a guide.

Snyder in his essay "Coming into the Watershed" asks the question, "What is California?" The common answer, he notes, would begin by looking at a state map. But that map fails to acknowledge that "landscapes have their own shapes and structures, centers and edges, which must be respected."[9] Every landscape has a bounded shape and structure—a watershed—that situates natural communities within the surrounding bioregion. This ecological reality is seldom mirrored in modern political boundary lines. The first step toward reinhabitation is thus to identify the watershed and bioregion in which we live and to come to know the creatures we share it with. We must ask ourselves to consider, "Where are we?"

I live in the Little Campbell River Watershed. This river is just thirty kilometers long. It crosses four modern municipal jurisdictions, transgresses the traditional territories of Semiahmoo First Nation, and is located within the province of British Columbia and the country of Canada, which have their respective laws governing streams and waterways, not to mention the rare species-at-risk that live here such as the red-legged frog and the Pacific water shrew. Into this river flow two additional streams that originate south of the US border in Whatcom County, Washington. All told, this thirty-kilometer creek that runs through my backyard is implicated in over ten different political jurisdictions, yet the salmon that return to spawn every fall have yet to carry a passport. Nor is the red-listed Oregon forest snail given a vote in important land use decisions affecting its multiple municipalities.

Moving beyond my own watershed, the keystone species of our bioregion—the salmon—connects me to a broader membership still. The Little Campbell River drains into Boundary Bay, a nationally significant marine ecosystem that serves as a habitat for migratory birds. Boundary Bay connects the borders of Washington and British Columbia and forms part of the Salish Sea. The Salish Sea stretches from south of Seattle northward, past the Gulf and San Juan Islands and then around the Western tip of Vancouver Island to as far north as the end of the Straight of Georgia, which is the body of water passing between the mainland of British Columbia and Vancouver Island. The Little Campbell River Watershed drains seventy-four square kilometers; the Salish Sea covers over 18,000 square kilometers. Further afield, the same salmon that spawn in the Little Campbell River travel along the Western Coast of our continent, as far north as Alaska and as far south as the Ventura River Watershed in southern California.

9. Snyder, *Place*, 221–22.

A watershed can be thought of as one big bathtub, an area within which all the water drains to a common point. And that flowing course of water links together the health of the human community with the nonhuman creation. We can't become fully human without recognizing this fundamental fact—we belong to the community of creation. Or, as Larry Rasmussen put it, "The 'createds' are all 'relateds.'"[10] One way to think of such a community is in terms of membership, following Saint Paul and Wendell Berry: I am a member of Christ's body; I am a member of the Little Campbell River Watershed.

Getting to know this geography and recognizing my membership in this bioregion has proven indispensable in my deepening efforts at caring for my place. Such a localized membership does not limit or prohibit my care for other places—quite the opposite. By first locating myself within the membership of the Little Campbell River, I find I am practically implicated in a web of relationships that span from the Puget Sound to the Georgia Straight, from southern California to the coast of Alaska, and thus I am called to work toward the health and restoration of those places as well. As Snyder writes, a community working to rehabilitate a salmon stream, as my community is, "might find itself combating clear-cut timber sales upstream, water-selling grabs downstream, Taiwanese drift-net practices out in the North Pacific, and a host of other national and international threats to the health of salmon."[11] This is where the church, whose citizenship is not in the first instance tied to any kingdom of this world, can and should organize its efforts to promote the integrity of creation. To do so, we must first explore how the biblical story depicts the concept of place.

The concept of place is foundational to the development of narrative in the Hebrew Bible. As Walter Brueggemann notes in his classic text *The Land*, "Land is a central, if not *the central theme* of biblical faith."[12] More recently, Ellen Davis has argued that whenever biblical scholarship directs its attention to land, it has been concerned primarily with "*possession of land* as a national territory." Davis argues, in contrast, that the concern for land care is as essential to the narrative as land tenure: "The biblical writers themselves consistently regard the two matters as related; land tenure is conditional upon proper use and care of land in community."[13] It is this concept of conditional tenure that is so thoroughly exercised throughout the Hebrew Bible and merits closer examination here.

10. Rasmussen, *Earth Community*, 262.
11. Snyder, *A Place*, 230.
12. Brueggemann, *The Land*, 3.
13. Davis, *Scripture, Culture, and Agriculture*, 2.

God's promises to Abraham and his descendants are finally realized (after a complex history and formation) in the promised land. And the land of promise is routinely framed in the language of gift—this particular land is *given* to this particular people that they might follow the ways of this particular God and be a blessing to all the nations. But the fact that the land is a gift reinforces its conditional nature. In Deut 8:1 we read, "Be careful to follow every command I am giving you today, so that you may live and increase and may enter and possess the land the Lord promised on oath to your ancestors."[14] Israel's obedience to the ways of YHWH ensures the flourishing of the land itself as stated in Lev 26:3–5: "If you follow my decrees and are careful to obey my commands, I will send you rain in its season, and the ground will yield its crops and the trees their fruit. Your threshing will continue until grape harvest and the grape harvest will continue until planting, and you will eat all the food you want and live in safety in your land." Safety in the land, an abundant harvest, and dependable rains—all of these are premised upon Israel's commitment to follow the decrees of YHWH. Of the Hebrew Bible as a whole, Davis writes, "human righteousness is the one condition that invites and even makes possible God's continued presence in the land."[15]

Hebraic law in several places is written to ensure the safekeeping of the land and the people living within it, with particular attention paid to the poor and marginalized. In Leviticus, for example, the people are commanded, "Do not reap to the very edges of your field or gather the gleanings of your harvest. Do not go over your vineyard a second time or pick up the grapes that have fallen. Leave them for the poor and the foreigner. I am the Lord your God" (Lev 19:9b–10). Central to covenant obedience is upholding the Sabbath day, and this has important implications for all creatures, not just human beings: "Six days do your work, but on the seventh day do not work, so that your ox and your donkey may rest, and so that the slave born in your household and the foreigner living among you may be refreshed" (Exod 23:12). Faithfulness in keeping the Sabbath is as much about rest for the donkeys as it is rest for the slaves and all the people. What's more, after six years the land is given a Sabbath of sorts, a year when it is not planted, tended, or cultivated. This is indigenous wisdom—that we cannot work the soil perpetually without ruining it. Therefore, many traditional peoples the world over have practices of routinely fallowing their fields.

14. All Scripture quotations in this essay are from the NIV Bible unless otherwise indicated.

15. Davis, *Scripture, Culture, and Agriculture,* 26.

Finally, after seven cycles of seven, the Israelites are commanded to practice the Jubilee, the Sabbath of Sabbaths, when the debts are cancelled, the land given rest and returned to its original owner, and all those who have fallen into devastating debt are redeemed. What rationale is given for this radical program of communal redistribution? "The land shall not be sold in perpetuity, for the land is mine; with me you are but aliens and tenants" (Lev 25:23 NRSV). The anchor of what we might call the Old Testament land ethic is this understanding of conditional ownership: the land must only be used in a way that honors its true owner or else Israel's tenure can be revoked. Similarly, Israel's ethic of care for the marginalized is anchored in their memory and self-identity as those who were once living on the margins: "Do not oppress a foreigner; you yourselves know how it feels to be foreigners because you were foreigners in Egypt" (Exod 23:9). Because Israel has been exploited, they are called to actively resist exploitation in their land and to keep a special place for those who would otherwise fall into exploitation.

The prophets explicitly link Israel's exile from the land with their failure to obey God's law in the land. Isaiah states, "The earth lies polluted under its inhabitants; for they have transgressed laws, violated the statutes, broken the everlasting covenant" (24:5 NRSV). The prophet Jeremiah witnessed the same cascading breakdown of relationships:

> But this people has a rebellious and defiant heart, they have rebelled and gone their own way. They did not say to themselves, "Let us fear the Lord our God, who gives us the rains of autumn and spring showers in their turn, who brings us unfailingly fixed seasons of harvest." But your wrongdoing has upset nature's order, and your sins have kept from you her kindly gifts.[16]

Theologian Michael Northcott argues that prophetic witness to exile and destruction of the land is not the external imposition of a wrathful God, as often assumed.[17] Rather, God's judgment comes against human disobedience, and the effects of this disobedience have implications for the health of the ecosystems we inhabit. As Saint Augustine famously exclaimed, "The

16. Translation of Jer 5:23–25 by Northcott, *Environment*, 170.

17. Northcott, *Environment*. Beisner, in contrast to Northcott, argues: "Since God willingly causes devastation to the natural environment in response to man's sin . . . (a) God's highest priority must not be environmental preservation . . . (b) in God's grand purposes, human beings take precedence over the natural world, and (c) environmental degradation must sometimes be attributed to God's direct judgment" (Beisner, *Where Garden Meets Wilderness*, 49). For an alternative view of the Hebrew concept of the land and prophetic witness, see Brueggemann, *The Land*; Marlow, *Biblical Prophets*; and Fretheim, *God and World*.

punishment of every disordered mind is its own disorder."[18] The Hebrew prophets see the effects of this disorder not just in minds and hearts but also written across the landscapes in which we live. The disorder that the prophets witness is, in Northcott's words, "the consequence of the human rebellion against the created order and wisdom of nature," and as such, it reveals the failure of Israel to fulfill its vocation as light to the nations.[19]

By placing these themes from the Hebrew Bible alongside the bioregional framework I have already discussed, a number of important insights emerge. First, place is paramount to human identity and central to the people of God—and not just any place but a particular place and land that God calls the people of God to inhabit.[20] Second, the conditional nature of the human relationship to place is paramount. The Israelites' tenure in the land is the direct result of God's gift and their wise care for all its human and nonhuman inhabitants. If they fail to care for that land and its inhabitants, they lose the place they have been given. This is ancient wisdom: as goes the land, so too go we.

These sacred stories need to be read afresh as the church seeks to resist the widespread exploitation of both people and places and learns again how to reinhabit our places. Doing so demands that we first recognize and confess how we have been complicit in exploitation. Participation in a globally exploitative economy demands repentance and actively seeking to embody an alternative way of life that bioregionalists and others call reinhabitation. Doug Aberley writes, "*Reinhabitation* means learning to live-in-place in an area that has been disrupted and injured through past exploitation . . . It involves applying for membership in a biotic community and ceasing to be its exploiter."[21] As we apply for membership, we take up the church's historic practice of confession and repentance and in doing so demonstrate a patient willingness to change our course of action. This is what Franciscan theologian Keith Warner calls "eco-penance." Eco-penance, he writes, "promotes consistency between the statement of values we make about Creation and our behavior towards it . . . It includes a sense of personal responsibility for the environmental impact of our lifestyle, and that of our society, and will

---

18. Augustine, *Confessions*, 1.19.

19. Northcott, *Environment*, 171.

20. This insight must be nuanced against the more common restorationist or Zionist reading, which overlooks the real ways in which land tenure is always conditional, a point upon which Ellen Davis elaborates (Davis, *Scripture, Culture, and Agriculture*). It is beyond the scope of this essay, however, to engage further with Zionist readings of these texts. See Munayer and Loden, *Land Cries Out*, for a helpful introductory collection to these matters.

21. Aberley, "Interpreting Bioregionalism," 23.

lead to efforts to reduce the harmful effects that we have on other forms of life."[22] The complex nature of the ecological crisis now before us easily traps us in unhealthy patterns of denial, detachment, despair, and desperation.[23] Confession is a practice where we admit our waywardness honestly before God, receive grace and forgiveness, and recognize how we are failing to inhabit the world God has made. Penance demands we commit ourselves to positive and restorative practices that seek to bring about God's dream for this world—on earth as it is in heaven. We must do the self-work necessary to become effective workers in God's world. Thus, penance is not just *personal* work but also political and, indeed, ecological.

Theologian Philip Sheldrake writes, "Theological reflections on place can no longer ignore that the world of concrete places is full of exiles, displaced peoples, diaspora communities, increasingly inflamed border disputes and the violent struggles by indigenous people and cultural minorities to achieve liberation."[24] This makes it imperative that faith-based initiatives of placemaking attend carefully to their disputed places and to the people groups who have been historically deprived of place. Here there are no quick or easy answers. Instead, we have the practices of confession and penance: confessing our complacency in acts of displacement to others, and committing penance as we work with others in the hard work of reconciliation, restoration, and reinhabitation. This is essential to bioregional discipleship.

Israel suffers a shattering event in 597 BCE, when Nebuchadnezzar captures Jerusalem and sends many of the Israelites into exile in Babylon. Now scattered and bereft of their land and place, Israel struggles to understand what it means to be a people in a foreign land. The prophet Jeremiah instructs them:

> Build houses and settle down; plant gardens and eat what they produce. Marry and have sons and daughters; find wives for your sons and give your daughters in marriage, so that they too may have sons and daughters. Increase in number there; do not decrease. Also, seek the peace and prosperity of the city to which I have carried you into exile. Pray to the Lord for it, because if it prospers, you too will prosper. (Jer 29:5–7)

Here Jeremiah makes clear that the work of placemaking extends far beyond the boundaries of the promised land. This is not just work for Israel in its particular place and time. Rather, this is basic human work; it is reminiscent of what Adam and Eve were called to do in the beginning: inhabit the place

---

22. Warner, "Get Him Out," 372.

23. These four responses were first pointed out to me by Byron Smith.

24. Sheldrake, *Spaces for the Sacred*, 22.

you are given, tend the garden, be fruitful and multiply, and contribute to the flourishing of all who reside there. Having failed to do this in their own place, Israel now must relearn the path of reinhabitation in the land of their enemies. Working to "seek the peace and prosperity of the city" while in exile is a daily practice that teaches Israel that land use is in fact more vital to their identity than is land ownership. The health and well-being of any place is bound up with the health of all its creatures, and the human community plays an essential role in placemaking whether we are in Israel, in exile, or in all of the various places now inhabited by human communities.

The prospect of exile is one way of framing our present human predicament. We have failed to recognize that "the earth is the Lord's and everything in it" (Ps 24:1). We have too readily exploited both the land and its inhabitants for our benefit, and it now lies polluted. Yet this is precisely the reality within which we must begin the vital work of bioregional discipleship. McGinnis writes, "This is the condition within which the restorationist works: We are disabled creatures dislocated in a wounded landscape."[25] The world is wounded and deeply needs a people who are committed to reinhabiting their places and actively resisting all the forces that would continue to exploit creation and its vulnerable members—whether marginalized human beings or other species at risk. The church is a body that spans both space and time and, as such, forms a membership that spans all modern political boundaries. The call to bioregional discipleship, for this membership, is therefore a call to anchor our common life and spiritual practices in the particularity of place, no matter where we find ourselves or for how long. Foremost, a Christian ethic of placemaking must always recognize that we have no real claim to the land under foot except to receive it as God's gift. "If the ground can be our common ground," writes Snyder, "we can begin to talk to each other (human and nonhuman) once again."[26]

It is my conviction that rediscovering "the ground as our common ground" is crucial to discipleship today. This could begin in a community garden, a riverside cleanup, a march to save the wetlands, or a protest against a pipeline. It will undoubtedly require listening to the indigenous peoples who have inhabited our land as well as standing alongside them in efforts to care for it presently. If the bioregionalist authors are correct, as I suspect they are, we must confess we cannot care for the planet. Yet by joining together with our families, neighbors, churches, and communities, we can effectively begin to care for all of our places right now. As Berry has written, "The question that *must* be addressed, therefore, is not how to care for the

25. McGinnis et al., "Bioregional Restoration," 206.

26. Snyder, *Place*, 235.

planet, but how to care for each of the planet's millions of human and natural neighborhoods, each of its millions of small pieces and parcels of land, each one of which is in some precious way different from all the others."[27] May the church seek to join in this important work of reinhabitation and in so doing become the ambassadors of reconciliation that we are called to be.

BIBLIOGRAPHY

Aberley, Doug. "Interpreting Bioregionalism." In *Bioregionalism*, edited by Michael V. McGinnis, 13–42. New York: Routledge, 1999.

Augustine of Hippo. *The Confessions of St. Augustine*. Translated by Henry Chadwick. Oxford: Oxford University Press, 1992.

Bartholomew, Craig. *Where Mortals Dwell: A Christian View of Place for Today*. Grand Rapids: Baker Academic, 2011.

Beisner, E. Calvin. *Where Garden Meets Wilderness: Evangelical Entry into the Environmental Debate*. Grand Rapids: Eerdmans, 1997.

Berry, Wendell. "Out of Your Car, off Your Horse." In *Sex, Economy, Freedom, Community: Eight Essays*, 19–26. New York: Pantheon, 1992.

———. "Word and Flesh." In *What Are People For?*, 197–203. San Francisco: North Point, 1990.

Brueggemann, Walter. *The Land: Place as Gift, Promise, and Challenge in Biblical Faith*. Minneapolis: Fortress, 2002.

Davis, Ellen F. *Scripture, Culture, and Agriculture: An Agrarian Reading of the Bible*. Cambridge: Cambridge University Press, 2009.

Durning, Alan. *This Place on Earth: Home and the Practice of Permanence*. Seattle: Sasquatch, 1996.

Fretheim, Terence. *God and World in the Old Testament*. Nashville: Abingdon, 2005.

Lane, Belden. *Landscapes of the Sacred: Geography and Narrative in American Spirituality*. Baltimore: Johns Hopkins University Press, 2001.

Marlow, Hilary. *Biblical Prophets and Contemporary Environmental Ethics*. Oxford: Oxford University Press, 2009.

McGinnis, Michael V., et al. "Bioregional Restoration: Re-establishing an Ecology of Shared Identity." In *Bioregionalism*, edited by Michael V. McGinnis, 203–22. New York: Routledge, 1999.

———. "A Rehearsal to Bioregionalism." In *Bioregionalism*, edited by Michael V. McGinnis, 1–9. New York: Routledge, 1999.

Munayer, Salim J., and Lisa Loden, eds. *The Land Cries out: Theology of the Land in the Israeli-Palestinian Context*. Eugene, OR: Cascade, 2012.

Northcott, Michael S. *The Environment and Christian Ethics*. New Studies in Christian Ethics. Cambridge: Cambridge University Press, 1996.

Rasmussen, Larry. *Earth Community, Earth Ethics*. Maryknoll, NY: Orbis, 1996.

Sale, Kirkpatrick. *Dwellers in the Land: The Bioregional Vision*. Athens, GA: University of Georgia Press, 1985.

Sheldrake, Philip. *Spaces for the Sacred: Place, Memory, and Identity*. Baltimore: Johns Hopkins University Press, 2001.

27. Berry, "Word and Flesh," 200.

Snyder, Gary. *A Place in Space: Ethics, Aesthetics, and Watersheds.* Washington, DC: Counterpoint, 1995.

———. *The Practice of the Wild: Essays.* San Francisco: North Point, 1990.

Warner, Keith. "Get Him out of the Birdbath! What Does It Mean to Have a Patron Saint of Ecology?" In *Franciscan Theology of the Environment: An Introductory Reader*, edited by Dawn M. Nothwehr, 361–75. Quincy, IL: Franciscan, 2002.

11

The Theological Place of Land

Watershed Discipleship as Re-*placed* Cultural Vision

Laura Schmidt Roberts

Watershed discipleship asserts the centrality of land in the disciples' identity and vocation as "citizen inhabitants of specific places."[1] The church as
an intentional community of disciples is called to a journey of "re-*placement*"[2] (italics added) in which every aspect of the community's life and
commitments is reconfigured as disciples in and of the local environmental
watershed. This essay explores the theological place of land in watershed
discipleship by placing it in conversation with Mennonite theologian
Duane K. Friesen's theology of culture and with the theological grounding of a Great Plains land ethic co-developed by Friesen and environmental
educator Bradley Guhr. I begin by first sketching watershed discipleship
as articulated in the work of Ched Myers, moving next to examining the
theology of land present within Friesen's theology of culture and Friesen
and Guhr's land ethic. Engagement with these authors extends a watershed
discipleship theology in Anabaptist directions and explores ways in which
this radically contextual paradigm presents an alternative cultural vision of
re-*placed* ecclesial communities of disciples.

1. Myers, "Creation Care Watershed Discipleship," 266.
2. Ibid., 256.

WATERSHED DISCIPLESHIP

As Ched Myers points out, the watershed discipleship movement capitalizes on the triple entendre of its name in first identifying this point in history as a watershed moment.[3] Watershed discipleship insists that this crisis moment calls for "deep paradigm shifts *and* broad practical changes"[4] in Christian understandings of ecological justice and sustainability. These shifts in understanding find practical expression in a radical discipleship focusing on place—that is, the actual environmental watershed in which disciples are located. This second sense of the term points to the fact that "our discipleship and the life of the local church take place *in* a watershed context,"[5] knowingly or not. As a result, in the third sense of the term, it is imperative to become disciples *of* the watershed also, learning by observing, serving, and preserving.[6]

Myers calls for a shift to a re-placed discipleship model that takes bioregionalism as its paradigm. Bioregionalism helps move beyond a theology of stewardship of the earth "to a theology of *interrelationship*, which stresses the inherent value of creation over its utility value."[7] Creation care movements help recalibrate Christian theology in this direction, but Myers insists that a more radical response is necessitated by the current crisis. What we need is a conversion to place, a reclamation of incarnational faith in localized settings. Especially at this crisis moment in history, Myers argues, "the best way to orient the church's work and witness is through *bioregionally-*grounded [emphasis mine] planning and action which focuses on the actual *watersheds* [emphasis in original] we inhabit."[8] In this way, the watershed paradigm "roots [broader notions of] Creation Care in place, offering a radical yet practical approach."[9] Central to this paradigm is the recognition that watersheds are themselves communities. Myers employs Brock Dolman's analogy of a "cradle" into which water flows from the high places and ridges. For Dolman, this cradle is best construed as a "basin of relations"[10] in which, Myers explains, "every living organism is interconnected and dependent on

---

3. Ibid., 265–66.
4. "What is Watershed Discipleship?," line 8.
5. Myers, "Bartimaeus Letter."
6. Myers, "Reflection on Isaiah 5," 11.
7. Myers, "Theologies of the Land," lines 39–41.
8. "What is Watershed Discipleship?," lines 19–20.
9. Myers, "Creation Care to Watershed Discipleship," 265.
10. Dolman, *Basins of Relations*, 6.

the health of the whole."[11] The community of disciples must be reoriented in their basin of relations as disciples *in* and *of* their environmental watershed.

Myers explains that such reorientation requires "education, advocacy, and organizing in four key areas": first, a re-placed theology and spirituality that "reclaims symbols of redemption indigenous to the bioregion in which the church dwells";[12] second, ecological readings of Scripture; third, a watershed ecclesiology in which communal identity and practices are reshaped by the local landscape (from architecture to Eucharistic elements to retreat topics to mission trip destinations); fourth, solidarity with traditional people of place. For Myers, watershed discipleship bears "a special responsibility" to connect justice and peacemaking concerns to the "ongoing story and struggle of the original inhabitants" of the watershed.[13]

Such intentional strategies to nurture consciousness and action are necessary, Myers observes, because of the Western church's complicity in the current ecological crisis. He traces this reality to what he identifies as three interrelated theological errors: first, a "functional docetism" that has "numbed [us] to the escalating horrors of both social and ecological violence";[14] second, an "anthropological presumption that humans rule over Creation . . . [which] rationalizes how modern technological development has exploited and re-engineered nature to benefit human settlement alone";[15] third, "a theology and/or politics of 'divinely ordained' entitlement to land and resources,"[16] that rejects any limits on production or consumption and denies any responsibility for restoration when harm is done. All three errors share what Myers terms "a fantasy of human autonomy that refuses the imperative of creatureliness—to live within the limits *of* the earth."[17]

In response and in contrast, Myers calls for an eco-theology that is thoroughly incarnate, symbiotic, and sustainable. The return to the earth—to our watershed—as disciples, is the only way forward in the present crisis for Myers. This return is a conversion to *place*, a journey of "re-*place*-ment" (italics added) reflected in every aspect of disciples' lives and commitments.[18]

---

11. Myers, "Creation Care to Watershed Discipleship," 258.

12. Myers, "Creation Care to Watershed Discipleship" (presentation)

13. Ibid.

14. Myers, "Creation Care to Watershed Discipleship," 253.

15. Ibid.

16. Ibid.

17. Ibid., 253–54.

18. Ibid., 256.

THEOLOGICAL PLACE OF LAND IN WATERSHED DISCIPLESHIP

The foregoing brief sketch begins to make evident the centrality of land in watershed discipleship, despite the paradigm's "water" framework. Myers insists that "the most important theological and practical journey of our time is to reclaim and restore our sense of place in and on the land."[19] This journey stands in sharp contrast to the "dominant culture of urban modernity" whose characteristics are "displacement and alienation from land and place."[20] Urban modernity has "built a culture which defies the land and its limits,"[21] normalizing patterns of domestic life, work, and leisure that are unnatural to the land on which they take place. In the words of Wendell Berry, we must rather "[re]construct our economic life upon the 'demands of affection' for the land, cognizant of our place in the Great Economy [of nature]."[22]

The journey of re-*place*-ment denies the "fantasy of human autonomy," instead embracing "the imperative of creatureliness [striving] . . . to live within the limits *of* the earth."[23] It calls for a theological re-grounding in which the land itself is central. For Myers, this re-grounding is *radical* in the sense of returning to roots at the heart of the biblical tradition: creation, covenant, and incarnation. In terms of *creation*, "watershed discipleship asserts the priority of Creation over all ideological or hegemonic claims."[24] The intrinsic (vs. utilitarian) value of creation, and of the land in turn, fundamentally recasts human identity and role. Asserting the priority of creation "re-centers anthropology in placed creatureliness, defined by symbiosis and servanthood, not by objectification and domination," according to Myers. Rather, this re-grounding in creation shifts the primary human vocation from re-engineering creation for human benefit to "rediscover[ing] communion with, and our proper place in, the community of earth."[25]

In terms of *covenant*, "a watershed hermeneutic remembers that the core narrative of the Hebrew Bible concerns a people covenanting with God and with specific land as caretakers of the divine gift."[26] The call is, in a sense,

19. Myers, "Reflection on Isaiah 5," 7.
20. Ibid.
21. Myers, "Economics of Place," lines 15–16.
22. Ibid., lines 19–20.
23. Myers, "Creation Care to Watershed Discipleship," 253–54.
24. Ibid., 267.
25. Ibid., 267–68.
26. Ibid., 267.

to view the land in/on which we find ourselves as land to which our identity as God's people, and our well-being, are inextricably linked. Our task is to re-inhabit our own location *as church*.[27] Covenant reminds us that human culture is "dependent upon the hospitality of the land that both constrains it and sustains it," the land that is divine gift.[28] In his extended reflection on the Song of the Vineyard from Isa 5, Myers explains that "without deep affection for our place and people, we can hardly be part of the vast work of healing and reconstruction that faces us."[29] Affection, healing, reconstruction—these reflect a covenant with the land.

Recalling the covenant narrative builds toward the notion of *incarnation*. The biblical witness attests to a God present, active, and known in history, most fully and completely in Jesus, who is "Emmanuel . . . God is with us" (Matt 1:23)[30]—"a terrestrial Jesus,"[31] as Myers calls him. Incarnation points to the fundamentally located nature of human existence. We are born and live and take a stand some place. Jesus is born into and walks the land. He teaches from it. He washes it from the disciples' feet. Jesus was located, a person inhabiting a place. Myers insists Jesus's followers today continue the incarnational reality of the gospel witness through embrace of a similar locatedness: "Personal and political disciplines of re-place-ment are key for both Christian identity re-formation and the church's gospel witness to be truly contextual today."[32] Ecclesial and missional conversations most often focus on questions of contextualization in terms of human culture and language. Watershed discipleship presses for recognition that culture develops in a place, and it calls for reconstructions of contextualization from the ground up. Along similar lines, theologians and biblical scholars have for some time now emphasized the fact that we understand God, articulate our faith, and read and interpret the Bible from a particular location. But this, too, is usually cast in terms of a social location focusing on cultural ethnic, gender, socioeconomic, and ecclesial situatedness. Watershed discipleship calls for theologizing not just *about* the land but *from* it. It calls for drawing imagery and analogies and yes, even lessons, from the chapter and verse of the Book of Creation in which we find ourselves; to theologize as true inhabitants, as ones among the earth community, as disciples *in* and *of* a

27. Ibid., 272.

28. Myers, "Economics of Place," lines 13–14.

29. Myers, "Reflection on Isaiah 5," 1.

30. All Scripture quotations in this essay are from the NRSV Bible unless otherwise indicated.

31. Myers, "Creation Care to Watershed Discipleship," 267.

32. Ibid., 256.

watershed. Myers's refrain is that "we have lost our way as creatures of God's biosphere [as ones among and dependent on it] and only the map woven into Creation can lead us home." The way is the journey of re-*place*-ment.[33]

FRIESEN'S THEOLOGY OF CULTURE

In his book *Artists, Citizens, Philosophers: Seeking the Peace of the City*, Duane Friesen locates his work on ethics and theology of culture in the "culturally engaged" stream of Anabaptist-Mennonite tradition.[34] His theology of culture reflects a historical consciousness characterized by tension, ambiguity, and polarity, and an acute awareness that cultural and autobiographical experiences shape one's viewpoint. Thus, he insists that Christian traditions are best understood as presenting various *cultural visions*, meaning they fundamentally orient the lives of their participants. This orientation is learned, practiced and negotiated. And it is not singular. Friesen explains his own boyhood experience in the Mennonite community as "not against culture (as if [the church community] were some entity separate from culture)" but rather as entailing "a cultural vision that was both in harmony with and in tension with other cultural perspectives."[35] The image he employs for this is that of *dual citizenship*. "Christian existence was for us life on the edge," he explains "at the boundary, not between this world and another world but on the [overlapping] boundaries between a variety of cultural alternatives."[36] Dual citizenship calls for both embodying an alternative cultural vision and engaging the larger culture; it calls for living in the overlap. The community of faith takes on an alternative (but not exclusive) identity distinct from the dominant culture while also participating in society. This seems an apt description of the watershed discipleship call for re-placed ecclesial communities marked by a conversion to place, living out an incarnational faith in localized settings to counter the placelessness and alienation of the dominant culture. The watershed paradigm presents an alternative vision that requires a journey of re-orientation and re-*place*-ment as disciples in and of the watershed.

So how might these ideas of dual citizenship and a community oriented by an alternative cultural vision help further develop a theology of watershed discipleship? In part, they locate watershed discipleship as an approach resonant with a believers church ecclesiology. Friesen's dual

33. Ibid., 256. For Myers's discussion of the journey of re-place-ment, see 254–56.

34. Friesen, *Artists, Citizens, Philosophers*, 15.

35. Friesen, "Anabaptist Theology of Culture," 36.

36. Ibid.

citizenship draws on three elements of historical Anabaptism—elements particularly relevant for the twenty-first-century church and core to a watershed theology:

> (1) the emphasis on voluntary commitment to an alternative value system defined by commitment to Jesus Christ as the central loyalty for Christian existence; (2) a community defined by mutual support for each other and committed to a process of disciplined discernment about what it means to be faithful in ethical practice; and (3) a community oriented toward mission to the larger world, engaged within the wider culture in sharing in word and deed a vision for the shalom (well-being) of the city wherever the church dwells.[37]

The notion of dual citizenship, grounded in the above elements, helps clarify the centrality of the re-placed ecclesial communities that watershed discipleship calls for. Cultural visions fundamentally orient the lives of their participants. The orientation is learned, practiced, and negotiated. The community is central because watershed discipleship, as an alternative vision, requires re-formation of lifeways. An alternative vision must be cultivated and sustained in contrast to but also in engagement with other visions. In cultural anthropology language, the community's *focal practices* do this. These practices center, sustain, and order the community's ways of being, living, and behaving. They provide the observable expressions of the vision. These visible, concrete ways of living are defined by a community of practitioners over time. Focal practices are taught to and learned from others, as persons are socialized or catechized into the disciplined community of the alternative vision.[38] When Myers describes a watershed ecclesiology in which "the natural landscapes . . . shape our symbolic life, social engagements, and material habits,"[39] he is talking about the focal practices of the alternative community that make the alternative vision observable.[40]

37. Ibid., 37. Myers himself articulates the "Anabaptist resonances" of watershed discipleship along similar lines, arguing the paradigm is congruent with Anabaptist vision and faith. See Myers, "Creation Care to Watershed Discipleship," 272–75.

38. Friesen, *Artists, Citizens, Philosophers*, 139–41.

39. Myers, "Creation Care to Watershed Discipleship," 272.

40. Friesen discusses several kinds of focal practices in considerable detail. Process practices include a dialogical process of discernment, the practice of reconciliation, and the recognition of gifts. Pastoral care practices, engaged by all in the community, may be characterized broadly as mutual aid reflecting the sense that all in the community are brothers and sisters in the household of faith. Practices of service to the wider community include voluntary service, the development of alternative organizations, and peacemaking. Friesen, *Artists, Citizens, Philosophers*, 139–66.

The idea of "practices" denotes intentionality and formation, and ritual practices of moral formation are particularly important for Friesen. In rituals, "the church is reoriented with reference to its ultimate center of concern (Tillich) and by the vision of life reflected in its view of reality (Geertz)."[41] Rituals such as baptism and the Lord's Supper, whether viewed sacramentally or more symbolically, link the ordinary and the extraordinary. They provide a visible marker and tangible sign of things that are central to the church's faith and identity but are often difficult to grasp or articulate—things like grace, and incarnation, and new life. The watershed invitation to use local waters, bread, and wine for baptism and the Lord's Supper, makes tangible the vision of life re-orienting the community of disciples. This vision insists that our identity and well-being are inextricably linked to the rest of the creation community, specifically the chapter of the Book of Creation we actually inhabit. A theology of culture approach provides a framework for what watershed disciples already know practically: at this crisis moment in history, the necessary change will not come by chance. It requires a cultural shift, a conversion, and intentional practices of formation and witness.

FRIESEN AND GUHR'S LAND ETHIC

One other aspect of Friesen's work presents theological resources for building a watershed discipleship theology, including a theology of land. In a piece entitled "*Metanoia* and Healing: Toward a Great Plains Land Ethic," Friesen and co-author Bradley Guhr argue for the necessity of developing a localized "land ethic from knowing intimately the rich texture of the ecology" of a region.[42] They use the classical Greek elements of earth, wind, water, and fire to explore "the long, slow, dynamic evolutionary process"[43] of the region's geological history. Then, they use the same four elements to identify concrete practices "that address threats to the Great Plains ecosystem, and that offer alternative paths to healing between we humans and the earth community." These "practices of *metanoia* and healing"—practices born of conversion and re-orientation to place—are carefully set in a theological framework.[44] I want to comment on two of the most important theological assertions in Friesen's land ethic: first, the idea of "seeing as sacramental

---

41. Friesen, *Artists, Citizens, Philosophers*, 141.
42. Friesen and Guhr, "*Metanoia* and Healing," 727.
43. Ibid., 733.
44. Ibid., 735–36.

presence"; and second, the convictions grounding his explicitly theocentric framework.[45]

1. Seeing as Sacramental Presence

Drawing on Gospel texts such as Luke 8:10, Friesen and Guhr recall Jesus's words: "Looking they may not perceive, and listening they may not understand." They characterize the notion of learning to see as central to the life and teachings of Jesus. More specifically, they argue that "one who sees well is passionately oriented to 'place,' not just any place, but the wonder and mystery of the particular place where she lives." This passionate orientation, this "seeing," generates passionate action rooted in feelings of belonging and loyalty to place. The "wonder and mystery" of that particular place indicate the presence of the sacred for the authors.[46] Resonances with watershed discipleship's emphasis on the intrinsic value of the land, the deep affection for the land and its people, and Myers's notion of the land as divine gift are evident here. In terms of fruitful generative possibilities for expanding watershed theology, I will note three things briefly.

First, these reflections remind watershed disciples of a rich storehouse of biblical imagery for framing and fueling watershed literacy and advocacy efforts. How do we move ourselves, our congregations, our communities from blindness to sight, from deafness to hearing, from silence to speech? Disciples *of* the watershed must learn to see what's really going on in their basins of relation. Friesen and Guhr remind us that to do so is central to following Jesus's life and teaching.

Second, for the authors, part of learning to see (following Martin Buber) entails recognizing the land as a "Thou" versus an "it."[47] This means we are in a relationship with an other—as opposed to observing an object—when we encounter the land and the earth community as a whole. This assertion advances Myers's critique of a "presumptive superiority"[48] that objectifies and dominates the land. Land as "Thou" provides another conceptual framework for an alternative understanding of our relationship to the land as a relationship *with* the land. Myers's insistence on restorative justice as central to a watershed ethos, and Elaine Enns's work applying

45. Ibid., 727. Friesen and Guhr also explore several guiding metaphors for a land ethic that are largely tied to biblical imagery: (1) covenant, (2) restoration of broken relationships, (3) cultivating as serving the land, (4) various meanings of *oikos* and terms related to this root (earth as God's home or household, ecology, economics, ecumenical). See Friesen and Guhr, "*Metanoia* and Healing," 734–35.

46 Friesen and Guhr, "*Metanoia* and Healing," 727–28.

47. Ibid. For Buber, see *I and Thou.*

48. Myers, "Creation Care to Watershed Discipleship," 267.

restorative justice principles to the victimization of non-human creation,[49] already move in this direction, as does Myers's insistence that "the land itself is an historic subject whose story must be learned."[50] What might it mean to more clearly elaborate a watershed and its land as a "Thou" that disciples are in relationship with? The I-Thou notion presents a fruitful model for building the relational interdependence central to recasting human role and self-understanding as "placed creatureliness."[51]

Third, and perhaps most significantly, the wonder and mystery that is part of seeing well for Friesen and Guhr indicates the presence of the sacred. They link this awareness with "sacrament," "the sense that we are in the presence of the sacred as we commune in the presence of soil, wind, water, and fire. As we experience and ponder our relationship to the earth community that is in us and we in it, at a deep level we come to know a profound mystery, a sense that we are in the presence of God."[52] What might it mean to think of *sacramental presence* as basic to what the land is *as land*? Or to consider land itself as sacrament? The emphasis on the intrinsic value of the land in watershed discipleship is clear, as is the sense of our dependence on it. How might these be built to clarify the sacramental nature of land as a visible, efficacious sign of invisible grace (to use one traditional Roman Catholic description)? Or as a "sign" or symbol that dispenses life?[53] How might watershed discipleship practices be framed in relation to an understanding of land as sacrament or sacramental presence, or as symbol? These notions are both grounded in the material and assume that encounter with the sustaining presence of the divine is part of the land's very being.

2. A Theocentric Framework

Lastly, Friesen and Guhr identify four interrelated convictions at the core of the explicitly theocentric framework for their land ethic: a) a necessary humility on the part of humans, as coming from and returning to the dust; b) recognition that earth is a community of which humans as earth-lings are an integral part; c) recognition that as part of creation, humans are in a covenant relationship with the God on whom we also utterly depend; and d) a necessary balance between humans "being *of* the earth and ethically

49. Enns, "Relevance of Restorative Justice."

50. Myers, "Creation Care to Watershed Discipleship," 264.

51. Ibid., 267.

52. Friesen and Guhr, "*Metanoia* and Healing," 727–28.

53. Tillich's understanding of a symbol is (a) something that participates in the reality it represents but also points beyond it; (b) something that opens up levels of reality that otherwise are closed for us; and (c) something shared or communal that provides many related avenues for development. Tillich, *Dynamics*, 41–43.

accountable to God *for* the earth."[54] They summarize a theocentric ethic as an alternative to an anthropocentric worldview and a biocentrism "that simply locates human beings as one species among others on earth, and that reverences nature as holy in and of itself."[55] They argue that a theocentric ethic best addresses the need for balance in the understanding of humanity's place as being both *of* the earth and accountable *for* the earth.

As watershed discipleship gains momentum as a movement, it is important to think carefully about its theological assumptions and assertions; to cultivate understanding and articulation of these (as well as of practices), in a way that is rooted in the biblical narrative. Friesen and Guhr's articulation of theocentrism and the clarity of humanity's dual role (a different kind of dual citizenship?) are particularly promising for further developing a watershed discipleship theology. Their explanation of the dual human role of belonging to the earth community of a particular place, and inheriting and perpetuating a human culture that has transformed the earth community's ecosystems, underscores the need for an adequate theological anthropology. Such an understanding of the human person must address human capacity for self-transcendence—the capacity "to view from outside . . . the earth community," to learn "to see, to know in an intimate way what is going on."[56] For Friesen and Guhr, humanity's unique relationship to the rest of creation yields a unique ethical responsibility.[57]

In a similar vein, watershed discipleship asserts the centrality of land and the "priority of Creation over all ideological or hegemonic claims,"[58] insisting on the intrinsic (vs. utilitarian) value of creation. Myers, too, makes evident the widespread necessity of a deconstructed and reconstructed anthropology and view of creation. These are profoundly theological issues. Our understanding of creation, our identity as part of it, and the insistence on our unique responsibility in relationship with it, are grounded in a Creator God who makes a person out of dirt to be *placed* in a harmonious community of life with the charge to cultivate and serve (Gen 2). Our understanding of the intrinsic value of creation is rooted in a Creator God who in Gen 1 declares each precious part of the emerging community of life to be good in and of itself, just as it is.

54. Friesen and Guhr, "*Metanoia* and Healing," 728–29.

55. Ibid., 733.

56. Ibid., 730, 727.

57. Ibid., 729–30.

58. Myers, "Creation Care to Watershed Discipleship," 267.

THE GROUND AHEAD

In terms of theological agenda, two working fronts emerge from the above explorations: (1) A theology of creation that adequately recognizes the intrinsic, innate value of creation. As "cultivators," we still tend to think in utilitarian terms vs. aesthetic. (2) A theological anthropology that frames humanity's unique role in a way that still asserts and values our full creatureliness. Aspects of a theology of culture model and Friesen and Guhr's land ethic present fruitful ground for further developing a watershed discipleship theology in these directions.

BIBLIOGRAPHY

Buber, Martin. *I and Thou*. New York: Scribner's Sons, 1958.

Dolman, Brock. *Basins of Relations: A Citizen's Guide to Protecting and Restoring Our Watersheds*. Occidental, CA: Water Institute, 2008.

Enns, Elaine. "The Relevance of Restorative Justice to Ecotheology." Paper presented at the Mennonite Scholars & Friends Forum, American Academy of Religion Meeting, Baltimore, MD, November 23, 2013.

Friesen, Duane K. *Artists, Citizens, Philosophers: Seeking the Peace of the City: An Anabaptist Theology of Culture*. Scottdale, PA: Herald, 2000.

———. "An Anabaptist Theology of Culture for a New Century." *Conrad Grebel Review* 13 (1995) 33–53.

Friesen, Duane K., and Bradley Guhr. "*Metanoia* and Healing: Toward a Great Plains Land Ethic." *Journal of Religious Ethics* 37 (2009) 723–53.

Myers, Ched. "Bartimaeus Cooperative Ministries Partner Letter." May 2014.

———. "Economics of Place and the Problem of Environmental 'Greenwashing.'" *Ched's Blog*, September 9, 2011. Ched's Blog, http://chedmyers.org/blog/2011/09/09/economics-place-and-problem-environmental-greenwashing (accessed September 14, 2014).

———. "From 'Creation Care' to 'Watershed Discipleship': An Anabaptist Approach to Ecological Theology and Practice." Paper presented at the Mennonite Scholars & Friends Forum, American Academy of Religion Meeting, Baltimore, MD, November 23, 2013.

———. "From 'Creation Care' to 'Watershed Discipleship': Re-Placing Ecological Theology and Practice." *Conrad Grebel Review* 32 (2014) 250–75.

———. "A Reflection on Isaiah 5, Ecological Solipsism, and 'Watershed Discipleship.'" http://chedmyers.org/system/files/watershed%20discipleship%20Isaiah%20%20 solastalgia.pdf (accessed September 5, 2014).

———. "Theologies of the Land." Ched's Blog, April 22, 2011. http://chedmyers.org/blog/2011/04/22/theologies-land (accessed September 14, 2014).

Tillich, Paul. *Dynamics of Faith*. New York: Harper & Row, 1957.

"What is Watershed Discipleship?" Watershed Discipleship: The Creation Waits, http://watersheddiscipleship.org/ (accessed July 15, 2015).

12

A Curse More Ancient?

J. Matthew Bonzo

Most of us who work from within the Christian tradition understand Gen 3 as the dividing point between things as they should be and when things go awry. Those among us who spend time in gardens other than Eden cringe when we hear "both thorns and the thistles it shall grow" (Gen 3:18 NASB) listed within the implications resulting from the fall of humanity. The emphasis on the curse leading to frustrating work is no surprise to us. Hard work itself, even when it causes us to taste the sweat of our brow, is not the problem. We do not easily grow weary or frustrated when preparing the soil to receive the seed, or in digging the furrows and placing chunks of potatoes just so; everything is too new, too clean, too ordered and full of potential. The field lying ready for planting beckons us to productive work.

The curse described in the Gen 3 account is not experienced on our soil until a couple of weeks later when the disorder of weeds and volunteer plants starts to make a mockery of the ideal garden we had imagined just days before. Our souls and bodies tire as we labor to keep the wrong things from growing. If you are like my wife, for whom any weed in her garden is a sign of weakness in her character, you take the endless threat of errant green appearing between your rows as a constant spiritual challenge. This struggle against disorder continues beyond even the productive season of the garden as we plot and work toward minimizing next year's weeds. The curse exhausts us not simply because it makes us work but because it threatens to overwhelm our work that is ordered toward an end.

But as we become increasingly aware of the degradation of the environment linked with our demand for more energy and more stuff, as we feel the loss of green space resulting from the never-ending expansion of the suburbs into farmland, and as we deal with the negative impacts of increased mechanization and technological mediation of agriculture itself, we are left to wonder if it is not the very presence of human beings that is the true scourge within creation—a curse more ancient than Gen 3. Or to state the problem more precisely, it may be that the issue is not our presence but the way we attempt to impose our order on the land itself. The pristine garden may have cured one scourge, but in implementing the cure, it may have revealed a deeper affliction.

Several of the essays in Wes Jackson's *Nature as Measure* investigate the impact of agricultural activity upon the land. His "Living Nets in a New Prairie Sea"[1] repeats a story told by Joseph Kinsey Howard that gave me pause last spring at about the time I was planning our community supported agriculture garden for the year. Jackson, of the Kansas Land Institute, is concerned with the health and sustainability of the soil, especially given the toll that contemporary agricultural practices take upon the land. In these essays, Jackson reiterates a couple of accounts that highlight the tension between the human ordering of the soil and the long-term well-being of the soil. As retold by Jackson, Howard describes a scene from 1883 when the plows of the settlers first broke open the rich soil of the plains. The virgin ground yielded under the force of the plow as it ripped through the thick prairie grass, exposing what was beneath almost like opening a zipper. This new ordering revealed a new kind of power being exercised upon this particular plot of earth. Apparently, a Native American watching from a point nearby quipped to the farmer, "Wrong side up."[2] The fertility of the plain that had been naturally maintained by the cycle of grasses growing and decaying and the soil being stirred up by passing bison was now being threatened by a disruption of that rhythm. Indeed, the world was being turned upside down as the old order was giving way to a new order that depended upon human powers being used to overcome the wildness of the land. Was irreparable harm being done to the soil? Would this disruption make sustaining the vitality of the land dependent upon external additives? Would it threaten the very existence of the soil? Does nature intend soil to be this way? History suggests we know some of the answers to these questions and that this reordering by agriculture has done damage to both soil and water. Turning the world upside down produces a field whose benefit has an expiration date.

1. Jackson, "Living Nets," 139.
2. Ibid.

In Jackson's second anecdote, he makes the case that some human ordering in a particular place may affect the natural cycle in such a fundamental way that it becomes impossible to imagine the way in which the soil could be repaired.[3] Jackson tells of walking in a forested area with colleagues who were also interested in the health and sustainability of the soil. In this instance, they were walking around old trees that had contributed their leaves and roots to the surrounding soil for years. His colleagues described how long it had taken for the leaves from these trees to form such fertile soil. The soil was nearly perfect in its content and structure. Its life-yielding nature needed no enhancement from human activity. Yet in its vitality, the soil was also fragile. The ease with which one could weaken this soil was alarming but not nearly as alarming as the hopeless task of trying to replicate or repair that soil. To cut down those trees and to plow that soil would interrupt the life-yielding cycle. The attempt to enhance the productivity of this particular soil through human ordering might not lead to immediate devastation, but it would break the natural rhythm between life and death and offer an inferior rhythm in its place.

Jackson's short narration about the condition of the soil in these places prompted me to question once again if I was doing the right thing in preparing our farm's land for planting. Was the curse of weeds and sweaty work hiding from me the curse more ancient? Would my farm, my place, be better off without me? If any human agricultural activity, no matter how carefully attended to, can degrade a rich, vital soil that got that way without human intervention, why did I think I was improving it? It seemed that Jackson was leading me to conclude that the good of agriculture always came at the cost of the soil. I am not thinking of soil here as some sort of platonic, static ideal that change fundamentally corrupts. For, as Jackson's descriptions of soil show, soil is dynamic by nature. An unchanging soil is a dead soil. The soil of the plains grew rich, in part, because the bison trod over it, mixing in organic material, and the forest soil gained health as the decomposed leaves blended with the existing soil. Healthy soil is the result of a process, and the presence of humans can interrupt the process. I seemed to be trapped between farming the land—with the threat of leaving the place worse off upon leaving it—or simply letting the land return to the wild and losing a sustaining connection to the land.

In thinking about human ordering within creation and the impact that human presence has on soil, it is easy to become overly nostalgic or even romantic, possibly to the point of agricultural existential paralysis. Imagining a time when the earth was untouched by human hands, with

3. Jackson, "Nature as Measure," 75.

the result of layer upon layer of rich humus, may tell us something about our world, but it is of limited value in helping us think about what we are to do when we humans do show up on the scene. And, of course, there is the puzzling question of which "pure" state of affairs we are trying to preserve. As mentioned, the dynamic nature of nature can produce radical changes in a place over time. There is little justification to privilege a particular time.

Even though trying to reclaim or return a time past offers little direction, we do still have experiences of wild soil. These virgin soils have either never been tilled or disturbed by agriculture, or have been allowed to re-wild for whatever reason. The ideal of soil untouched by human hands is a little too optimistic, for the touch of our hands has so expanded that we sometimes have an unintended global presence. The spread of chemicals in air and water has been thoroughly researched and has revealed that human-made chemicals produced in North America show up, for instance, in Antarctica by accident. It may be that there is no earthly place beyond the reach of our industrial practices. In spite of our inadvertent spread of our technological presence, wild soil does remain and offers a standard by which we can measure the health of our activity. We do not have to try and get behind what I have called the "more ancient curse of human existence" in order to ground a set of norms for our interactions with the earth.

Wendell Berry is right in describing the soil itself as wild.[4] You do not have to go to a state park or even out of the city to experience soil as wild. In part, what Berry means by "wild" is that the soil is beyond being understood in a reductionistic, scientist way. There is always more to the soil than its chemical makeup or pH level. So, as important as taking these measurements may be for some understanding of the health of a soil and what it can grow, not everything can be learned about soil by putting it under the microscope or in a test tube. The soil needs to be watched and slowly observed within the context in which it "lives." Berry goes as far as to say that the soil needs to be known in love by a sympathetic mind.[5] This mind asks not only, What can I get from the land? but also, What does the land need from me?

Any soil worthy of its name is wild when understood sympathetically. But I would add the assertion that in order to know soil in its wholeness, rather than trying to know it completely, we need some soil to be left in the wild. In the wild, we can perhaps see the natural processes more clearly. And from these processes, we can learn the soil's way of health, and, maybe most importantly, we can learn the limits of the soil so as to farm in an

4. Berry, "Preserving Wildness," 140.
5. Berry, "Two Minds," 88.

anticipatory way rather than simply trying to repair the damage once it has been done. We need unattended wild growth soil as much, if not more, than we need old growth trees. And we need this soil in both large and small scales.

Though I have not done a large-scale survey of soil to see how much soil remains untilled or untouched in the world, I do not think I am being overly optimistic to suggest that there is enough wild land to preserve in the face of the dire predictions regarding the increased need for food production. Even if the assertion that one-fifth of the land in China is undeveloped is an overstatement, there seems to be enough land to protect for the purpose I am suggesting. Many protected areas already exist throughout the world, and these areas function as more than places to escape from the noise and stress of urban life. While there may be some question regarding how analogous the protected lands are to the land where we do much of our agriculture, we can compare our observations of the wild soil of the protected places with the wild soil surrounding our own gardens and fields. When Berry proposes that farmers should leave the fence rows around their fields undeveloped, he does so not simply to allow a place for wildlife but also to leave a place for the wild life of the soil. The fence or a fallow field is a place where the farmer can study the soil and use that knowledge for her nurturing of the land.

When we first moved to our farm, our fence row was dominated by sumac trees. The sumac is often dismissed as a weed tree, and I must admit that I was not a big fan of it. I'm still not enthralled by it, but it is starting to grow on me. I have come to realize that when the soil is stripped of vegetation, it requires some type of plant to help hold its structure—and the quicker the better. In our sandy soil, the sumac is one of the first plants to appear after the soil has been cleared, and so there was evidence that our fence row had been cleared not too long before we bought the farm. But now along our fence line, the sumac have slowly started to die off as more "preferable" trees (oaks, poplars) start to mature. While I won't be planting sumacs in my garden any time soon, I have learned something about the damage done by leaving the soil exposed and about how I can change my practices to keep from overexposing the soil in my garden. Nor will I let the willows spread from our wetland into the hayfield. The order of a farm field is threatened by the wild disorder of an undeveloped fence line or swamp unless the field approaches infertility through chemical control. Only by the sweat of our brow do we maintain order in the hayfield and garden, but even as we do so, we learn lessons from the wild soil on the boundaries of our work.

So we can protect small wild spaces on our own. But the need remains for bigger spaces such as the forest and the plains. These need to be protected so that we can learn how the natural health of soil is sustained and even restored. We need the wild spaces not only so we can experience the difference of a wild setting but also to teach how to be in the tamed places.

The ideal of a pure soil that exists before the curse of human existence can offer us a caution and a reminder that creation is not dependent upon us for its life. But awareness of this limit is not sufficient in and of itself to guide our practices of agriculture. Rather, we must get our hands dirty, as it were, in order to know which soil should be nurtured for agriculture, in what ways it can replicate the natural process, and what it needs from its caretakers. In such questions we do not encounter the limits that prevent agriculture; rather, these limits guide our stewarding of the land. I playfully suggested earlier that nature intended soil to be a certain way. This could not be further from the truth. As a confessing Christian, I don't believe that nature "intends" anything. Creation's purpose does not lie within itself. Simply protecting the original state of soil, or anything else for that matter, is not the end of the biblical narrative. While other than human creation may be able to sing its praises to its creator without a human presence, human beings play a vital role in nurturing and developing and adding our voice to the song of creation.

To imagine a past creation where human beings are absent, and to project a future where creation is restored without human beings, is not the biblical vision. Nor does such a vision ground hope for us as we live in a creation increasingly populated by human beings. Immediately preceding the account of the curse in Gen 3 is, of course, the mandate given in Gen 1–2 to be God's image bearers. Human beings are called not only to populate the earth but also to make it their place by nurturing and cultivating creation. The initial language of human activity is agricultural. Making our home in this creation and unfolding the possibilities of creation in our daily activities is at the heart of who we are and what we do.

To state my point a little differently, while we may be able to make the distinction between nature and culture, the biblical story knows nothing of an opposition between nature and culture. The cultural mandate is not meant as undertaking the task to make nature submit to the rule of culture. Rather, I would describe the human calling to know the world in such a loving, sympathetic way that we see its particular potentialities and recognize ways that allow those potentialities to develop. I think parenting is a great analogy here. To love your child is not to remain ignorant of her talents and desires but to help her find faithful ways to live them out. Just as the great lie for our children is "you can be anything you want to be," so also the great lie for our soil is that it can be used in any way we want.

As we know all too well, soil can be used and abused. From nearly the beginning of agriculture, the production of food has been linked with violence. The way the stories of agriculture have been told has helped to make this violence possible. When the story of our relationship to the soil begins with the idea that soil is a scarce resource that we must somehow tightly control, what usually follows is a plan for its use that is more rooted in what we want from the land rather than the possibilities that the land holds. And depending on the agenda, we begin by simply asserting that we need to use more land or less land; we need more production or less production. Here, like a bad parent who crafts her child's future to meet the parent's desire, we simply read our expectations onto the soil. Such expectations can easily become justification for manipulation.

Within the biblical narrative of God's provision for human flourishing through plentitude, expectations that lead to manipulation that seeks to guarantee the outcome are viewed as idolatrous. Cultivating creation is not a fight for limited resources but a partnering with God that creatively recognizes limits. Coming to understand that not all our efforts bear the results we desire or need is a hard lesson to learn. Flood, drought, cool weather are all reminders that human culture begins in dependence. The fact that lack is sometimes the result even though we have been faithful, never allows for hoarding or withholding in the biblical story. Lack is shared, as is excess.

So soil can—must—be nurtured properly through close attention to its life and its possibility. While agriculture can be just as damaging and death-bringing as other human activities, it can also work in a rhythm with the natural processes of the soil. The soil can yield its bounty without sacrificing the good of the soil. But even in aligning our agriculture with the needs of the soil, we do not control the outcome. Limits point to dependence.

In the biblical tradition, dependence is found in both the order of nature and the order of culture, of the wild and the tamed. These are not opposing orders. To deny the natural is often to miss the thing itself. To see soil only as a medium to grow our crops treats the soil as a mirror for reflection. But the ideal of a wild soil draws us back to the soil itself, its limits, and its potential. To deny the cultural is to lose meaning as humanity is pushed to the margins of creaturely existence. The human calling encompasses both the good of the city and the stewarding of land, water, and air that makes the development of civilization a possibility.

The threat of the curse remains. As we gather on our farm to harvest the final crops of the season, I must turn my gaze from the bounty that has been produced this year back to the soil. As I carefully observe the soil, I will be led to think about how this year's activities have helped or harmed its health. In humility, I will look at the seeming disorder of my fence rows and try to learn the lessons being taught. And in this wild space of gratitude, I will ponder whether my attempts to fight the curse of weeds and unproductivity have felt more like a curse that is more ancient to the land.

BIBLIOGRAPHY

Berry, Wendell. "Two Minds." In *Citizenship Papers*, by Wendell Berry, 85–105. Washington, DC: Shoemaker & Hoard, 2003.

———. "Preserving Wildness." In *Home Economics*, by Wendell Berry, 137–51. New York: North Point, 1987.

Jackson, Wes. "Living Nets in a New Prairie Sea." In *Nature as Measure: The Selected Essays of Wes Jackson*, by Wes Jackson,139–46. Berkeley, CA: Counterpoint, 2011.

———. "Nature as Measure." In *Nature as Measure: The Selected Essays of Wes Jackson*, by Wes Jackson, 59–80. Berkeley, CA: Counterpoint, 2011.

13

Eschatology Shapes Ethics

New Creation and Christian Ecological Virtue Ethics

Steve Bouma-Prediger

But lacking the qualities of virtue, can we do the difficult things that will be necessary to live within the boundaries of the earth?[1]

"I believe the kind of stuff I'm writing about [all saved Christians, dead and alive, get snatched into heaven; those with weak faith get left behind to fight the antichrist; a seven-year tribulation of plagues ravages the earth] is going to happen some day."[2] So spoke Jerry Jenkins, co-author of the wildly popular Left Behind series of books, in an interview published some years ago in the *Chicago Tribune*. In other words, while the books may be fiction, the basic plot is not fiction but fact, based on the authors' interpretation of the Bible. Given this future, Jenkins implied with his message, Christians need not worry about the earth or its plethora of creatures. These nonhuman creatures will, after all, be incinerated in the (soon) coming apocalypse. Christians need not worry about porcupines or pine trees or tall grass prairies. These are of no value to a god who cares only for human souls, and therefore they should be of no value to us.

1. Orr, *Earth in Mind*, 62.
2. Jenkins, Interview, 2002.

This view of the future is powerfully captured by noted environmental historian Roderick Nash in his book *The Rights of Nature: A History of Environmental Ethics*. In a chapter on "The Greening of Religion," Nash comments on "the pervasive otherworldliness of Christianity."[3] He writes: "Christians' aspirations were fixed on heaven, the supposed place of their origins and, they hoped, their final resting. The earth was no mother but a kind of halfway house of trial and testing from which one was released at death . . . Indeed Christians expected that the earth would not be around for long. A vengeful God would destroy it, and all unredeemed nature, with floods or drought or fire."[4] Nash's concluding comments are telling: "Obviously this eschatology was a poor basis from which to argue for environmental ethics in any guise. Why take care of what you expected to be obliterated?"[5]

Unfortunately, social science data reveal that many Christians today hold this view of the future and exhibit the behavior one would expect from such a view. For example, in a study entitled "End-Times Theology, the Shadow of the Future, and Public Resistance to Addressing Global Climate Change," political scientists David Barker and David Bearce conclude that beliefs among Christians about the second coming of Jesus are a major factor underlying the resistance to addressing global climate change in the US.[6]

ESCHATOLOGY SHAPES ETHICS

These introductory remarks illustrate my central thesis: eschatology shapes ethics. How we view the future affects what we do (or don't do) in the present. And for critics of Christianity (and Nash is only one of many), this means that an escapist eschatology implies an ethic of neglect and exploitation. In other words, in seeking the cause of contemporary ecological degradation, one need look no further than religion, and Christianity in particular. We are in the ecological mess we are in, it is argued, largely because the vast majority of Christians do not care about creation. And they don't care about creation because they believe God doesn't care about creation. Indeed, the created world, they believe, will be destroyed. So why care for something that (soon) will be obliterated? Ethicist James Nash identifies

---

3. Nash, *Rights of Nature*, 91.

4. Ibid., 91–92.

5. Ibid., 92.

6. Barker and Bearce, "End-Times Theology," 267–79.

escapist eschatology as one of the four main planks in what he calls the "ecological complaint against Christianity."[7]

All of the above prompts the question of this essay: How would an earth-affirming eschatology change our ethic? How would a properly biblical Christian view of God's good future—of heaven and earth renewed as vividly described, for example, in Rev 21–22—reshape our actions in the present? My answer is that a truly biblical view of God's good future would shape our ethic so that more of us would become earthkeepers.

An important related question has to do with what kind of ethic. More exactly, what virtues might a theology of renewed creation require? In the remainder of this paper, I explore these two questions. In other words, this is an attempt to take seriously David Orr's question in the epigraph, by showing how a Christian virtue ethic rooted in a biblical eschatology of renewed creation can help us "do the difficult things that will be necessary to live within the boundaries of the earth."[8]

RENEWED CREATION ESCHATOLOGY

Since there is not enough space here to exegete biblical texts, allow me merely to summarize a biblical view of God's good future.[9] Reflecting on the mind-boggling vision in Rev 21–22 of an earthy and earthly future, Eugene Boring comments:

> Even though the first earth and the first heaven have passed away, the scene continues very much as a this-worldly scene . . . [This] is an affirmation of the significance of this world and history, even after the new heaven and new earth arrive . . . [God] does not junk the cosmos and start anew—he renews the old and brings it to fulfillment . . . God does not make "all new things," but "all things new."[10]

George Caird summarizes the gist of John's vision:

> John's heaven is no world-denying Nirvana, into which men may escape from the incurable ills of sublunary existence, but the seal of affirmation on the goodness of God's creation. The treasure that men find laid up in heaven turns out to be *the treasures and wealth of the nations*, the best they have known and

---

7. Nash, "Ecological Complaint," 68.

8. Orr, *Earth in Mind*, 62.

9. For more on my own views, see chap. 4 of my book *For the Beauty of the Earth*.

10. Boring, *Revelation*, 220.

loved on earth redeemed of all imperfections and transfigured by the radiance of God . . . Nowhere in the New Testament do we find a more eloquent statement than this of the all-embracing scope of Christ's redemptive work.[11]

This conclusion has been more recently echoed by N. T. Wright:

> We thus arrive at the last and perhaps the greatest image of new creation, of cosmic renewal, in the whole Bible. This scene, set out in Revelation 21–22, is not well enough known or pondered . . . This time the image is that of marriage. The New Jerusalem comes down out of heaven like a bride adorned for her husband.
>
> We notice right away how drastically different this is from all those would-be Christian scenarios in which the end of the story is the Christian going off to heaven as a soul, naked and unadorned, to meet its maker in fear and trembling. As in Phil 3, it is not we who go to heaven, it is heaven that comes to earth; indeed, it is the church itself, the heavenly Jerusalem, that comes down to earth. This is the ultimate rejection of all types of Gnosticism, of every worldview that sees the final goal as the separation of the world from God, of the physical from the spiritual, of earth from heaven. It is the final answer to the Lord's Prayer, that God's kingdom will come and his will be done on earth as in heaven.[12]

In short, from Genesis to Revelation, the Bible teaches an earth-affirming eschatology.[13]

VIRTUE AND THE VIRTUES: A (VERY) BRIEF OVERVIEW

What does all this reflection on eschatology have to do with ethics? And what is the connection with virtue ethics? First, some background on virtue ethics, and then a brief foray into ecological virtue ethics in particular.

In my view, the most pressing ethical question is not "What are my duties?" or "What would be the consequences?" but "What kind of person should I be?" While obligations and consequences are important in ethics, concern for virtue (or the virtues) is even more important.[14] In short, I wish to emphasize character rather than conduct, though I full well realize

11. Caird, *Revelation of St. John*, 279–80.

12. Wright, *Surprised by Hope*, 104.

13. See Middleton, "New Heaven and a New Earth," 73–97.

14. For a masterful combination of all three, see Smedes, *Choices*.

that each shapes the other. I also realize that this emphasis on virtue goes against the grain of much ethical theory, which typically focuses on duties or consequences.[15] Nevertheless, my claim is that areteology—the study of *arêtē*, or virtue—is more basic than deontology or teleology.

My reason, in brief, for adopting a virtue-based approach to ethics is quite simple: what we do depends on who we are. Doing is contingent upon being. To a large extent, our actions arise from our desires and affections, our dispositions and inclinations—in short, our character. Jamie Smith captures this point well:

> Much of our action is not the fruit of conscious deliberation; instead, much of what we do grows out of our passional orientation to the world—affected by all the ways we've been primed to perceive the world. In short, our action emerges from how we *imagine* the world. What we do is driven by who we are, by the kind of person we have become.[16]

And the kind of person we have become is best described by traits of character such as virtues and vices. This approach implies a critique of much contemporary ethics as too intellectualistic, too focused on rational principles and conscious deliberation. Such ethical theory has failed to notice or understand the pre-reflective basis of (moral) action. While rational reflection is important, the simple fact is that most of our actions are pre-reflective and pre-conscious, a result of having an intuitive and embodied feel for the world—a kinesthetic way of being in the world, shaped over time by habits, rituals, and routines.

So what is a virtue? A virtue is a story-shaped, praiseworthy character trait formed by practices over time, that disposes us to act in certain ways. It is a habitual disposition to act with excellence, molded by the narrative(s) we identify with and in which we dwell. We know how to live well by soaking in certain stories of particular communities, with their corresponding practices, and by looking to people of virtue as role models.

---

15. As Taylor, among others, notes: "The dominant philosophical ethics today, divided into the two major branches of Utilitarianism and post-Kantianism, both conceive of morality as determining through some criterion what an agent ought to do. They are rather hostile to an ethics of virtue or the good, such as that of Aristotle." See Taylor, *A Secular Age*, 282.

16. Smith, *Imagining the Kingdom*, 31–32.

ECOLOGICAL VIRTUE ETHICS

In the last three decades, serious work has been done on ecological virtue ethics (EVE). Beginning with Thomas Hill's pivotal 1983 essay, "Ideals of Human Excellence and Preserving Natural Environments,"[17] and with subsequent work by Bill Shaw, Geoffrey Frasz, Ronald Sandler, and Philip Cafaro—to name only a few of the principal contributors—the field is now well established. Evidence for this includes the publication of anthologies such as *Environmental Virtue Ethics* by Sandler and Cafaro in 2005, and monographs such as *Character and Environment: A Virtue-Oriented Approach to Environmental Ethics* by Sandler in 2007.

Contributors to the new field of EVE develop and explicate various virtues. For example, Frasz speaks of benevolence as an environmental virtue.[18] This virtue is the active concern for the flourishing of both humans and nonhumans. The expansion of the sphere of concern to include whole species and particular places, large ecosystems and local watersheds, is what distinguishes benevolence as an environmental virtue from benevolence as such. Following Aldo Leopold, Frasz expands the concept of community to include nonhuman entities, both living and nonliving. He also argues that the environmental virtue of benevolence implies the related virtues of proper humility, patience, and perseverance, as well as the character traits of imagination and attentiveness.

On his short list of virtues, Cafaro includes care, patience, persistence, self-control, humility, respect, and self-restraint.[19] Along with these moral virtues, Cafaro lists intellectual virtues such as attentiveness and wonder, aesthetic virtues such as appreciation and creativity, physical virtues such as stamina and hardiness, and what he calls "overarching virtues" such as wisdom and humility.

This is not the place to extensively review these various proposals. I merely wish to make two observations. First, much solid work has been done to establish the importance of ecological virtue ethics. Most of this work has involved a retrieval and appropriation of the Greco-Roman traditions of virtue ethics. Second, there has been precious little attention given to EVE by Christians, and yet we Christians have a rich tradition of virtue ethics from which to draw.[20]

17. Hill, "Human Excellence," 211–24.

18. Frasz, "Benevolence," 121–34.

19. Cafaro, "The Naturalist's Virtues," 85–99.

20. In one of the few explicitly Christian forays into EVE, van Wensveen mentions care and compassion as ecological virtues. See van Wensveen, "Ecological Virtue Language" (adapted from chap. 1 of her book *Dirty Virtues: The Emergence of Ecological*

In chapter 6 of my book *For the Beauty of the Earth*, I have developed a set of fourteen ecological virtues.[21] For example, the virtue of courage is moral strength in the face of danger. As one of the four cardinal virtues for the Greeks, courage implies firmness of mind and resoluteness of spirit despite the fearful awareness of risk. In the Christian tradition, courage was transmuted into fortitude.[22] Fortitude is tenacity in the face of opposition, or stubborn persistence in the face of adversity. Ecological courage is a kind of fortitude or perseverance. In the face of apathy or ignorance or fear, ecological courage is the dogged determination to persevere in caring for the earth.

The vice of deficiency is cowardice, or the inability to overcome fear without being reckless. Paralyzed by fear, the coward lacks the ability to act when the situation calls for decisive or swift action. The ecological coward fails to properly care for pine tree, mountain meadow, or planet earth because of some overwhelming fear. The vice of excess is rashness. While courageous people honestly face their fear and persevere in spite of its sometimes paralyzing effects, rash people refuse to acknowledge their fear and thus act hastily or without proper caution. The ecologically rash stuff their fear and rush off to "save the earth," but in so doing they often do more damage than good.

A VIRTUE ETHIC FOR RENEWED CREATION

With respect to eschatology, three virtues are especially germane: justice, love, and hope. Why these three? In brief, they name central features of a properly biblical eschatology. It is difficult to envision God's good future of shalom without speaking of justice, love, and hope. As Martin Luther King Jr. famously put it, "There is something in the universe that unfolds for justice."[23] That is its trajectory. The ultimate *telos* of creation is that state in which wrongs are put to right and equity reigns supreme. So also with love. The biblical vision of the future cannot be described except by reference to

---

Virtue Ethics [Amhurst, NY: Humanity, 2000]). See also Deane-Drummond, "Environmental Justice," 294–310; and Bible, "Pursuing Ecological Virtue."

21. My argument, in brief, for referring to these virtues as *ecological* virtues is quite simple. While similar in many ways to the virtues as usually conceived, for example, as naming a particular disposition, these virtues are sufficiently different to warrant the term "ecological virtues" because they have either an expanded scope (e.g., a focus on nonhuman creatures or a particular place) or a distinct meaning (e.g., courage as ecological courageous endurance) or both.

22. See, e.g., Aquinas, *Summa Theologiae, I-II*, question 61.

23 King, *Testament of Hope*, 14; see also 20, 257.

love—the kind of love manifest in the life, death, and resurrection of Jesus. Love is, as Jesus teaches, the summary of the law and the prophets. And hope is an essential ingredient in biblical eschatology. Hope is the lifeblood of that yearning for shalom that marks those who follow Jesus. In sum, justice, love, and hope are central to the biblical vision of the future. Given the limits of this essay, I will address only justice and hope.

First, justice. For the Greeks, justice is rendering to each his or her due—rendering to each that to which they have a right. More exactly, as Nicholas Wolterstorff cogently argues, justice is what due respect for the worth of someone requires.[24] It is treating someone as befits her or his worth, and as such involves respecting the rights of that person.[25] So justice, at its core, is about respect—respect for rights. Justice is also about fairness. In whatever form—commutative, distributive, or retributive—justice concerns equity. For example, distributive justice has to do not only with the determination and rendering of goods based on legitimate claims to those goods, but also with the equitable allocation of goods. Justice means not playing favorites; it means being impartial. Justice is the equitable respect for rights.

Thus, the virtue of justice is the habitual disposition to act fairly. It is the ability to make decisions with equity, which is not to be confused with equality. The virtue of justice involves the ability to discern when to treat equals equally and unequals differentially; thus, it implies the virtue of practical wisdom. So the virtue of justice implies respect—respect for the rights of others—and the just person knows how to respect the rights of others even when faced with competing rights. The virtue of ecological justice names the settled disposition to act fairly when faced with the competing rights or legitimate claims of creatures both human and nonhuman. It is a cultivated fairness with respect not only to oppressed people but also to domestic animals and wild plants, endangered species and damaged ecosystems. Ecological justice is the steady disposition to render with equity to human and nonhuman alike that which their worth requires.

In my view, the virtue of justice is not a mean, and thus has only one vice—namely, injustice. Injustice is the propensity to be partial—to play favorites for no good reason or, more perversely, for personal gain. The vice of injustice names a disinclination to be evenhanded, impartial, or fair-minded. As such, it fails to give others their due; it fails to respect their rights. Ecological injustice names the willingness to violate the rights

---

24. Wolterstorff, *Justice in Love*, 85–92.

25. Ibid., 85–87. For a brief mention of the rights of nonhumans, see 138, 146.

of others, including the rights of nonhuman creatures.[26] Or if you think that nonhuman creatures have no rights, ecological injustice is the failure of human moral agents to properly exercise their duties to those creatures whose intrinsic value makes them objects of concern.[27] Ecological injustice is the habitual disposition to do wrong to creatures—human and nonhuman—whose worth calls for our respect.

Second, hope. Hope is confident expectation of future good. It involves imagining some good future, believing that such a future is possible, and acting in such a way as to bring this good future to fruition.[28] So the act of hoping involves three things—imagining, believing, and willing. For example, I imagine my local lake purged of all invasive species and free of water contaminated by harmful bacteria. I believe such a future is actually obtainable, especially given the watershed-wide cleanup effort named "Project Clarity." And I will to act in such a way that this vision of the local watershed becomes a reality. For Christians, the expectation of a good future is based on God's promises and God's character as a keeper of promises.[29] Christians hope because they worship a God who raised Jesus from the dead as a sign of the future restoration of all things.

Thus, the virtue of hope is the settled disposition to act with confidence to bring about some imagined good future. It is an inclination to live into an imagined world that is really possible, no matter how improbable. Ecologically speaking, hope names the settled disposition to yearn for God's good future of shalom, rooted in confidence that such a future lies in God's good hands. Ecological hope remembers the rainbow promise made to Noah, celebrates the resurrection. Resurrection anticipates the new Jerusalem.

There are two vices that correspond to the virtue of hope. The vice of deficiency is despair. Despair is the absence of any expectation of a good future. As its etymology suggests, it is the loss of all hope (*de-sperare*). Despair is cynicism of a profound kind, for it signals a failure or inability to trust. Ecologically speaking, despair is hopelessness in the face of our aching earth. It is the inability to imagine or believe, in the face of pervasive ecological degradation and intractable ecological problems, that any liveable future on earth is possible. Despair is an abandonment of belief in the ultimate redemption of all things.

---

26. Haught, "Environmental Virtues and Environmental Justice."

27. Rolston, *Environmental Ethics*, chaps. 1, 6.

28. Smedes, *Standing on the Promises*, chaps. 2–4.

29. Hope is different from optimism since optimism is an inclination to put the most favorable face on actions or events, without adequate warrant or reason. See Wright, *Surprised by Hope*, chap. 5.

The vice of excess is presumptuousness. This can take two forms. Sometimes it has to do with what is called a presumptuous attitude. In contrast to the confident expectation of genuine hope, this kind of false hope exudes an overconfidence that takes the good future for granted. It is an unwarranted audacity of belief. Another kind of presumptuousness concerns the grounds for belief rather than the level of confidence. Not all objects of hope are worthy of trust. There are pretenders of hope in our anxious world. This species of false hope presumes that ecological healing will be pain free and/or won't demand much from us.

CONCLUSION

Eschatology shapes ethics. And a truly biblical eschatology of creation renewed should inspire us to be earthkeepers. Such a view of the future should shape us into people who embody ecological virtues such as justice, love, and hope. While many people of late have spoken of this, none has done so as eloquently as Wendell Berry. I conclude with some words of his:

> The ecological teaching of the Bible is simply inescapable: God made the world because He wanted it made. He thinks the world is good, and He loves it. It is His world; He has never relinquished title to it. And He has never revoked the conditions, bearing on His gift to us of the use of it, that oblige us to take excellent care if it. If God loves the world, then how might any person of faith be excused for not loving it or justified in destroying it?[30]

BIBLIOGRAPHY

Aquinas, Thomas. "God and the Order of Creation" (*Summa Theologica*, Part 1). Vol. 1 of *Basic Writings of St. Thomas Aquinas*. Edited by Anton C. Pegis. New York: Random House, 1945.

Barker, David C., and David H. Bearce. "End-Times Theology, the Shadow of the Future, and Public Resistance to Addressing Global Climate Change." *Political Research Quarterly* 66 (2012) 267–79.

Berry, Wendell. *What Are People For?: Essays*. New York: Northpoint, 1990.

Bible, Seth. "Pursuing Ecological Virtue: A Critical Analysis of the Environmental Virtue Ethics Models of Ronald Sandler, Louke van Wensveen, and Philip Cafaro." PhD diss., Southeastern Baptist Theological Seminary, 2011.

Boring, M. Eugene. *Revelation*. Interpretation: A Bible Commentary for Teaching and Preaching. Louisville: John Knox, 1989.

30. Berry, *What Are People For?*, 98.

Bouma-Prediger, Steven. *For the Beauty of the Earth: A Christian Vision for Creation Care*. Rev. 2nd ed. Grand Rapids: Baker Academic, 2001.

Cafaro, Philip. "The Naturalist's Virtues." *Philosophy in the Contemporary World* 8 (2001) 85–99.

Caird, George B. *A Commentary on the Revelation of St. John the Divine*. New York: Harper & Row, 1966.

Deane-Drummond, Celia. "Environmental Justice and the Economy: A Christian Theologian's View." *Ecotheology* 11 (2006) 294–310.

Frasz, Geoffrey. "Benevolence as an Environmental Virtue." In *Environmental Virtue Ethics*, edited by Ronald D. Sandler and Philip Cafaro, 121–34. Lanham, MD: Rowman & Littlefield, 2005.

Haught, Paul. "Environmental Virtues and Environmental Justice." *Environmental Ethics* 33 (2011) 357–75.

Hill, Thomas, Jr., "Ideals of Human Excellence and Preserving Natural Environments." *Environmental Ethics* 5 (1983) 211–24.

Jenkins, Jerry. Interview. *Chicago Tribune*, March 13, 2002.

King, Martin Luther, Jr. *A Testament of Hope: The Essential Writings and Speeches of Martin Luther King, Jr*. Edited by James Washington. New York: HarperOne, 2003.

Middleton, J. Richard. "A New Heaven and a New Earth: A Case for a Holistic Reading of the Biblical Story of Redemption." *Journal for Christian Theological Research* 11 (2006) 73–97.

Nash, James. "The Ecological Complaint against Christianity." In *Loving Nature*, 68–92. Nashville: Abingdon, 1991.

Nash, Roderick. *The Rights of Nature: A History of Environmental Ethics*. Madison: University of Wisconsin, 1989.

Orr, David W. *Earth in Mind: On Education, Environment, and the Human Prospect*. Washington, DC: Island, 1994.

Rolston, Holmes, III. *Environmental Ethics: Duties to and Values in the Natural World*. Philadelphia: Temple University Press, 1988.

Sandler, Ronald. *Character and Environment: A Virtue-Oriented Approach to Environmental Ethics*. New York: Columbia University Press, 2007.

Sandler, Ronald, and Philip Cafaro, eds. *Environmental Virtue Ethics*. Lanham, MD: Rowman and Littlefield, 2005.

Smedes, Lewis B. *Choices: Making Right Decisions in a Complex World*. San Francisco: Harper & Row, 1986.

———. *Standing on the Promises: Keeping Hope Alive for a Tomorrow We Cannot Control*. Nashville: Nelson, 1998.

Smith, James K. A. *Imagining the Kingdom: How Worship Works*. Cultural Liturgies 2. Grand Rapids: Baker Academic, 2013.

Taylor, Charles. *A Secular Age*. Cambridge, MA: Harvard University Press, 2007.

van Wensveen, Louke. "The Emergence of Ecological Virtue Langauge." In *Environmental Virtue Ethics*, edited by Ronald Sandler and Philip Cafaro. Lanham, MD: Rowman and Littlefield, 2005.

Wright, N. T. *Surprised by Hope: Rethinking Heaven, the Resurrection, and the Mission of the Church*. New York: HarperCollins, 2008.

Wolterstorff, Nicholas. *Justice in Love*. Grand Rapids: Eerdmans, 2011.

14

Holy Ground

Considering a Sacramental Ecclesiology in Berry's Port William

Winn Collier

Wendell Berry's religious readers often reach a moment of consternation when we attempt to make sense of the ambiguity of Berry's themes. While his work comes laced with themes of Christian faith and exhibits rich theological sensibilities, Berry's rebuke can be blistering:

> Christian organizations, to this day, remain largely indifferent to the rape and plunder of the world and of its traditional cultures ... The certified Christian seems just as likely as anyone else to join the military-industrial conspiracy to murder Creation.[1]

This rebuke continues in his fiction, where the church sits awkwardly at the edge of the community and often seems to have little to do with the actual membership (a term rich with church imagery) of Port William. Are we to understand Berry to believe that the church will inherently ruin goodness while degrading communities and creation? Does Berry envision no hope for the church?

I suggest that a short tour of Berry's fictional Port William provides the possibility of reading Berry more in the lineage of biblical prophets who

1. Berry, *Art of the Commonplace*, 305–6.

lament the failure of God's community to live at the center—her failure to be a people of shalom for, and presence, in the world. The barber, Jayber Crow, seems to offer a voice for Berry's own inclinations: "The belief has grown in me," Jayber says, "that Christ did not come to found an organized religion but came instead to found an unorganized one. He seems to have come to carry religion out of the temples into the field and sheep pastures, onto the roadsides and the banks of rivers, into the houses of sinners and publicans, into the town and the wilderness, toward the membership of all that is here."[2] Berry's consternation centers on how the church has not wedded herself to the world God loves and to the people and the land God loves. There is too great a gulf between church and world. Heaven and earth do not meet as they should. There is a failure to see grace in each tall oak and every clod of red dirt, a failure to receive God's stunning image in every worn and fair body. If we were to put this in theological terms, Berry's critiques might be understood as a failure to receive God's world as sacramental ground where divine grace courses through each river and at each table and in each place of friendship and where all of creation finds itself drawn together in God.

I should make it clear that I'm not suggesting this reading provides some explicit meaning Berry encoded into the text. Rather, I am reading with a generous eye, and what I suggest here should be understood as the appropriation of useful metaphors, not the unearthing of implicit analogies. In Berry's terms, I'm seeking the "kindly use" of the possibilities I believe Berry has made available to us.[3] While Berry never uses the language of *sacrament*, he does ground his work in the belief that God truly loves the world and as such infuses the world with "inherent goodness."[4] Further, in his seminal theological essay "Christianity and the Survival of Creation" published in 1992, Berry quotes both the poet Blake ("everything that lives is holy") and the Greek Orthodox theologian Philip Sherrard ("Creation is nothing less than the manifestation of God's hidden Being") to establish a posture that, so far as I can tell, can only be understood as sacramental.[5]

---

2. Berry, *Jayber Crow*, 321.

3. Berry uses this language in relation to agricultural concerns (see, for example, *Unsettling of America*, 30), but it fits well as a description of his posture toward literature, land, community, friendship, etc. Oehlschlaeger makes this connection well in *Achievement of Wendell Berry*.

4. Berry, *Art of the Commonplace*, 308.

5. Berry, "Survival of Creation," 98.

A SPECIFIC PLACE ON EARTH

One of Berry's first novels, *A Place on Earth*, imagines Port William as a "kind of Heavenly City . . . [where] . . . all the houses would be bound together in friendships, and friendliness would move and join among them like an open street."[6] Port William, in some sense, models an eschatological vision where grace is tied to history, place, neighborliness—and to the art of presence.

People familiar with Berry's writings would not be surprised to hear that the word *presence* appears thirty-three times in *A Place on Earth*, carrying one of Berry's familiar themes—presence to the dirt and the flesh that forms one's life. Berry, like his crusty character Old Jack, is one who "has lived his all his life loving solid objects."[7] Refusing abstractions, Berry envisions the good life as one where a person lives and dreams and dies in the world in front of her, the world that simply (and splendidly) exists in bone and sod, in handshakes and heartbreaks, in death and life. As such, whatever ecclesial vision one might encourage via Berry, it must possess concrete connection to a specific place and a specific people. So, to the people we'll turn—to three of Port William's characters.

BROTHER PRESTON: ISOLATION

Brother Preston, Berry's most prominent pastoral figure, embodies isolation and distance, a failure to belong to the people and the place of Port William. When news arrives that the Feltner's son Virgil is missing in action, Brother Preston knows his duty and makes his way toward the Feltner homestead. As rain deluges Port William, we discover an omen in the observation that Brother Preston "meets no one along the road."[8] Brother Preston has never really met anyone in this town, never truly seen them.

Brother Preston steps onto the Feltner's front porch, a telltale description since Berry writes that in Port William, only salesmen and ministers knock on the front door, while neighbors and friends use the side entrance—a sign of familial belonging. Berry describes Preston's knock, perfectly timed and modulated, as "an act of ministerial discretion."[9] Margaret Feltner led Brother Preston into the parlor where he sat "erect in the chair, holding the Testament in his lap." Berry observes how "the attitude of his body seems to

---

6. Berry, *Place on Earth*, 72.

7. Ibid., 51.

8. Ibid., 95.

9. Ibid.

isolate him from the room, to hold out to it a formality alien to it. Some part of his presence is withheld from it; he might [as well] be sitting in the tall-backed chair behind his pulpit."[10] Isolation. Formality. Alienation. Preston was not a part of that room, not a part of the family, not really a part of this community. If Brother Preston did not know his people well enough to be present with them in their grief, could he possibly know them well enough to speak a good word from God to them on Sunday? If a pastor cannot join his people in tears, can he really join them in prayers?

When Mat Feltner enters the parlor, the distance expands. Brother Preston does not ask neighborly questions or express the quietness required for human comfort. Rather, he waits for a break in the conversation so he can unload the theological words he has come to deliver. His oration moves him further from this grief, further from these wounded souls. Berry describes the cold estrangement: "His eyes have become detached from his hearers; [Brother Preston] might be speaking down from his pulpit now, looking at all, seeing none."[11]

And so the preaching continues. Berry describes the disembodied exercise: "The preacher's voice, rising, rides above all chances of mortal and worldly hope, hastening to rest in the hope of Heaven."[12] Indeed, Berry observes, "This is the preacher's hope, and he has moved to it alone, outside the claims of time and sorrow." And then, words of true Berry-damnation strike Brother Preston: "He is free of the world."[13] Brother Preston stands absent from these people, absent from Port William.

Brother Preston evidences one of Berry's core judgments against the church—that the church has too often untethered herself from the concrete realities and localities of this world, rejecting her call to ally with "light, air, water, earth; plants and animals; human families and communities; the traditions of decent life, good work, and responsible thought; the religious traditions; the essential stories and songs."[14] The church, if it is true to itself, exists as a community concretely wedded to specific people and locales, her language evoking a deeply imbedded sacramental existence.

---

10. Ibid., 96.
11. Ibid., 98.
12. Ibid.
13. Ibid., 99.
14. Berry, *What are People For?*, 102.

WILLIAMS MILBY: WITH THE PEOPLE

Though Port William's pastoral characters are often the ones most at the fringes of the town's membership, Berry's short story "A Desirable Woman," originally published in the Summer 2008 issue of the *Hudson Review* and recently collected (2012) in the hardback edition *A Place in Time*, offers an dissenting view. Laura Milby is the story's central character, but her husband Williams Milby, the pastor of Little Flock in the ramshackle village of Sycamore, looms large as well. Sycamore belongs to the broader Port William community, but their respective pastors—Williams Milby and Brother Preston—are worlds apart.

The stark difference between the two pastors centers on the attentiveness Williams gives to the particularities of life within Sycamore. He surrenders himself to these people and this place. He stays attuned to the common talk that many would have considered inconsequential to lofty pastoral work. Berry tells us that "it was to this subsurface current of gossip that Williams Milby learned to listen with greatest care, for it told him where needs were."[15] Williams gathers the stories of the Wallis twins (with their weekly Saturday night drives in their Model A), Mrs. Etta Mae Berry (who always looks for germs in the well's dipper before drinking), Uncle Lute Wisely (the last black man left in Sycamore) and Lizard Eye and Zinnia Creed (who butchers virtually every word of the King's English). Williams is "given knowledge" of his neighbors, his congregation.[16]

Williams takes great joy in the Sunday ritual of "feeding the preacher," where the Milbys join different parishioners each week for the long stretch of Sunday lunch and early dinners before the evening church service, a hospitality Williams considers "a dear privilege . . . for it opened up the countryside to them as it was opened otherwise only to the veterinarian."[17] These afternoons allow Williams to cross the barrier between church and farm, the worlds so many of his parishioners believe hold little in common. Rather than allowing his pastoral vocation to set him apart from the folks in his care, "Williams's ministry carried him always along the seams of the community where the people were joined to one another and to the place."[18] These seams reveal the marginal and commonplace as essential parts of the whole—a sacramental truth.

15. Berry, *Place in Time*, 50.
16. Ibid., 41–52.
17. Ibid., 56.
18. Ibid., 58.

JAYBER CROW: BARBER-PRIEST

I believe, however, that Berry provides his most substantive reflection on ecclesial life through an unexpected character—Jayber Crow, a barber who I would argue represents Port William's true priestly presence. Jayber lives among the people, listens well, knows his neighbors. He takes confession from the barber chair. Jayber inhabits monk-like simplicity in his simple cell above his shop. He takes vows of chastity. Unlike Brother Preston, who attempted a role he could never manage, Jayber was a pastor without ever receiving the title.

Sensing a call to ministry, Jayber (and we should remember Jayber's real name is Jonah, another divine spokesperson in the Bible) enrolls in Pigeonville College as a ministerial student. Pigeonville never suited him, however. "The place had a pious atmosphere," Jayber remembered. "It was soapy and paperish and shut-in and a little stale. It didn't smell of anything bodily or earthly. A little whiff of tobacco smoke would have done wonders for it. The main thing was that it made me feel excluded from it, even while I was in it."[19] This is a religious community at odds with the flesh and bone of this world.

Bewildered, Jayber leaves Pigeonville and commences the long trek afoot, toward home. During his traverse, however, a catastrophic flood ravishes Kentucky, and Jayber has to walk through those waters, which serve as his baptism, his sacramental entrance into a new life. The biblical Jonah drowns in the deep waters in order to arrive at his ministry. Berry's Jonah drowns so he can enter his new life, his ministry in Port William.

Jayber serves as Port William's confessor, with the rows of chairs in his shop serving as pews for his congregation. One evening, Fee Berlew, the old "ramshackledy" town drunk, gets hold of a pint of whiskey from his nephew, and, as anyone who knew Fee would have predicted, the whiskey sends Fee on a bender. Fee stumbles to Jayber's shop one night "completely sodden, bewildered, half-crazy, and full of the foulest kind of indignation." Fee grows more vulgar in his abuse, calling Jayber an "orphan three days shy of a bastard" and a "damned low-down hair barber."[20] The next day, Fee returns, penitent and seeking pardon.

> "Jayber," [Fee] said, "Could you forgive an old son of a bitch?"
> "I could," [Jayber] said, "Yes I can. I do."[21]

---

19. Berry, *Jayber Crow*, 48–49.
20. Ibid., 7.
21. Ibid., 8.

The priest has spoken. Grace is present. The sacrament of confession en-
acted. Absolution declared.

Jayber does have an official church job. Two, in fact. He is the church
gravedigger and the church janitor. This means he serves the congregation
in the most tender and human ways, always preparing for his neighbor's
gathered presence and tending to his neighbor's bodies. Jayber presides over
life's closing moments, the last one to bid a parishioner farewell and the one
who will pass final dirt over their bodies. It is at another gravesite, on the
evening that the war ends and Jayber, Burley, and Big Ellis find Whacker
drunk on the curb, that Jayber's priestly role becomes most vivid. As a
prank, the trio carry Whacker to a fresh grave Jayber had dug for a funeral
the following day. They lower Whacker, snoring like a baby, into the cool
ground. In mock funeral, Jayber begins to speak a litany as he stoops down
and cups dirt from the grave's edge. In Berry's description, the farce trans-
figures into grace:

> Overtaken and sobered by Jayber's words . . . they stand with
> their heads bowed after he has finished. Apart from anything
> any of them could have intended or expected, Jayber's words
> have transcended drunkenness and farce. The meaning of the
> time has been lifted far above the snores that come with aston-
> ishing power out of the grave.[22]

Jayber understood the church as a "gathered community," a visible,
united membership that he served and of which he was a part.[23] Jayber's
ecclesiology may be best reflected here:

> What gave me the most pleasure of all was just going up there,
> whatever the occasion, and sitting down with the people. I al-
> ways wished a little that the church was not a church, set off as
> it was behind its barriers of doctrines and creed, so that all the
> people of the town and neighborhood might two or three times
> a week freely have come there and sat down together—though
> I knew perfectly well that, in the actual world, any gathering
> would exclude some, and some would not consent to be gath-
> ered, and some (like me) would be outside even when inside.[24]

And Jayber's criticism of Port William's pastors followed the same lines:

> What they didn't see was that [Port William] is beautiful, and
> that some of the greatest beauties are the briefest. They had

22. Berry, *Place on Earth*, 301.

23. Berry, *Jayber Crow*, 205.

24. Ibid., 164.

imagined the church, which is an organization, but not the world, which is an order and a mystery. To them, the church did not exist in the world where people earn their living and have their being.[25]

Jayber rejected the dichotomy between spiritual and physical, between life with God and life with one's community. Jayber, it seems, did not so much desire less church but, rather, less disconnection between church and *life*.

SCHMEMANN AND SACRAMENT

In *What are People For?*, Berry acknowledges his frustration with the church, yet he refuses to ultimately give up on her. "I acknowledge that I feel deeply estranged from most of the manifestations of organized religion," Berry confesses. "Yet I am far from thinking that one can somehow become righteous by carrying protestantism to the logical conclusion of a one-person church."[26] After all, how can Berry hold a privatized vision of the community of faith and remain true to everything else he holds dear?

Berry's concerns are, of course, by no means unique. Many ecclesial voices have raised alarm over the dichotomous severing of church from creation, the life of faith from . . . *life*. A sacramental vision of the world, rightly understood, melts these false dichotomies. Eastern Orthodox theologian Alexander Schmemann bemoans how so often "liturgy is neither explained nor understood as having anything to do with 'life' as above all, an *icon* of that new life which is to challenge and renew the 'old life' in us and around us."[27] Schmemann, through a liturgical lens, levels a similar critique as Berry. What the church offers, Schmemann insists, is "an all-embracing vision of life, a power meant to judge, inform and transform the whole of existence, a 'philosophy of life' shaping and challenging all our ideas, attitudes and actions."[28] There is no retreat here, no parochial concern here. In *For the Life of the World*, Schmemann takes aim at so-called "spiritual" theologies that carry little regard for creation and cultures—for the human order as such. These theologies give shape, in disastrous ways, to a religious life that (in Schmemann's words) "makes the secular one—the life of eating and drinking—irrelevant, deprives it of any real meaning save that of being

---

25. Ibid., 160–61.

26. Berry, *What are People For?*, 101.

27. See Schmemann, "Liturgy and Theology," 52.

28. Ibid., 51–52.

an exercise in piety and patience."[29] In other words, a church life that fails to be present with the concerns, sorrows, and joys of our actual human existence is a betrayal of the incarnational and sacramental nature of Christian faith. We are to see the world, in all of its glorious particularity—and to name it, to see its uniqueness and its beauty, to truly *know* it. One might stretch so far as to combine Schmemann and Berry with a bit of paraphrase: to fail to be *present* to our life, in its comprehensive and concrete totality, is to fail to be the church.

Schmemann believed we should understand ourselves as priests in God's world, both offering the world to God and receiving the gifts of grace from God via the world. The world is a Eucharistic reality, brimming with splendor and glory. The church's vocation is to participate in announcing the truth—everything belongs. Perhaps we could say that everyone and everything, every person and community, every beast and seedling, is invited into the membership. To this, I believe Berry could say, "Amen."

BIBLIOGRAPHY

Berry, Wendell. *The Art of the Commonplace: The Agrarian Essays of Wendell Berry*, edited by Norman Wirzba. Berkeley, CA: Counterpoint, 2002.

———. "Christianity and the Survival of Creation." In *Sex, Economy, Freedom and Community: Eight Essays*, 93–116. New York: Pantheon, 1992.

———. *Jayber Crow: A Novel*. Washington, DC: Counterpoint, 2000.

———. *A Place in Time: Twenty Stories of the Port William Membership*. Berkeley, CA: Counterpoint, 2012.

———. *A Place on Earth: A Novel*. Berkeley, CA: Counterpoint, 1983.

———. *The Unsettling of America: Culture and Agriculture*. Berkeley, CA: Counterpoint, 1996.

———. *What are People For?* Washington, DC: Counterpoint, 2010.

Oehlschlaeger, Fritz. *The Achievement of Wendell Berry: The Hard History of Love*. Lexington: University Press of Kentucky, 2011.

Schmemann, Alexander. *For the Life of the World*. Crestwood, NY: St. Vladamir's Seminary Press, 1973.

———. "Liturgy and Theology." In *Liturgy and Tradition: Theological Reflections of Alexander Schmemann*, edited by Thomas Fisch, 49–68. Crestwood, NY: St. Vladamir's Seminary Press, 2003.

29. Schmemann, *Life of the World*, 12.

15

Cultivating Right Desire

Wendell Berry's Economic Vision

Richard J. Klinedinst

"You cannot know that life is holy," Wendell Berry writes, "if you are content to live from economic practices that daily destroy life and diminish its possibility."[1] Increasingly, members of the Christian tradition have heeded Berry's bold warning that if creation is to survive, religious faith must account for both the theology and practice needed to sustain its renewal. Wendell Berry's agrarian economic philosophy aids us in recovering both in theory and practice the important attachments to land and place that capitalism, and late modern culture, so unreservedly eschews. Berry's vision reminds us that the triumph of the ethos and ethics of economic liberalism is not inevitable, at least not in our own local communities and particular neighborhoods.

In bringing Berry's thought into conversation with Adam Smith and Smith's intellectual heirs, one begins to see the myriad ways in which liberal economic theory leads to environmental destruction. Central to this discussion will be an exploration of the important differences between freedom as commonly defined in the liberal tradition, and the distinctly Christian understanding of freedom evident in the writings of Augustine. Berry's agrarian economic vision offers a fruitful model of Christian exchange that

---

1. Berry, *Sex, Economy, Freedom and Community*, 99.

reflects both Augustine's insight and the witness of the biblical tradition, including such contemporary thinkers as Albert Borgmann and William Cavanaugh. Berry's body of work offers a striking vision of how we might cultivate right desire and bear good fruit, as creatures at once fallen and redeemed, in the paradise of God's creation.

CLASSICAL LIBERAL ECONOMICS

The rise of liberal economic theory is inextricably bound to the story of the rise of the nation-state—both are simply "surface manifestations of a more fundamental change of thought."[2] Hence the claim of Donald Worster, the eminent environmental historian, that the roots of the current environmental crisis lie "in modern culture itself, in its world-view that swept aside much of the older religious outlook."[3] Key to this modern culture is an economic and scientific materialism notable for its secular, progressive, and rational outlook. Such materialism allows us, to quote René Descartes, to "make ourselves, as it were, the lords and masters of nature."[4]

Adam Smith is in many respects the seminal philosopher—"the representative modern man"—who emerges from this cultural shift to economic materialism.[5] In Smith's discussion of economic development, he argues that a nation's wealth results from humanity's self-interest, and so too the resulting propensity to barter and trade.[6] The division of labor allows for a surplus of goods, and as a result, a medium of exchange and method of valuation are established. Methods of distribution are necessitated by the exchange of goods and services, and this results in the further development and accumulation of capital.

With labor as the foundation of wealth, Smith argues for the interconnectedness and natural tendencies of economic development. According to Smith's economic model, the wealth created by one's self-interest acts as a benefit to others and contributes to the well-being of society as a whole. Wealth is best obtained, Smith argues, through a market free of government manipulation, and the invisible hand offers the best guide to continued

2. Worster, "Wealth of Nature," 167. While many economic historians share this reading, there are some who vehemently oppose it (Clark, *Farewell to Alms*, 208–29).

3. Worster, "Wealth of Nature," 167.

4. Cottingham et al., *Philosophical Writings*, 142–43.

5. Worster, "Wealth of Nature," 171.

6. Smith discusses economic development in the first half of *Wealth of Nations*, and political economy in the second.

development. Thus, labor acts as the basis of all economic development, and liberty as the means of sustaining and continuing such growth.

Central to Smith's system of "natural liberty," then, is a curtailment of all external interference (whether from the state or the church) and an insistence that the "natural world" has worth only if we (productively) labor to extract value from it.[7] The defining characteristic, though, and likely the most influential legacy of the liberal tradition, is its conception of individual freedom. In the wake of liberal economic theory, "people's moral actions are no longer intelligible because of their role within a community, but people are reconstituted as *individuals* who through their autonomous activities give value to the things in the world."[8] Freedom, according to Adam Smith and other economic liberals, consists of pursuing individual desires apart from the interference of other persons or groups. As Milton Friedman suggests, it is only through the free market that individual autonomy is maintained:

> So long as effective freedom of exchange is maintained, the central feature of the market organization of economic activity is that it prevents one person from interfering with another in respect to most of his activities. The consumer is protected from coercion by the seller because of the presence of other sellers with whom he can deal; the seller is protected from coercion by the consumer because of other consumers to whom he can deal. The employee is protected from coercion by the employer because of other employers for whom he can work, and so on. And the market does this impersonally and without centralized authority.[9]

Central, then, to this economic tradition is an insistence on the absolute value of individual autonomy, regardless of familial, communal, ecclesial, or political attachments. As theologian William Cavanaugh suggests, "all that matters for a market to be free is that individuals have real wants and can pursue them without the interference of others, especially the state."[10]

7. Worster, "Wealth of Nature," 173–74.

8. Long, *Divine Economy*, 188.

9. Friedman, *Capitalism and Freedom*, 14–15.

10. Cavanaugh, *Being Consumed*, 7.

RETHINKING FREEDOM

According to philosopher James K. A. Smith, one finds in the history of philosophy and theology "two dominant, and competing, concepts of freedom."[11] The first, outlined in the preceding discussion of liberal economic theory,

> is a "libertarian" understanding of freedom that equates freedom with *freedom of choice* or the power to do otherwise . . . To be free is to have (a) options to choose and (b) the ability to choose, uncoerced and unrestrained, among these options. On a certain version of this, the more options, the more free one is. Any specified telos for human agency would constitute a restraint on legitimate options and therefore a restriction of freedom. Even the articulation of a normative good would constitute a restriction on options and therefore a restriction of freedom. To be free, then, is equated with a state of *autosovereignty*, with respect to both the power to choose and the freedom to determine one's own good.[12]

Wendell Berry and other agrarians note that it is precisely this understanding of freedom—a "credo of limitlessness" that "does not allow for any question about the *net* good of anything proposed"—that underwrites our destructive economic system, and so too the pervasive belief that "*all* are entitled to pursue without limit whatever they conceive as desirable."[13]

Berry argues that, "in the phrase 'free market,' the word 'free' has come to mean unlimited economic power for some, with the necessary consequence of economic powerlessness for others."[14] There is, by all agrarian accounts, an obvious and radical disconnect between the promises and realities of economic liberalism. Though in theory the self-interest—the greed and the freedom—of one works for the benefit of all, Berry suggests that in practice "the defenders of the ideal of competition have never known what to do with or for the losers."[15] Berry's exposition offers a glimpse at a stark reality:

> The losers simply accumulate in the human dumps, like stores of industrial waste, until they gain enough misery and strength to overpower the winners. The idea that the displaced and

11. Smith, "Gospel of Freedom," 80.
12. Ibid., 80–81.
13. Berry, *What Matters?*, 42–43.
14. Ibid., 48.
15. Berry, *Art of the Commonplace*, 208–9.

dispossessed "should seek retraining and get into another line of work" is, of course, utterly cynical; it is only the hand-washing practiced by officials and experts. A loser, by definition, is somebody whom nobody knows what to do with. There is no limit to the damage and suffering implicit in this willingness that losers should exist as a normal economic cost.[16]

A fundamental aspect of the agrarian critique of liberal economic freedom, then, is making clear its oft-denied costs, both human and ecological. For it is only by some form of false accounting—some false notion of freedom and good—that "we have before us the spectacle of unprecedented 'prosperity' and 'economic growth' in a land of degraded farms, forests, ecosystems, and watersheds, polluted air, failing families, and perishing communities."[17] An economy built upon self-interested competition, in the end, can guarantee only that some will win and, inevitably, that some will lose.

James Smith reiterates that in the liberal account of freedom, "the only 'Good' that can be specified is the good of prosperity, which requires precisely that we bracket any specification of 'the Good' and let many *teloi* bloom (which really amounts to none)."[18] It is precisely this vague promise of the "good of prosperity" that Wendell Berry describes as "sentimental capitalism."[19] Such forms of political economy may properly be called sentimental, he suggests, because "they depend absolutely upon a political faith for which there is no justification."[20] In its propaganda, this form of "free-market" capitalism attempts to "justify violent means by good ends, which always are put beyond reach by the violence of the means."[21] The ends, the many *teloi*, Berry argues, are always defined vaguely—"the greatest good of the greatest number" or "the benefit of the many"—and so always kept at a safe distance.[22] Yet, ironically, "the only future good that [the free-market] assuredly leads to is that it will destroy itself."[23]

It is in the attempt to define freedom as "escape from all restraint," Berry argues, that we cease "to understand ourselves as beings specifically human."[24] In essence, we break ties with our religious and cultural tradi-

---

16. Ibid.
17. Berry, *Citizenship Papers*, 66.
18. Smith, "Gospel of Freedom," 81.
19. Berry, *Citizenship Papers*, 65.
20. Ibid.
21. Ibid.
22. Ibid.
23. Ibid., 66.
24. Berry, *What Matters?*, 45, 47.

tions that insist we are autonomous only in small part and only in a qualified way, as we are forever limited by our status as creatures, not Creator. Thus the formulation of autonomy inherent in the liberal economic vision, according to Berry, is an "illusory condition" that implies one "can be self-determining and independent without regard for any determining circumstance or any of the obvious dependencies."[25] Berry insists that, "there is, in practice, no such thing as autonomy," but rather "only a distinction between responsible and irresponsible dependence."[26] As earthly creatures, Berry writes,

> we live, because we must, within natural limits, which we may describe by such names as "earth" or "ecosystem" or "watershed" or "place" or "neighborhood." But as humans, we may elect to respond to this necessary placement by the self-restraints implied in neighborliness, stewardship, thrift, temperance, generosity, care, kindness, friendship, loyalty, and love.[27]

Thankfully, Augustine of Hippo offers a deeply instructive, radically Christian account of freedom that challenges many of the basic assumptions of the reigning economic paradigm.[28] For Augustine, "freedom is not simply a negative freedom *from*," Cavanaugh notes, "but a freedom *for*, a capacity to achieve certain worthwhile goals."[29] These worthwhile goals do not entail maximization of choice or liberation from all restraint, but rather "are taken up into the one overriding *telos* of human life, the return to God."[30] For Augustine, then, "autonomy in the strict sense is simply impossible, for to be independent of others and independent of God is to be cut off from being, and thus to be nothing at all."[31] Berry, along with contemporary agrarians generally, makes a strikingly similar point: "We must have limits or we will cease to exist as humans; perhaps we will cease to exist, period."[32] And further:

> In our limitless selfishness, we have tried to define "freedom" . . . as an escape from all restraint. But . . . "free" is etymologically related to "friend." These words come from the same Germanic and Sanskrit roots, which carry the sense of "dear" or "beloved."

25. Berry, *Unsettling of America*, 111.

26. Ibid.

27. Berry, *What Matters?*, 45.

28. Augustine, *Confessions*.

29. Cavanaugh, *Being Consumed*, 7–8.

30. Ibid. 8.

31. Ibid.

32. Berry, *What Matters?*, 47.

We set our friends free by our love for them, with the implied restraints of faithfulness or loyalty. And this suggests that our "identity" is located not in the impulse of selfhood but in deliberately maintained connections.[33]

For Augustine, like for Berry, "others are in fact crucial to one's freedom," as human beings "need a community of virtue in which to learn to desire rightly."[34] Augustine insists that desire is social, and so also reiterates the importance of community for the cultivation of right desire and fruitful practice. This is clearly demonstrated early in *Confessions*, as Augustine recounts a childhood crime:

Yet had I been alone I would not have done it—I remember my state of mind to be thus at the time—alone I would never have done it. Therefore my love in that act was to be associated with the gang in whose company I did it. Does it follow that I loved something other than the theft? No, nothing else in reality because association with the gang is also a nothing.[35]

Because there exists both true and false desires—desires deeply shaped by the communities to which we belong—"we need a *telos* to tell the difference between them."[36] For Augustine and agrarians alike, "the key to true freedom is not just following whatever desires we happen to have, but cultivating the right desires."[37] For Berry, then, to cultivate "right desire" necessarily means that one must "reexamine the economic structures of our life, and conform them to the tolerances and limits of our earthly places."[38] It is to this effort, the effort to cultivate right desire amid earthen community, which we now turn.

THE KINGDOM OF GOD AND AGRARIAN ECONOMICS

A fundamental problem of the industrial economy is "that it is not comprehensive enough," and further, that "it tends to destroy what it does not comprehend, and that it is *dependent* upon much that it does not comprehend."[39] The free-market, try as it might, cannot make a commodity of—it cannot

33. Ibid., 45.
34. Cavanaugh, *Being Consumed*, 9.
35. Augustine, *Confessions*, 33.
36. Cavanaugh, *Being Consumed*, 10.
37. Ibid.
38. Berry, *What Matters?*, 52–53.
39. Berry, *Art of the Commonplace*, 219.

quantify or account for—love of neighbor, of land, or of God. According to the agrarian mindset, the *only* economy that is comprehensive enough is the kingdom of God, or what Berry calls the "Great Economy."

Berry suggests several overarching principles of the kingdom of God, and they are worth juxtaposing with our current economic structure. First, the kingdom of God "includes everything; in it, the fall of every sparrow is a significant event."[40] All humans are in it, "whether we know it or not and whether we wish to be or not."[41] Second, everything in the kingdom of God is interdependent, and thus autonomy is never a moral absolute. Third, "humans do not and can never know either all the creatures that the Kingdom of God contains or the whole pattern or order by which it contains them."[42] In short, we can never conquer nature and its inhabitants, for though we live within order, "this order is both greater and more intricate than we can know."[43] Fourth, if we do attempt to master that which we do not fully comprehend—if we presume upon it or violate it—"severe penalties are in store for us."[44] And finally, because as creatures we do not control history, "*we* cannot foresee an end to it," and thus must tend creation to the best of our limited knowledge and ability.[45] This kingdom of God, the Great Economy, Berry concludes,

> is indeed—and in ways that are, to some extent, practical—an economy: it includes principles and patterns by which values or powers or necessities are parceled out and exchanged. But if the Great Economy comprehends humans and thus cannot be fully comprehended by them, then it is also not an economy in which humans can participate directly. What this suggests, in fact, is that humans can live in the Great Economy only with great uneasiness, subject to powers and laws that they can understand only in part. There is no human accounting for the Great Economy.[46]

Though all creatures are dependent on the Great Economy, it is also the case that humanity must have "a little economy," or "a narrow circle within which things are manageable by the use of our wits."[47] Berry suggests

40. Ibid., 220.
41. Ibid.
42. Ibid.
43. Ibid.
44. Ibid.
45. Ibid., 223.
46. Ibid., 221.
47. Ibid., 222.

that the proper relationship between the Great Economy and all smaller economies might be found in the sixth chapter of Matthew:

> After speaking of God's care for nature, the fowls of the air and the lilies of the field, Jesus says: "Therefore take no thought, saying, What shall we eat? or, What shall we drink? or, Wherewithal shall we be clothed? . . . But seek ye first the kingdom of God, and his righteousness; and all these things shall be added unto you."[48]

Berry interprets this text not as a summons to abandon all worldly economies but rather as an indication of the *telos* of all exchange. We must seek *first* the kingdom of God—a kingdom that includes the fowls and the lilies—thus giving "an obviously necessary priority to the Great Economy over any little economy made within it."[49] It is the Great Economy that must direct, must push and pull, our smaller economy. And when this smaller economy turns "in sympathy with the greater, receiving its being and its motion from it," the implications are profound:

> Then, because in the Great Economy *all* transactions count and the account is never "closed," the ideal changes. We see that we cannot *afford* maximum profit or power with minimum responsibility because, in the Great Economy, the loser's losses finally afflict the winner . . . Thus, it is not the "sum of its parts" but a *membership* of parts inextricably joined to each other, indebted to each other, receiving significance and worth from each other and from the whole. One is obliged to "consider the lilies of the field," not because they are lilies or because they are exemplary, but because they are fellow members and because, as fellow members, we and the lilies are in certain critical ways alike.[50]

AGRARIAN ECONOMIC PRACTICE

According to Wendell Berry's agrarian philosophy, love must always be incarnated in the small economy, in one's own neighborhood and household. For love "is not just a feeling but is indistinguishable from the willingness to help, to be useful to one another."[51] Thus the way of love leads inevitably to economic practice and "is indistinguishable, moreover, from the way of

48. Ibid.
49. Ibid.
50. Ibid., 233.
51. Berry, *Way of Ignorance*, 134.

freedom."[52] The vision of freedom Jesus offers in the Gospels—freedom from hatred, enmity, indifference, and violence—must guide us in our effort to "live and work so as not to be estranged from God's presence in His work and in all His creatures."[53] Berry insists that Jesus's teachings about love must constantly inform our economic lives. The question the agrarian mindset forces upon us, then, is at once profoundly simple and utterly challenging: "How are we to make of that love an economic practice?"[54]

One way Christians might begin such public offering is through a commitment to, and embodiment of, what philosopher Albert Borgmann calls "focal things and practices."

> A focal thing is something that has a commanding presence, engages your body and mind, and engages you with others. Focal things and the kinds of engagement they foster have the power to center your life, and to arrange all other things around this center in an orderly way because you know what's important and what's not. A focal practice results from committed engagement with a focal thing.[55]

The cultivation of focal practices enables precisely the sort of neighborhood Berry advocates, as they are "habits and events that bring people together in regular, sustained ways so that they can achieve an understanding of and participation in a common good."[56] Moreover, while commodities "are sharply defined and easily measured," focal things resist such reductive measurement.[57] As Borgmann notes,

> We can count the number of fast food outlets, the hamburgers sold, the times a family eats out. And such a measurement of eating understood as consumption can with some additional data capture its commodity. But how can we begin to measure a family meal, thoughtfully prepared and celebrated at home? Again we can measure highway miles; we can count cars per population and scenic resting places. But how does one determine and quantify the essential dimensions of a hike in the wilderness? . . . When value talk is about [focal] things, it falters, and the object of discourse slips from our grasp. Discourse that is appropriate to things must in its crucial occurrences abandon

52. Ibid.
53. Ibid., 137.
54. Ibid.
55. Borgmann, "Taming Technology," 23.
56. Wirzba, "Economy of Gratitude," 154.
57. Borgmann, *Technology*, 81.

the means-ends distinction. It must be open to and guided by the fullness of the focal thing in its world, and it can communicate the thing only through testimony and appeal.[58]

Focal things, then, "engage us in so many and subtle ways that no quantification can capture them."[59] They are "not at the mercy of how you feel at the moment" or "whether the time is convenient"; rather, "you commit yourself to it come hell or high water."[60] And such focal things naturally lead to practices—meals, festivals, sports leagues, community events, church services—that, however simple, enable us "to feel once again the eloquence and the loveliness of reality," of our own local and particular neighborhoods and households.[61]

Of all the focal practices Christians might develop, however, the most important may be the breaking of bread together. For it is this practice, the Eucharistic act, that "is the sign that gives all other signs their significance because it is the repetition of the moment of *ultimate exchange* between God and humanity that Christians cannot but claim to be the basis for all other exchanges."[62] It is this practice, finally, that must orient all other economic thinking and practice, for it is in breaking bread that we give thanks and provide for all members of our community, weak and strong alike.

"The Eucharist," John Howard Yoder noted, "is an economic act." When we join in the fellowship of Christ's table, we reaffirm that the kingdom of God sustains all smaller economies. And so also we witness to the profound freedom of a community shaped by mutual love and sharing, by concern for those a disordered economy forgets, by deep care for the land and its creatures, and by gentle loving-kindness for all in its membership. Thus "to do rightly the practice of breaking bread together is a matter of economic ethics"—the moment of ultimate exchange between God and humanity must impact the ordering of our lives and the lives of others.[63]

It seems unavoidable that Berry's daunting question—How are we to make of Jesus's love an economic practice?—proves essential to Christian communities attempting to live and act faithfully in a violent, fragmented, and seemingly limitless world. It is a question that, when carefully considered, forces us to abandon the dodges of political and economic abstraction and take up the practical, communal, and often difficult effort of cultivating

58. Ibid.
59. Ibid.
60. Borgmann, "Taming Technology," 23.
61. Wirzba, "Economy of Gratitude," 154.
62. Long, *Goodness of God*, 236.
63. Yoder, *Body Politics*, 21.

right desire in a disordered world. "What is most important," Cavanaugh concludes, "is the direct embodiment of free economic practices," and so too the fostering of "economic practices that are consonant with the true ends of creation."[64] Thankfully, Berry offers us a striking vision of how we might cultivate right desire and bear good fruit, as creatures at once fallen and redeemed, in the paradise of God's creation.

BIBLIOGRAPHY

Augustine. *Confessions*. Edited by Henry Chadwick. Oxford: Oxford University Press, 1991.

Berry, Wendell. *The Art of the Commonplace: The Agrarian Essays of Wendell Berry*. Edited by Norman Wirzba. Washington, DC: Shoemaker and Hoard, 2002.

———. *Citizenship Papers*. Washington, DC: Shoemaker and Hoard. 2004.

———. *Sex, Economy, Freedom and Community*. New York: Pantheon, 1993.

———. *The Unsettling of America: Culture and Agriculture*. 3rd ed. San Francisco: Sierra Club, 1996.

———. *The Way of Ignorance: And Other Essays*. Washington, DC: Shoemaker and Hoard, 2005.

———. *What Matters? Economics for a Renewed Commonwealth*. Berkeley, CA: Counterpoint, 2010.

Borgmann, Albert. "Albert Borgmann on Taming Technology." *Christian Century*, August 23, 2003.

———. *Technology and the Character of Contemporary Life: A Philosophical Inquiry*. Chicago: University of Chicago Press, 1984.

Cavanaugh, William T. *Being Consumed: Economics and Christian Desire*. Grand Rapids: Eerdmans, 2008.

Clark, Gregory. *A Farewell to Alms: A Brief Economic History of the World*. Princeton: Princeton University Press, 2007.

Cottingham, John, Robert Stoothoff, and Dugald Murdoch, trans. *The Philosophical Writings of René Descartes*. Cambridge: Cambridge University Press, 1985.

Friedman, Milton. *Capitalism and Freedom*. Chicago: University of Chicago Press, 1962.

Long, D. Stephen. *Divine Economy: Theology and the Market*. London: Routledge, 2000.

———. *The Goodness of God: Theology, the Church, and Social Order*. Grand Rapids: Brazos, 2001.

Smith, Adam. *An Inquiry into the Nature and Causes of the Wealth of Nations*. 1776. Edited by R. H. Campbell, Andrew S. Skinner, and W. B. Todd. Indianapolis: Liberty Classics, 1981.

Smith, James K. A. "The Gospel of Freedom, or Another Gospel? Theology, Empire, and American Foreign Policy." In *Evangelicals and Empire: Christian Alternatives to the Political Status Quo*, edited by Bruce Ellis Benson and Peter Goodwin Heltzel, 79–92. Grand Rapids: Brazos, 2008.

Wirzba, Norman. "An Economy of Gratitude." In *Wendell Berry: Life and Work*, edited by Jason Peters, 142–55. Lexington: University Press of Kentucky, 2007.

64. Cavanaugh, *Being Consumed*, 32.

Worster, Donald. "The Wealth of Nature." In *The New Agrarianism: Land, Culture, and the Community of Life*, edited by Eric T. Freyfogle, 161–77. Washington, DC: Island, 2001.

Yoder, John Howard. *Body Politics: Five Practices of the Christian Community Before the Watching World*. Scottdale, PA: Herald, 1992.

INTERLUDE TWO

Adam M. L. Tice

The Earth Belongs to God Alone

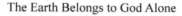

MORNING SONG (CONSOLATION) CM

1. The earth be - longs to God a - lone; hard clay, rich soil, fine sand.
2. The fer - tile ground through years of toil has cried for sab - bath rest—
3. All life be - longs to God a - lone— in wil - der - ness and fields.
4. 'Till God en - dows the earth once more with E - den's state of grace,

Give thanks wher - ev - er food is grown on bor - rowed ho - ly land.
a time of peace for worn - out soil so land can be re - freshed.
From fal - low land, or plowed and sown, God gives the good it yields.
may we en - deav - or to re - store all land as sa - cred space.

Text: Adam M. L. Tice, 2006; ©2011 by GIA Publications, Inc., 7404 S. Mason Ave., Chicago, IL 60638; www.giamusic.com; 800-442-1358
All rights reserved. Used by permission.
Music: anonymous, John Wyeth's *Repository of Sacred Music, Part Second,* 1813.

We Dream of a Turning

LOCH LOMOND 11.10.13.10 with refrain

1. We dream of a turn-ing from a - ges of wrong, Earth to
2. We dream of a feast where there's no - one out - side, turned a -
3. We dream of a moun - tain where no harm is done, where the

E - den re-stored, and our par - don. Like Eve and A - dam, join in a
way due to dif - f'rence or la - bel, when all the wea-pons forged to de-
wolf and the lamb lie to - geth - er. A lit - tle child shall dance, lead-ing

sto - ry and a song as we wan - der with God through the gar - den.
stroy or to di - vide turn to rust far from God's ho - ly ta - ble.
all the crea-tures on, as we join hand to hoof, claw and fea - ther!

Where true peace is shin - ing as hate rolls a - way, see, God's

bright new cre - a - tion is gleam - ing. The mor - ning rays that dawn on our

wea - ry, wak - ing day bring a hope far be - yond all our dream - ing.

Text: Adam M. L. Tice, 2008
Tune: Scottish traditional, arr. Adam M. L. Tice
Text and arrangement ©2009 by GIA Publications, Inc., 7404 S. Mason Ave., Chicago, IL 60638; www.giamusic.com; 800-442-1358

PART THREE

Historical Reflections

16

On Hollowed Ground?

The Ambivalent Territoriality of Saint Justin's
Interpretation of the Kingdom of God and Its Implications
for Contemporary Christian Theological Reflection

Nicholas R. Brown

One of the notable trends to emerge from recent theological reflection is a
renewed focus on Jesus's proclamation of the kingdom of God. In particular,
leading scholars from a variety of fields have argued that Jesus's kingdom
vision expressed a widely-shared first-century Jewish eschatological hope
for Israel's national restoration.[1]

At the same time, however, several scholars have also argued that Jesus
deterritorialized the kingdom. More specifically, they have claimed that Jesus decoupled the kingdom from Israel's territorial borders and *transformed*
Jewish national existence from a geographic state into a universal religio-
ethical praxis.

John Howard Yoder, for instance, has argued that Jesus's announce-
ment of the kingdom is "a visible socio-political, economic restructuring

---

1. A representative but by no means exhaustive list of works advancing some
variation of this thesis includes Borg, *Conflict, Holiness, and Politics*; Hauerwas, *Peaceable Kingdom*; Horsley, *Jesus and the Spiral of Violence*; McKnight, *New Vision For Israel*;
Moxnes, *Putting Jesus in His Place*; Sanders, *Jesus and Judaism*; Stassen and Gushee,
Kingdom Ethics; Wright, *Jesus and the Victory of God*; and Yoder, *Politics of Jesus*.

of relations among the people of God."[2] However, he has also suggested that "the universality of God's kingdom contradicts rather than confirms all particular solidarities and can be reached only by first forsaking the old aeon."[3] Accordingly, Jesus's kingdom proclamation confirms that statelessness is the normative sociopolitical posture for Christians.[4]

These arguments are striking not only for their internal tensions—the discomfiture between a political yet landless kingdom—but also because they are juxtaposed against a burgeoning discourse on the theological importance of place and placedness.[5] There is tension, then, between those who emphasize the placedness of the kingdom and those who obscure or ignore Israel's landedness.

Where does this ambivalence about the kingdom's territorial placement arise? Is it simply consistent with newer trends of post-territorial and post-national politics? Or is it more pervasive and enduring, a sensibility intrinsic to the pilgrimage that is Christian existence?

A good place to begin answering these questions is Saint Justin Martyr (c. 100–165 CE) and his interpretation of the kingdom of God. Before delving into the specifics of his interpretation, it is important to first highlight the theological crucible from which it emerged. Particularly pertinent are St. Justin's chiliastic eschatology and the theological error with which he was most consistently and passionately consumed: the heresy of Gnosticism.

The term *chiliasm*, from the Greek word *chilioi* meaning "one thousand," refers to the future thousand-year, global kingdom established by Christ at his second coming described in Rev 20:1–6. Yet as Robert Louis Wilken observes, for early theologians like St. Justin, chiliasm emphasized less "the idea of [Christ's] thousand-year reign" and more "the belief that Christian hope is centered on a glorified Jerusalem that will come down from the heavens."[6]

It is this attention to the kingdom's territorial placement that puts St. Justin at odds with the gnostics. It would be reductionistic to claim Gnosticism is summed up by its denial of embodiment, but its ontological quest to be liberated from corporeal existence certainly makes it incompatible with orthodox Christianity, and more distantly, St. Justin's view of the land.

2. Yoder, *Politics of Jesus*, 32.

3. Yoder, *Original Revolution*, 58.

4. Yoder, *For the Nations*, 51–78. See also Yoder, *Jewish-Christian Schism*.

5. Such works that have received more critical attention and acclaim are Bartholomew, *Where Mortals Dwell*; Brueggemann, *Land*; Gorringe, *Theology of the Built Environment*; Llywelyn, *Catholic Theology of Nationality*; and Jennings, *Christian Imagination*.

6. Wilken, *Land Called Holy*, 56.

Thus, whereas a gnostic soteriology presupposes disembodiment, an orthodox account of salvation asserts the exact opposite, inasmuch as Jesus's incarnation testifies to the reality that "there is no accessing . . . the supramaterial apart from its revelation, and thus mediation, in the materiality of creation and the flesh."[7] Christ's incarnation, in other words, not only refutes the gnostic impugnation of corporeality, but it also reaffirms that "Christ's flesh as Jewish, covenantal flesh is a social-political reality displayed across time and space into which the Gentiles are received in praise of the God of Israel."[8]

Having reviewed St. Justin's critiques of Gnosticism, we can better understand his interpretation of the kingdom. Indeed this interpretation incorporates the countergnostic principles described above—that is, it generally affirms material existence and, more specifically, the concrete, historical continuity of Christianity and Judaism.

Consider, for example, St. Justin's description of the kingdom in *Dialogue with Trypho*.[9] When asked by his Jewish interlocutor whether he, a Christian, "really believe[s] that this place Jerusalem shall be rebuilt, and do you actually expect that you Christians will one day congregate there to live joyfully with Christ, together with the patriarchs, the prophets, the saints of our race, or even those who become proselytes before your Christ arrived?," St. Justin responds as follows:

> If you have ever encountered any nominal Christians who do not admit of this doctrine, but dare to blaspheme the God of Jacob by asserting that there is no resurrection of the dead, but that their souls are taken up to heaven at the very moment of their death, do not consider them to be real Christians. . . .
>
> Whereas I, and all other wholeheartedly orthodox Christians, feel certain that there will be a resurrection of the flesh, followed by a *thousand years in the rebuilt, embellished, and enlarged city of Jerusalem,* as was announced by the prophets Ezekiel, Isaiah and others.[10]

This response is remarkable for its depth and complexity; nevertheless, three aspects stand out. First, St. Justin rather begrudgingly concedes there is a group of "nominal Christians" who reject the coincidence of the kingdom's full eschatological consummation with a physically restored Jerusalem. Of course, it would be overly speculative to presume these "nominal

7. Carter, *Race*, 25.

8. Ibid., 30.

9. Martyr, *Dialogue with Trypho*.

10. Ibid., 80.3–5.

Christians" were, in fact, gnostics given that St. Justin offers no further clue about their identity. Nonetheless, even if not gnostic by name, the spirit (if not the letter) of their beliefs comport with a gnostic penchant for rejecting the body.

Secondly, St. Justin notes an interdependence between the bodily resurrection of the dead and the territorial restoration of the kingdom. The two are inextricably linked, as a human soul cannot be fully resurrected apart from a human body any more than a resurrected body can fully dwell in the kingdom of God apart from its being replaced in a territorially restored Jerusalem. In St. Justin's mind, both are predicated upon the fully restored materiality of the other.

Finally, there is St. Justin's insistence that a denial of a territorially restored kingdom is blasphemous because such a kingdom is foretold by the prophets. Thus, not only does Justin reiterate the canonicity of the Hebrew Scriptures but he also reaffirms Christianity's unbreakable continuity with Judaism. This does not mean, however, that Justin views Jesus simply as another Jewish prophet. Nor does he think Jesus is wholly disinterested in the kingdom's territorial restoration. Instead, Justin views Jesus, in some sense, as repeating, yet also bringing into fuller completion, the prophetic promises of the kingdom's eschatological restoration. Hence, he also writes in *Dialogue with Trypho*,

> And just as [Joshua], not Moses, conducted the people into the Holy Land and distributed it by lot among those who entered, so also will Jesus the Christ gather together the dispersed people and distribute the good land to each, though not in the same manner.
>
> For, Joshua gave them an inheritance for a time only, since he was not Christ our God, nor the Son of God; but Jesus, after the holy resurrection, will give us an inheritance for eternity . . . After his coming the Father will, through [Jesus], renew heaven and earth.
>
> This is he who is to shine in Jerusalem as an eternal light.[11]

In juxtaposing Christ's allocation of the land with Joshua's, it is not the physical quality of the land that is being compared but the permanence of its distribution. Christ's allocation is final and eternal whereas Joshua's is considered temporary. Nevertheless, St. Justin is still convinced that Christ's restoration of the kingdom entails nothing less than a physical return to Israel's land.

---

11. Ibid., 113.3–5.

Thus, St. Justin is sure that the future consummation of Christ's eschatological kingdom will be firmly entrenched within a Palestinian territorial locale. Furthermore, his emphasis on the materiality of the kingdom directly coincides with his commitments to preserve the materiality of creation and the concrete connection between Christianity and Judaism.

Nevertheless, St. Justin also undermines the concrete realities of Israel, the body, and the land. Consider, for example, the relationship he sees between Gentile Christians and the Abrahamic and Mosaic covenants. His first move is to once again affirm the continued legitimacy of those covenants and their complementarity with Christianity. "But," he continues with a caveat that portends significant departure, "our hope is not through Moses or through the Law, otherwise our customs would be the same as yours."[12] On the contrary, he concludes that not only is the "law promulgated at Horeb . . . already obsolete," but it is also nullified since "a later law in opposition to an older law abrogates the older." [13] That being the case, Gentile Christians "have been led to God through this crucified Christ, and *we are the true spiritual Israel* (emphasis added), and the descendants of Judah, Jacob, Isaac, and Abraham."[14]

In one fell swoop, Justin has gone from resolutely affirming Christianity's dependency on Israel to not only calling that dependency into question but also, in fact, declaring it defunct. The previous carnal and historical dependence on Israel has thus suddenly given way to spiritual independence.

This independence takes on an even sharper edge when St. Justin considers the Jews' denial of Jesus's lordship, an intransigence that according to St. Justin ultimately causes YHWH to replace carnal Israel with the church. As he writes:

> Since God blesses and calls this people [Gentile Christians] Israel, and announces aloud that it is his inheritance, why do you not feel compunction both for fooling yourselves by imagining that you alone are the people of Israel, and for cursing the people whom God has blessed? Indeed when he spoke to Jerusalem and its surrounding communities, he said, *And I will beget men upon you, my people Israel, and they shall inherit you, and you shall be their inheritance, and you shall no more be bereaved by them of children.*[15]

12. Ibid. 11.1
13. Ibid., 11.2.
14. Ibid., 11.5.
15. Ibid., 123.6.

Absent here is any sense of the historical and material continuity that previously permeated St. Justin's discussions of the kingdom.

Of course, such a provocative and defamatory claim elicits no small measure of incredulity and indignation from Trypho. "Do you mean to say," he asks of St. Justin, "that you [Gentile Christians] are Israel and that God says all this about you?"[16] Lest Justin's previous statement let any doubt linger, he doubles down with emphatic boldness:

> If you have ears to hear it, in Isaiah, God, speaking of Christ in parable, calls him Jacob and Israel. This is what he says: *Jacob is my servant, I will uphold him; Israel is my elect. I will put my spirit upon him and he shall bring forth judgment to the Gentiles. He shall neither strive nor cry, nor shall any one hear his voice in the streets. The bruised reed he shall not break, and smoking flax he shall not quench, but he shall bring forth judgment unto truth. He shall shine, and shall not be broken, till he set judgment in the earth; and in his name shall the Gentile trust.*
>
> Therefore, as your whole people was called after that one Jacob, surnamed Israel, so we who obey the precepts of Christ, are, through Christ who begot us to God, *both called and in reality are, Jacob and Israel and Judah and Joseph and David and true children of God* (emphasis added).[17]

Hence, a deep-seated ambivalence marks St. Justin's interpretations of the kingdom as well as his understanding of Judaism. As Paula Friedreksen notes, from one side St. Justin's thought is thoroughly Jewish "to the degree that [he] insisted that Christ had had a fleshly body, that he had indeed descended from the house of David, and that the entirety of the Septuagint, understood correctly, actually referred to Christ and his church."[18] Furthermore, because St. Justin did not think creation "itself was evil," he insisted it was just as essential to envision the kingdom's eschatological restoration as "a thousand-year-long Sabbath in a renewed and resplendent Jerusalem" as it was to envision a bodily resurrection.[19]

At the same time, however, St. Justin continued to view Jewish obduracy toward Christ as symptomatic of a larger, congenital defect, namely a Jewish insistence to read both the Scriptures and the kingdom "in a carnal way," such that both were "interpret[ed] . . . literally rather than

---

16. Ibid., 123.7.

17. Ibid., 123.8–9. Justin quotes portions of Isaiah 42 here.

18. Friedreksen, "Birth of Christianity," 25.

19. Ibid.

allegorically."[20] Accordingly, while St. Justin's millennialism reiterated a territorial interpretation of the kingdom, his quasi-gnostic reading of YHWH's covenants with Israel ultimately interjected a theological and material fissure between Christianity and Judaism, as well as between the kingdom and the *eretz* Israel.

Recognizing this cleavage allows us to observe how Justin's critique of Gnosticism fails to carry over and inform his chiliasm and eschatology. For on the one hand, he believed that God's kingdom had always been and would always remain landed. On the other hand, however, the territorial particularity of Israel no longer held any theological significance by virtue of Christ's "greater" revelation. The kingdom had already been replaced, both theologically and geographically, by the catholic Christian community known as the church.

To conclude, I will now briefly address how St. Justin's interpretation of the kingdom foregrounds contemporary theological discussions about land and place. Two lines in particular stand out. One is the recognition that Jesus's incarnation designates place and land not just as instrumental theological categories but as essential ones. Gary M. Burge makes this point persuasively:

> The Gospels do not talk about the revelation of Christ without referring to the place where it happened. Location is valuable because history is important. In the New Testament the incarnation is a genuine embrace of human life with all of its particularities. And what emerges is the wedding of theology and history, which together form the nexus of how Christians begin to think about their world and Christ.[21]

Another contemporary theological perspective on land is an increased awareness that Christian theology is so inescapably placed and landed that it cannot ignore or displace Israel. As Scott Bader-Saye argues, "The church looks to the Jews not just because they embody something that the church wants to imitate but more importantly because the church's own life and story are unintelligible apart from this people and their God."[22]

Thus, both Burge and Bader-Saye echo St. Justin's landed interpretation of the kingdom of God. Both possess a parallel commitment to preserve the historicity and materiality of Christian faith as well as its relationship with the ongoing reality of God's covenant with Israel. And yet, even as they affirm the theological importance of Israel's place in Christian theology, they

20. Ibid., 26.
21. Burge, *Jesus and the Land*, 126.
22. Bader-Saye, *Church and Israel*, 25.

also, like St. Justin, ultimately speak in ways that undermine the importance of a landed Israel, in a manner mimicking St. Justin's replacement logic.

For instance, when further exploring the implications Jesus's incarnation has for Christian theology of the land, Burge contends, "For a Christian to return to a Jewish territoriality is to deny fundamentally what has transpired in the incarnation. It is to deflect appropriate devotion to the new place where God has appeared in residence, namely, in his Son . . . He is the new spatiality, the new locale where God may be met."[23]

Bader-Saye offers a comparable sentiment when he examines the role of the Eucharist. For although the eucharistic celebration "does not *replace* the land," the body of Jesus nevertheless "becomes the material site of redemption."[24] Consequently, the "gift of eucharistic peace is a siteless participation in God's coming redemption . . . In this fleshly gift, this body that is the soil of God's redemption, Christians taste peace and are made into peaceful citizens in God's holy land."[25]

Once again then, Burge's and Bader-Saye's interpretations bear a strong family resemblance to Justin's conception of the kingdom. Positively, they all declare land, placement, and Israel to be essential for Christian theological reflection on account of the materiality and historicity of Jesus's incarnation. Negatively, however, all believe this same incarnation also replaces and, thus, removes the historicity and materiality of Israel's territorial particularity.

What, then, are we to make of these negative theological assessments regarding Israel's territoriality? More specifically, do they create a set of problems that not only undermine a proper theological interpretation of the kingdom, with respect to place and land in particular, but also Christian theology *in toto*?

As theologians James McClendon and Nancey Murphy have persuasively argued, while human embodiment is not, in and of itself, sufficient to the task of Christian ethical reflection, it is most undeniably necessary.[26] Furthermore, both McClendon and Murphy have acknowledged that a Christian moral agent exists as an embodied moral self, placed within a particular territorial locale. Indeed, if one grants the premise that Christian morality is always embodied, by virtue of the fact that both Christ and Christians are always embodied, then one must extend this logic further and admit that territoriality, too, is an essential Christian ethical modality

---

23. Burge, *Jesus and the Land*, 129–30.

24. Bader-Saye, *Church and Israel*, 144–45.

25. Ibid., 145.

26. McClendon Jr., *Ethics*; Murphy, *Bodies and Souls*.

insofar as both Christians and their embodied moral practices are always territorially placed.

Thus, to deny the territoriality of Israel deprives Christian theological reflection of the very historical and material sources required to be politically normative. Without access to such sources, not only does such an ethic run the risk of becoming something less than Christian, but it also loses its capacity to be political, as it fails to demonstrate to a watching and waiting world an alternative praxis for how places and land should be lived in and governed.

A dismissal of Israel's territoriality also further compounds the theological error that Kendal Soulen describes as structural supersessionism. Structural supersessionism claims that the Old Testament is rendered *"largely indecisive for shaping conclusions about how God's purposes engage creation in universal and enduring ways."*[27] In particular, it "drives an *historical* wedge between the gospel and the God of Israel *by collapsing God's covenant with Israel into the economy of redemption in its prefigurative form*" and thus "misinterprets redemption in Christ as deliverance from God's history with Israel and the nations."[28]

Accordingly, I would contend that the replacement of Israel's territoriality with the spatiality of Christ or the church is a corollary of structural supersessionism in two ways. First, such a hermeneutics is structurally closed off from not only the carnality of Israel's people but also their territoriality. Second, it also implies that *eretz* Israel has no lasting theological import for public and political life. In short, it is to recapitulate the gnostic error of wanting to separate Christianity's place in the economy of redemption to the placedness of Israel's covenant.

I began this essay with John Howard Yoder's observation that the radicality of Jesus's kingdom proclamation consisted in its opening up of Israel's covenant to make it more inclusive and universal. Yoder also articulated this sentiment in another way, by saying the gospel is good news "for the nations."[29] However, in light of the theological importance of place in general and Israel's land in particular, it is now necessary to recognize that

27. Soulen, *God of Israel*, 31.

28. Ibid., 110.

29. Yoder, *For the Nations*, 3. As Yoder writes in the volume's introduction, "Each of the following essays argues, though each in a somewhat different key, that the very shape of the people of God in the world is a public witness, or is 'good news,' for the world, rather than first of all rejection or withdrawal. Where the attitude to world needs to be rejection or retreat, that is determined contextually, because of the world's recalcitrant response to that initial noncoercive, yea vulnerable affirmation. I call these essays 'evangelical' in the root sense of the term, having to do with being bearers of good news for the world" (ibid., 6).

the very reason Jesus's kingdom vision was good news for the nations was because it was first good news for the nation of Israel.

BIBLIOGRAPHY

Bader-Saye, Scott. *Church and Israel after Christendom: The Politics of Election*. Eugene, OR: Wipf and Stock, 1999.

Bartholomew, Craig G. *Where Mortals Dwell: A Christian View of Place for Today*. Grand Rapids: Baker Academic, 2011.

Borg, Marcus. *Conflict, Holiness, and Politics in the Teachings of Jesus*. New York: Continuum, 1998.

Brueggemann, Walter. *The Land: Place as Gift, Promise, and Challenge in Biblical Faith*. 2nd ed. Philadelphia: Fortress, 2002.

Burge, Gary M. *Jesus and the Land: The New Testament Challenge to "Holy Land" Theology*. Grand Rapids: Baker Academic, 2010.

Carter, J. Kameron. *Race: A Theological Account*. New York: Oxford University Press, 2008.

Friedreksen, Paula. "The Birth of Christianity and the Origins of Christian Anti-Judaism." In *Jesus, Judaism, and Christian Anti-Judaism: Reading the New Testament after the Holocaust*, edited by Paula Fredriksen and Adele Reinhartz, 8–30. Louisville: Westminster John Knox, 2002.

Gorringe, Timothy. *A Theology of the Built Environment: Justice, Empowerment and Redemption*. Cambridge: Cambridge University Press, 2002.

Hauerwas, Stanley. *The Peaceable Kingdom: A Primer in Christian Ethics*. Notre Dame: University of Notre Dame Press, 1991.

Horsley, Richard A. *Jesus and the Spiral of Violence: Popular Jewish Resistance in Roman Palestine*. Philadelphia: Fortress, 1993.

Jennings, Willie James. *The Christian Imagination: Theology and the Origins of Race*. New Haven: Yale University Press, 2010.

Llywelyn, Dorian. *Toward a Catholic Theology of Nationality*. Plymouth, UK: Lexington, 2010.

Martyr, Justin. *Dialogue with Trypho (Selections from the Fathers of the Church)*. Edited by Thomas Halton. Translated by Thomas Halls. Washington, DC: Catholic University of America Press, 2003.

McClendon, James William, Jr. *Ethics: Systematic Theology*. Vol. 1. 2nd ed. Nashville: Abingdon, 2002.

McKnight, Scot. *A New Vision for Israel: The Teachings of Jesus in National Context*. Grand Rapids: Eerdmans, 1999.

Moxnes, Halvor. *Putting Jesus in His Place: A Radical Vision of Household and Kingdom*. Louisville: Westminster John Knox, 2003.

Murphy, Nancey C. *Bodies and Souls, or Spirited Bodies?* Cambridge: Cambridge University Press, 2006.

Sanders, E. P. *Jesus and Judaism*. Philadelphia: Fortress, 1985.

Stassen, Glen H., and David P. Gushee. *Kingdom Ethics: Following Jesus in Contemporary Context*. Downers Grove: InterVarsity, 2003.

Soulen, R. Kendall. *The God of Israel and Christian Theology*. Minneapolis: Fortress, 1996.

Wilken, Robert Louis. *The Land Called Holy: Palestine in Christian History and Thought.* New Haven: Yale University Press, 1992.

Wright, N. T. *Jesus and the Victory of God.* Christian Origins and the Question of God 2. Philadelphia: Fortress, 1996.

Yoder, John Howard. *For the Nations: Essays Public and Evangelical.* Grand Rapids: Eerdmans, 1997.

———. *The Jewish-Christian Schism Revisited.* Edited by Michael G. Cartwright and Peter Ochs. Grand Rapids: Eerdmans, 2003.

———. *The Original Revolution: Essays on Christian Pacifism.* Scottdale, PA: Herald, 2003.

———. *The Politics of Jesus.* 2nd ed. Grand Rapids: Eerdmans, 1994.

17

Extracting Faith, Cultivating Faith

Andean Lessons on Decolonizing Christian Environmentalism

Ryan M. Juskus

Mining has long been both a source of wealth and a topic of theological ambiguity. King Solomon, for instance, built the Jerusalem temple using his vast wealth, symbolized in the Old Testament by the gold he obtained from the land of Ophir (1 Kgs 10:11–12). Yet both he and his source of wealth draw prophetic critique.[1] Much later, medieval Christians in Europe, lured by popular tales of eastern sources of gold, associated this biblical reference to Ophir with eastern lands, so much so that when Christopher Columbus landed in the "West Indies," he and his men immediately began their search for the gold of Ophir.[2] In this way, the Spanish and Portuguese theologically interpreted their ventures in the "New World" as Christian mission. Spanish writer Pedro de Medina captured the thrust of this missiology in 1547:

> Just as God provided Solomon with that gold and silver brought
> to built [sic] the *material temple*, so that it was the richest and

1. See 1 Kgs 11:9–13 and Job 28, respectively. Regarding the latter, the author juxtaposes the gold mined in Ophir with the true source of wisdom, wealth, and understanding: it comes not from resource extraction but rather from YHWH.

2. Brown, *History of Mining*, 2–3.

most solemn in the world, he likewise wanted the Spaniards to bring from remote and distant places so much gold and silver and other riches to edify the *spiritual temple*, which is to bring the infidels to the society and council of the holy mother Church.[3]

"The deluge of American gold and silver," concludes historian Kendall Brown, "seemed an answer to Columbus's dream of finding a westerly route to Cipangu's mythical gold in order to finance the Last Crusade."[4]

What King Solomon, medieval Europeans, and modern mining-based development strategies share in common is what I call an extractive theology of mission. De Medina's missiological interpretation of European conquests in what is now Latin America reflects a more than five-hundred-year pattern of justifying the extraction of precious or industrial metals, and more recently oil and gas, in the name of greater human or divine projects. Justifications like de Medina's are explicitly theological: they equate God's project with that of the extractive enterprise to finance global mission or achieve other perceived goods, such as economic development. Other, less explicitly theological, approaches manifest an extractive paradigm through anthropocentric practices that instrumentalize the earth and its resources for various human projects. A contemporary example of this is neo-extractivism, a trend in Latin American growth-oriented development in which states nationalize and augment their extractive industries and primary exports, using extraction-derived rents to finance social and anti-poverty initiatives.[5] Whereas the beneficiaries and justifications of extractive industry have shifted considerably in five hundred years, Latin America's history of extraction mirrors the worldview and theologies that allowed such extraction-based paradigms to flourish.

Research suggests that greater levels and technologies of extraction have significantly contributed to today's socio-ecological crisis. While modern extractive industries may have many positive impacts, they negatively

---

3. Ibid., 12; emphasis mine. The Spanish monarchs at the time were engaged in a nearly 800-year *reconquista*, a Christian project to reconquer the Iberian Peninsula from the Muslims who had controlled it since the early eighth century.

4. Ibid., 12.

5. This can be seen in Venezuela, Ecuador, Bolivia, Peru, and Brazil, among other countries in the region. See Gudynas, "La Renovación," 71–83, or "La Ecología Política," 53–67. See also Burchardt and Dietz, "(Neo-) Extractivism," 468–86. The "neo-" signals that this model is both distinct from and yet similar to the now-waning neoliberal era of extractivism in Latin America, a period defined by privatization, free market ideology, and state policies, and the important role played by transnational corporations in the exploitation of raw materials and the appropriation of profits (ibid., 469–70). This was particularly seen in Peru, Argentina, and Chile in the 1980s and 1990s.

affect both regional and global ecologies, as well as the groups of people, such as indigenous peoples, most vulnerable to largely exogenous socioeconomic forces.[6] After briefly developing a juxtaposition between theologies of extraction and cultivation, I engage with the worldview and practices of Andean indigenous peoples to sketch a framework and agenda for identifying what Christian environmentalists can learn from indigenous peoples who have resisted extractivist paradigms for centuries and who are only recently starting to achieve measurable success at local and regional levels.[7]

In this postcolonial era, indigenous peoples are decolonizing their thought and socio-political life. Environmentally conscious Christians whose theological and practical imaginations have been formed by extractivist strains of Euro-American modernity are also engaging in a similar kind of decolonizing effort.[8] Building upon the environmental turn in Christian theology, Christian environmentalists must develop conceptual and practical resources for translating these theologies into communities of holistic gospel transformation that innovate new forms of faithfully, lovingly, and hopefully living together in shared spaces and among fellow creatures before God.[9] How can Christians formed by an extractive paradigm transform their extractive faith into a faith that cultivates *shalom*?[10] I argue that as Christians decolonize their environmental thought and develop the

---

6. Space does not allow for a summary of the socioecological impacts of modern extractive industries. These impacts are well documented by researchers and think tanks—such as the International Land Coalition, the FAO, CIRAD, CISEPA, IFPRI, the Blacksmith Institute, and many others—tracking the links between industry, environment, and social issues. See, for instance, research on the Peruvian Amazon by Dourejeanni et al., *Amazonía Peruana*.

7. Regarding "Christian environmentalists," I mainly have in mind North American Christians engaged in the environmental movement, including evangelicals, mainline Protestants, Orthodox, and Catholics.

8. I will not reiterate a biblical theology of environmental ethics or creation care here. For this, see the works of Calvin B. DeWitt, Christopher J. H. Wright, and Richard Bauckham. Their projects all entail some form of decolonizing biblical theologies of creation and environmental ethics from European cultural elements. For an excellent evangelical engagement with postcolonialism in the United States, see Smith et al., *Evangelical Postcolonial Conversations*.

9. In this paper, I use "Western" and "Euro-American" interchangeably.

10. *Shalom* refers here to the Hebrew notion of a whole and positive peace within the covenantal relationships between human beings, the earth, the other living creatures, and God; it signifies not only a restoration of relationships after a period of broken or skewed relationship but also the *enjoyment* of such relations. For a classic articulation of shalom in relation to Christian theories of development, see Wolterstorff, *Until Justice and Peace Embrace*. For an interaction between shalom theology and Native American belief and practice, see Woodley, *Shalom*.

imaginative practices necessary to cultivate *shalom*, they should learn from the experience of indigenous peoples.

The terms *extraction* and *cultivation* represent two patterns by which human beings relate to the nonhuman world, or what I refer to as the environment.[11] Undoubtedly, there are more than two ways of relating to the environment. However, there is heuristic benefit in using these two terms to signify two broad patterns of human-environment relations and, in the process, two general ways in which human beings relate to each other and to themselves through the environment. Whereas extraction denotes an anthropocentric pattern, cultivation refers to a communitarian one: humans are caretaking members of the community of creation.

A model for understanding the relation between today's socioecological crisis and human faithfulness to the Triune God comes from the Old Testament: Israel's socioeconomic relations measured the health of the nation's relationship to YHWH.[12] Unhealthy socioecological relations indicate a need for more faithful ways to relate to God vis-à-vis human relations to God's creation.[13] David Kelsey argues that God-human relations move in two directions: first, God's relating to humans, and second, our relating responsively to God.[14] My focus is on the latter—how human faith, love, and hope are expressed in terms of human beings' relating to God, each other, and the nonhuman world as patterned by either extraction or cultivation.

EXTRACTING FAITH

A people's practices are a form of speech that reveals their worldview and theology, particularly their understandings of God and humanity. I maintain that in the dominant worldview of the colonizers and the subsequent governments and business interests in Latin America, human beings are seen as separate from and superior to nature, instrumentalizing the earth and its resources for human or divine projects to achieve historical progress

11. While the shortcomings of the term "environment" are significant, I use it here as a placeholder for the nonhuman world, including animals, plants, the earth, and other living or nonliving creatures.

12. See Wright, *Old Testament Ethics*, 17–20.

13. This is not to suggest that by improving ecological or social relations human beings can somehow manipulate the saving grace of God—some notion of justification by works—thus changing how God relates to humanity; rather, it is to suggest that greater faithfulness to God, love toward God and neighbor, and hope in the already-but-not-yet kingdom will be indicated by healthy interactions between human beings and the environment.

14. Kelsey, "On Human Flourishing," 19.

or development.[15] This admixture of European Enlightenment philosophy and science, Christian theology, anthropocentrism, and a progressive view of history makes up an extractive paradigm. Its theological form is managerial stewardship, in which God's project in/for creation is closely related to human progress and development.[16] Human beings extract themselves from the rest of the biotic community and proclaim themselves God's managers over the rest of creation, which exists primarily for human benefit. An extracting faith is one that breeds or reinforces this competitive and instrumental human relation to the environment.[17]

The opening excerpt by de Medina is an historical example of extractive theology: he interprets Spain's new source of wealth in terms of its utility for financing the evangelization of nonbelievers. Columbus himself hoped that his efforts "would supply the gold needed to satisfy his view of humanity's greatest need: the wealth to launch the Final Crusade and usher in the end of time with Christ's return."[18] A contemporary example, managerial stewardship theology, mixes biblical, Greek, and Enlightenment sources to convert the biblical, theocentric concept of *dominion* into a modern, anthropocentric notion of *domination*.[19] Here, human responsibility toward nature involves managing it for God's purposes, which are closely identified with human progress.[20]

An historical example of this extractive paradigm and its socioecological impact is the central Peruvian region around Cerro de Pasco and La Oroya in the early twentieth century. For economic and ideological reasons, mining companies in Andean countries sought to sever the sociocultural, economic, and spiritual relationship between indigenous peasants and

15. The key word is "dominant" worldview. Clearly, there were and are subdominant people, institutions, and organizations that embodied/embody a cultivating paradigm in Latin America.

16. I specify *managerial* stewardship in recognition that not all stewardship theologies involve anthropocentric or Enlightenment conceptions of humanity or progress.

17. While human beings have been involved in forms of mining for thousands of years, including in pre-Columbian America, and while it would be unfair to equate all forms of extraction, the technologies of extraction and the scale of resource removal from the colonial era to today are in a category of their own, not only due to the processes involved, but also the scale of the damage done to individuals, societies, and the environment. Extractivism thus represents much more than just mining; it refers to a pattern of sociopolitical, ecological, psychological, and even spiritual relations in which resource extraction is a defining feature.

18. Brown, *History of Mining*, 192.

19. Bauckham, "Stewardship," 100–101.

20. One relevant example from early European modernity is John Locke, whose theology of human self-preservation closely links God's work in the world with human progress.

agrarian life. They needed peasants to abandon farming and work full-time in the mines, which they also expected would develop indigenous peoples by introducing them to modern labor, education, and social life.[21] Companies, therefore, devised strategies to sever the ties between peasants and the land, which, in Cerro de Pasco, largely failed. Eventually a smelter was opened in nearby La Oroya that so polluted the surrounding countryside that indigenous peasants resorted to working in the mines simply because the contaminated land could no longer support crops or livestock. More than their previous strategies, "contamination from the smelter caused the semi-proletarianization of the miners because by spoiling the village lands, the pollution made it impossible for the miners to obtain food and other necessities from their home communities."[22] In short, the Cerro de Pasco Corporation's profits depended on its ability to successfully sever the sociocultural, economic, and spiritual relationship between the indigenous peasants and their land. The company achieved this only after so polluting the land that it could no longer support life.

Ultimately, extractive paradigms create or reinforce a pattern of social, ecological, psychological, and spiritual relations that are fragmented, unhealthy, and distorted. Extractive theologies radically separate human beings from the rest of God's creation, setting them above and in competition with it, and seeking *human* flourishing over that of the environment. As such, extractive theologies tend to subordinate the value of nonhuman creatures to their use-value in achieving human ends rather than recognizing their intrinsic value as fellow creatures. Theologies that ossify the separation and superiority of human beings over the environment contribute to the effects produced by irresponsible extractive industries.

CULTIVATING FAITH

The second theological paradigm is what I call a cultivating faith. Cultivation denotes a careful process of production. It signifies the values and practices of reciprocity, restoration, care, sustainability, and mutuality. Cultivation is a creative act: it re-creates and sustains the processes of life. Cultivation does not entail perfection but rather a commitment to living within the limits of a place and, when those limits are transgressed, seeking restoration.[23] Con-

---

21. Brown, *History of Mining*, 139.

22. Ibid., 141.

23. It is important to note that I do not intend to convey that all forms of extraction qualify as an extractive paradigm. A cultivating paradigm does not necessarily exclude extractive industry. The relevant questions here revolve around scale, methods,

trasted with the image of polluted La Oroya is the agrarian vision given to Moses by YHWH just prior to the Israelites' settlement of Canaan. This was a vision sustained by sociolegal mechanisms, such as sabbatical institutions and the Jubilee, that recognized the inevitability of misfortunes, natural limits, and distorted social relations and yet instituted practices for social and ecological restoration.[24] For our purposes, the two crucial aspects of a cultivating faith revolve around a communitarian theological anthropology and a relational worldview that entails a reconciliation ethic.

In a cultivating faith, human beings are caretaking members of the "community of creation."[25] While there is a theological and moral distinction between humans and the nonhuman world, it remains a reciprocal relationship where the flourishing of both human beings and the environment are mutually bound. Humanity's caretaker role must be understood within this community and will therefore involve living within the limits of healthy relationship, largely through sociolegal institutions that recognize and uphold such limits.

Secondly, a cultivating faith entails what Arturo Escobar calls a "relational ontology" or worldview in which "all beings exist always in relation and never as 'objects' or individuals." Relational ontologies eschew the neat divisions "between nature and culture, between individual and community, and between us and them that are central to the modern ontology."[26] Rather, diverse creatures are bound together in dynamic relationship. A cultivating theology thus emphasizes the health of the relations between the things of creation. When relations are out of balance, broken, or distorted, then it is necessary to work toward their reconciliation. With a relational moral imagination, then, ecological and social health mirrors the health of human faithfulness to the Triune God.

Andean worldview and moral imagination overlap significantly with a cultivating faith, while the dominant paradigms of the various Latin American political and economic regimes largely reflect an extracting theology.

---

impact, and socioeconomic dependence on extraction or, in other words, the centrality of extraction for maintaining an unsustainable socioeconomic system.

24. Even though there is little evidence to suggest that practices like the Jubilee were fully implemented in history, the vision and practices of Leviticus 25 shape a pattern of values, morals, and the allocation of burdens of persuasion that continue to propel the Christian imagination toward a kingdom of God socioecological ethic.

25. Bauckham, *Bible and Ecology*, preface.

26. Escobar, *Encountering Development*, xxviii.

THE ANDEAN INDIGENOUS MOVEMENT

Indigenous peoples movements in Latin America, particularly in the Andean countries of Peru, Ecuador, and Bolivia, lead global efforts not only to resist an extractive paradigm but also to offer an alternative path of development that more closely reflects a cultivating paradigm.[27] Indigenous peoples experienced European institutions and ideas as exogenous cultural impositions that oftentimes conflicted with their worldview and values. Because of this, indigenous peoples starkly contrast Andean worldview with that dominant in the West.

Historically, discussions about indigenous peoples' common experiences led to concrete actions in the 1980s and 1990s in Ecuador, Mexico, Bolivia, and Peru.[28] In Ecuador and Bolivia, the movement's success partly culminated in constitutional reforms that recognize these countries as "plurinational states," incorporating indigenous values and understandings of the abundant life—variously called *Sumak Kawsay, Suma Qamaña*, or *buen vivir*[29]—into the legal code and political charter.[30] "[*Buen vivir*] is life in abundance. It is knowing how to live in harmony and balance: in harmony with the cycles of Mother Earth, the cosmos, life and history; and in balance with every form of existence with a never-ending respect."[31] According to Maria Ceci Misoczky, indigenous peoples articulate their worldview "with the production of social life, generating a coherent connection between the material and the sacred, the profane and the divine."[32] Ecuadorian economist Pablo Dávalos notes that indigenous explanations of life and nature became the basis for the emergence of a "cultural-political movement," the goal of which is "to reclaim the commons."[33] And while this movement is strongest in Latin America, its leaders are also set on reframing and reformulating development goals and objectives in the international

27. The Andean indigenous movement is best represented by the Andean Coordinator of Indigenous Organizations (CAOI) as well as a number of overlapping regional, national, and international networks, such as AIDESEP in Peru, CONAIE and ECUARUNARI in Ecuador, and CIDOB in Bolivia.

28. Misoczky, "Visions in Dispute," 352–53.

29. These have been variously translated into English as "the good life" or "living well."

30. In his systematic account of *buen vivir*, Fernando Huanacuni clarifies that the Quechua concept of Sumak Kawsay, the Aymara concept of Suma Quamaña and the Spanish translation, *buen vivir*, all mean the same thing—"life in plenitude," or, "abundant life." See Huanacuni, *Buen Vivir*.

31. Ibid., 32.

32. Misoczky, "Visions in Dispute," 353.

33. Ibid., 346, 353.

sphere, particularly to address global crises such as climate change.[34] This indigenous movement has produced remarkable agreement that local and global socioecological crises are the outcome of a Euro-American worldview and as such cannot be solved by Western institutions alone but must include substantial interaction with indigenous conceptions and practices such as *buen vivir*.

Buen vivir continues to gain resonance on a global scale, influencing "various groups and social movements that are looking for viable alternatives to the dominant discourse of development based on economic rationality and the Modern-European ideal of progress."[35] While some scholars, fearing co-optation by international institutions, hesitate to apply indigenous concepts to a broader audience, many see a dialogical relationship between indigenous notions of *buen vivir* and other discourses of sustainability and ecology in our contemporary era.[36] I share the conclusion of Vanhulst and Beling:

> The greatest potential of *Buen Vivir* lies in the opportunities it generates for dialog with other modern discourses and the current forms of development, by enlarging the frame of current debates and allowing for the potential emergence of novel conceptions, institutions and practices through collective learning.[37]

In short, without coopting indigenous thought and practice, those committed to finding sustainable ways of living and flourishing together on this earth should learn *from* and *with* indigenous peoples.

The former Minister of Foreign Relations of Bolivia, David Choquehuanca Céspedes, distinguishes "living well" (*buen vivir*) from "living better."[38] Living well has to do with communitarianism, harmony, and complementarity, whereas living better has to do with living *better than* others at the expense of nature and the other. He concludes that development initiatives have generally focused on living better rather than on living well. Living well

34. See, for instance, the efforts of Evo Morales, President of the Plurinational State of Bolivia, to provide an alternative approach to the climate crisis; Schipani, "Evo Morales' Message." See also Morales, "Speech at Climate Summit."

35. Vanhulst and Beling, "Buen Vivir," 60.

36. Latin American scholars who are engaging indigenous thought from this perspective, relating it to wider discourses of sustainability, include Alberto Acosta, Eduardo Gudynas, Arturo Escobar, and Pablo Dávalos. See, for instance, Gudynas, "La Ecología Política," 34–47; Acosta, "El Buen Vivir."

37. Vanhulst and Beling, "Buen Vivir," 61.

38. Céspedes, "Hacia la Reconstrucción," 8. The following references by Céspedes are translated by the present author.

is about recovering a "culture of life" in which "we are all part of nature."[39] "The living better approach," says Céspedes, "believes in *social* justice" even though in practice it only achieves justice for the few. However, an exclusive focus on social forms of justice also leaves the nonhuman world outside the moral frame. He continues, "Our struggle transcends social justice. We seek a balanced life . . . achieving balance among human beings and between humans and nature, a balanced life between men and women."[40] Likewise, where liberty means license to exploit, complementarity accounts for the harmony of relationships between members of the life community, and where democratic institutions perennially fail minorities, the indigenous movement instead seeks consensus. Céspedes concludes,

> With our own practices and resources drawn from the breast of our communities, we are compelled to reconstruct a 'living well' paradigm based on a complementarity in harmony with nature within the limits that the health of mother nature permits us, a 'living well' that points to living in community, in fraternity, and especially in complementarity.[41]

Aymara Bolivian historian Fernando Huanacuni, tasked with writing a systematic account of *buen vivir*, contends that the root of the global ecological crisis is a hierarchical anthropocentrism founded on the Christian doctrines of God and creation. He argues that a wider vision of life is required, one consistent with a "culture of life, which is naturally communitarian."[42] For Huanacuni, dominant twentieth-century reasoning was anthropocentric—it excluded the ethical status of the environment. This hierarchical anthropocentrism, he believes, stems from Judeo-Christian doctrine, particularly a "king of creation" anthropology, women's secondary status in creation, and the masculine, hierarchical relationship between the Father and the Son. Finally, he attributes Western homogenization and universalism to monotheism. Huanacuni concludes,

> These "sacred" conceptions mark and establish a whole process of interaction and relation of life that is machista-individualistic, merely humanistic, where the role of women is random

39. Ibid., 10.

40. Ibid., 11. While the indigenous values of complementarity and balance are derived from a primal duality in creation between the heavenly force and the telluric/earthly force—a duality not reflected in Christian traditions—the values are still relevant, particularly when incorporated within trinitarian theology.

41. Ibid., 12.

42. Huanacuni, "Paradigma Occidental," 17. The following references by Huanacuni are translated by the present author.

and secondary and, in addition, where human beings place themselves above other forms of existence, generating a pyramidal hierarchical structure in a subject-object relationship that gives power to humanity to use and abuse everything around [them].[43]

Huanacuni's scathing conclusion, although directly aimed at Christian doctrines, ultimately implicates the syncretism that I call extractive theology. He accurately diagnoses the problem but inaccurately identifies the theological origins. More accurate is to critique the extractive paradigm of Christian-Enlightenment synthesis.

The crisis brought about by this paradigm, according to Huanacuni, requires deep engagement with premodern, "ancestral principles" for communitarian living.[44] Communitarian living, however, also requires a communitarian cosmology that "conceives of life in a communitarian form, not only in terms of social relations, but also in terms of profound life relations."[45] In short, Huanacuni advances a relational worldview in which human and nonhuman life are understood to be dynamically, ontologically, and morally related to each other. Within this paradigm, the earth's "resources" instead become "vital systems" that support life. The emphasis is on life—both human and nonhuman—and the processes of life. This, I argue, is consistent with a cultivating theology in which human beings are considered caretaking members of the community of creation that produces and reproduces life. Additionally, a cultivating theology also overlaps with Huanacuni's communitarian cosmology: the Triune God, human beings, the earth, and all living creatures are bound together in creative relationship that was broken by sin and yet has been/is being restored to *shalom* through the work of Christ. Huanacuni's call to return to "ancestral principles" echoes Christian theologians engaged in decolonizing their faith from anthropocentric managerialism.[46]

43. Ibid.; Ever since Lynn White accused Christian eschatology of laying the theological foundations of the ecological crisis, it has become commonplace to focus on eschatology. However, it is notable that the indigenous movement critiques not Christian eschatology but rather the doctrines of God and creation.

44. Ibid., 19.

45. Ibid.,20.

46. While some scholars sharply juxtapose Judeo-Christian beliefs and Amerindian indigenous beliefs, it is important to note that many Andean indigenous peoples retain indigenous beliefs while also being active members of Christian churches and denominations. See, for instance, the Council of Evangelical Indigenous Peoples and Organizations of Ecuador (FEINE). Raúl Zibechi also notes the interpenetration of Christian, indigenous, and urban fringe practices. Zibechi, *Territories in Resistance*, 322.

Regardless of potentially significant differences between Andean and Christian understandings, the indigenous retrieval of pre/non-modern principles and values offers not only fresh imagination but also new social practices and institutions that significantly cohere with the nascent environmental aspirations of Western Christians. Only a brief sketch of some of the movement's practices is presented here.

1. Hybridization

Hybridization is a process by which indigenous peoples are decolonizing their thought and practices not by returning to a pre-modern way of life but by drawing from pre/non-modern principles and values within and for a context highly structured by modern institutions. Hybridization provides a model for engaging modern structures, ideas, and institutions through insight largely drawn from non-modern sources. Indigenous peoples' successful inclusion of their values and language within the constitutions of Ecuador and Bolivia is one example. A second is how indigenous peoples utilize the language of rights and thus employ Western legal mechanisms in new, unforeseen ways. For instance, Ecuador and Bolivia are the first countries to legally recognize the rights of nature. While these efforts are still very young, they signify the potential for creative hybridization of modern institutions and non-modern principles at multiple levels. Christian environmentalists, drawing on divine revelation and rich tradition, are similarly aiming to hybridize modern institutions.

2. Territoriality

A second feature of indigenous movements is their territoriality. Indigenous groups rarely refer to land but refer instead to geographic territory, "a wider concept which defines a collective good and its interdependency with nature."[47] Territories are indispensable for indigenous identity and vitality—sources of food, shelter, and cultural creation. Land can be bought and sold like any other commodity, but because a territory is infused with spiritual and cultural significance, it is inalienable. Political theorist Raúl Zibechi notes that indigenous movements territorialize spaces where communities live out alternative socioecological relations. "Territory becomes the place where counter-hegemonic social relations are deployed and where groups and collectives can practice different ways of living."[48] Rarely seeking change by fiat, indigenous movements instead occupy and reclaim spaces where they can both insert their practices into public life as well as model

47. Misoczky, "Visions in Dispute," 355.

48. Zibechi, *Territories in Resistance*, 209–11.

new forms of living together in territories with relative autonomy from state institutions.[49] Whether through community gardens, farmer's markets, land trusts, or other creative and cooperative uses of visible space, Christian environmentalists can create demonstration plots where alternative forms of living together influence the wider society.[50]

3. Consultation

Indigenous peoples achieved internationally recognized "consultation laws" requiring their inclusion in a consultation process regarding any initiatives that will affect their territories and livelihoods.[51] While accountability remains a struggle, consultation laws shift the burdens of persuasion in support of indigenous peoples—including their socioecological values—and away from purely extractive interests. Whereas indigenous peoples have rightly earned special legal status due to their unique history and vulnerability, Christians could strengthen existing consultative processes for development projects that will impact their local environments. The goal should be to shift the burdens of persuasion toward ventures that support, rather than jeopardize, socioecological health.

4. Spontaneous Change

A key distinction between today's indigenous movement and other social movements is that indigenous peoples are not limited by state-centered models of social change or bureaucratic organization. Whereas many social movements have sought state power—sometimes through violence—to effect change from above, indigenous peoples have often pursued change from below and within society. They have not rejected political power entirely but instead engage politics selectively as they enact new patterns of social relations as "societies in movement."[52] Organizationally, Zibechi ob-

49. Territorialization is also a key feature of indigenous mobilizations to protect territories. For instance, when legislation was decreed in 2008 in Peru that would significantly weaken indigenous territorial rights and grant greater powers to extractive industries, indigenous groups seized petroleum headquarters and blocked highways. After almost two months, the standoff ended with Peruvian army helicopters firing on strikers near the city of Bagua. While the strike ended in tragedy, the mobilization proved successful in that the most egregious decrees were overturned and the rest declared unconstitutional by a government committee. See Misoczky, "Visions in Dispute," 355–56.

50. The similarities with Anabaptist and neo-Anabaptist approaches are not lost on the author.

51. The most important is the International Labour Organization's Convention no. 168.

52. Zibechi, *Territories in Resistance*, 208.

serves that indigenous movements often reflect social forms of everyday life rather than hierarchical, bureaucratic models, oftentimes favoring familial consensus and spontaneity over democratic structures.[53] While enormous challenges like climate change require public policy changes, Christians can more effectively pursue cultural change at family, church, community, and regional levels.[54] A similar temptation is to seek change primarily through institutional models, such as the nonprofit organization, rather than through a groundswell of spontaneous and decentralized actions.[55]

5. Renaming

Finally, there is the powerful, symbolic practice of renaming. Indigenous peoples are renaming places and things as they decolonize their social institutions *and* their vocabulary. For instance, indigenous groups increasingly refer to Latin America as "Abya Yala," a term that pre-dates Columbus. Likewise, the earth is "Mother Earth," nature is "Pachamama" and resources are "vital sources." These semantic changes rhetorically signify a deeper shift in human-environment relations. Whereas "earth" may signify an Enlightenment notion of dead matter in space, "Mother Earth" connotes the connection between earth and life. Likewise, while "resources" denotes extractivism, "vital sources" signifies a web of life, including the human need to maintain its longevity. This symbolic action of renaming holds significant potential for re-shaping Christians' moral imaginations—from earth to creation, ownership to stewardship. Do we perpetuate words in our vocabulary of faith that implicitly sanction an extractive form of faith?[56] Renaming places, production processes, and things can valorize the interconnections between human, nonhuman, and divine life.

53. Ibid., 307–9.

54. The recent movement called "watershed discipleship" is one example of a creative, non-statist form of Christian environmentalism in the United States. See http://watersheddiscipleship.org/.

55. For a compelling perspective on spontaneous and "blessed unrest," see Hawken, *Blessed Unrest*.

56. I have sometimes wondered whether some methods of biblical exegesis and ethics operate as a form of extraction—mining scriptural texts for principles or propositions that can be extracted and repackaged for consumption. See Vanhoozer, *Drama of Doctrine*, for a non-extractive form of biblical interpretation that seeks to maintain the integrity of the form in which God's communication has been revealed.

CONCLUSION

While a deeper engagement is necessary, I have set out an agenda for further cross-pollination between indigenous peoples and Christian environmentalists as they decolonize human-environment relations. The indigenous movement insists that today's socioecological crisis will not be resolved by more extraction-based development because these models mis-identify the root problem. For indigenous peoples, the roots lie within the dominant Western worldview and values. If there is reason for Euro-American Christians to self-examine and repent of extractive faith—to recognize extractivism as a divergence from Christian faith—there is even greater reason to hope: Christians can learn from and join others, such as indigenous peoples, who are hybridizing modern institutions and creating spaces of alternative socioecological relations with a commitment to cultivating practices aimed at life in abundance.

BIBLIOGRAPHY

Acosta, Alberto. "El Buen Vivir en el camino del post-desarrollo: Una lectura desde la Constitución de Montecristi." Policy Paper 9. Quito, Ecuador: Fundación Friedrich Ebert Stiftung, October 2010.

Bauckham, Richard. *The Bible and Ecology: Rediscovering the Community of Creation*. Waco: Baylor University Press, 2010.

———. "Stewardship and Relationship." In *The Care of Creation: Focusing Concern and Action*, edited by R. J. Berry, 99–106. Downers Grove, IL: InterVarsity, 2000.

Brown, Kendall. *A History of Mining in Latin America: From the Colonial Era to the Present*. Albuquerque: University of New Mexico Press, 2012.

Burchardt, Hans-Jurgen and Kristina Dietz. "(Neo-)Extractivism: A New Challenge for Development Theory from Latin America." *Third World Quarterly* 35, no. 3 (2014) 468–86.

Céspedes, David Choquehuanca. "Hacia la Reconstrucción del Vivir Bien." *America Latina en Movimiento* 452 (2010) 8–13. http://www.alainet.org/es/revistas/531 (accessed September 22, 2015).

Dourejeanni, Marc, et al. *Amazonía peruana en 2021: Explotación de recursos naturales e infraestructuras*. Lima, Peru: ProNaturaleza, 2009.

Escobar, Arturo. *Encountering Development: The Making and Unmaking of the Third World*. 2nd ed. Princeton: Princeton University Press, 2012.

Gudynas, Eduardo. "La ecología política del giro biocéntrico en la nueva Constitución de Ecuador." *Revista de Estudios Sociales* 32 (2009) 34–47.

———. "La ecología política de la crisis global y los límites del capitalismo benévolo." *Revista de Ciencias Sociales* 36, (2010) 53–67.

———. "La renovación de la crítica al desarrollo y el buen vivir como alternativo." *Utopía y Praxis Latinoamericano* 16, no. 53 (2011) 71–83.

Hawken, Paul. *Blessed Unrest: How the Largest Social Movement in History is Restoring Grace, Justice, and Beauty to the World*. New York: Penguin, 2008.

Huanacuni Mamani, Fernando. *Buen Vivir/Vivir Bien: Filosofía, Políticas, Estrategias y Experiencias Regionales Andinas.* Lima, Peru: Coordinadora Andina de Organizaciones Indígenas, 2010. https://www.reflectiongroup.org/stuff/vivir-bien (accessed October 19, 2014).

———. "Paradigma Occidental y Paradigma Indígena Originario." *America Latina en Movimiento* 452 (2010) 17–22. http://www.alainet.org/es/revistas/531 (accessed October 19, 2014).

Kelsey, David. "On Human Flourishing: A Theocentric Perspective." Paper presented at the consultation on "God's Power and Human Flourishing" at the Yale Center for Faith and Culture, Yale Divinity School, New Haven, CT, May 23–24, 2008.

Misoczky, Maria Ceci. "World Visions in Dispute in Contemporary Latin America: Development X Harmonic Life." *Organization* 18, no. 3 (2011) 345–63.

Morales, Evo. "Speech at Climate Summit on Behalf of G77." *America Latina en Movimiento,* September 26, 2014. http://www.alainet.org/en/active/77464 (accessed September 22, 2015).

Schipani, Andres. "Evo Morales' Message to Grassroots Climate Talks—Planet or Death." *Guardian,* April 21, 2010. http://www.theguardian.com/environment/2010/apr/21/evo-morales-grassroots-climate-talks (accessed September 22, 2015).

Smith, Kay Higuera, et al., *Evangelical Postcolonial Conversations: Global Awakenings in Theology and Practice.* Downers Grove, IL: InterVarsity, 2014.

Vanhulst, J., and A. E. Beling. "Buen Vivir: Emergent Discourse within or beyond Sustainable Development?" *Ecological Economics* 101 (2014) 54–63.

"Watershed Discipleship." http://watersheddiscipleship.org/ (accessed June 18, 2015).

Wolterstorff, Nicholas. *Until Justice and Peace Embrace.* Grand Rapids: Eerdmans, 1983.

Woodley, Randy S. *Shalom and the Community of Creation: An Indigenous Vision.* Grand Rapids: Eerdmans, 2012.

Wright, Christopher J. H. *Old Testament Ethics for the People of God.* Downers Grove, IL: InterVarsity, 2004.

Zibechi, Raúl. *Territories in Resistance: A Cartography of Latin American Social Movements.* Translated by Ramor Ryan. Oakland, CA: AK, 2012.

Vanhoozer, Kevin J. *The Drama of Doctrine: A Canonical-Linguistic Approach to Christian Theology.* Louisville: Westminster John Knox, 2005.

18

"But It Is Nothing Except Woods"[1]

Anabaptists, Ambitions, and a
Northern Indiana Settlerscape, 1830–1841

D. Ezra Miller

In the spring of 1841, four Amish Mennonite families left their homes in Somerset County, Pennsylvania, in search of new homes in northern Indiana. Heading north after a two-week layover in Holmes County, Ohio, they followed trails across southern Michigan until they reached White Pigeon, Michigan. From there they turned south and entered northern Indiana, setting up temporary homes on the Elkhart Prairie, south and east of present-day Goshen, Indiana. Discovering the prairie land to be more expensive than they had anticipated, they soon found suitable locations for settlement in the western part of LaGrange County and the eastern part of Elkhart County.

Unfortunately, there are few known documents that state directly why these families chose to leave the familiarity of their homes and venture into unfamiliar territory. Much of what we do know of this event comes from an account written by Hansi Borntreger seventy years later. An Amish

1. This paper benefited from research funded by the Newberry Consortium for American Indian Studies Short Term Fellowship during August 2014 in the Mennonite Historical Library, the Mennonite Church USA Archives-Goshen, and the Northern Indiana Amish Library.

historian, Borntreger was the three-year-old son of one of these first four Amish Mennonite families at the time of their migration to northern Indiana. Other than noting that a "feeling" arose in the community, Borntreger fails to elaborate on why they chose to move to Indiana.[2] Were they simply drawn by the appeal of cheaper land? Had congregational disputes and tensions grown to such an extent that dissolution became more feasible than conciliation? Did they seek political isolation to buffer themselves against potential threat of military conscription by the United States government? Most likely, all of these factors contributed at some level to their decision to migrate. Yet, none of these explanations adequately account for how Amish Mennonite settlers perceived the places and people they encountered in migration. For example, how did they reconcile their migration in the Great Lakes region with the displacement of Native communities, considering their pacifist ideologies rooted in religious beliefs and the memory of their own disenfranchisement throughout Europe? Others have posed similar questions, yet with few exceptions, this dilemma remains largely unexplored.[3] A look at the impact religion has upon the way humans interact with unfamiliar landscapes contributes to the understanding of the "motives, intentions, and imaginings" of Anabaptist settlers in the Great Lakes region during the nineteenth century.[4]

Over the past several decades, anthropologists and historians have recognized the diversity and fluidity of the cultural relations in the Great Lakes region during colonization and settlement.[5] Much of this research has grown out of Richard White's seminal work *The Middle Ground.*[6] White's book focuses on the fur trade in the region from the middle of the sixteenth century to the early part of the nineteenth century with an emphasis on the alliances, accommodation, and new meaning produced by the various scales of agency within European colonial structures and the Algonquin nations in the Great Lakes region. The concept of "middle ground" has given complexity and texture to Indigenous-white relations, which have often been oversimplified as linear narratives of either acculturation or persistence. However, according to White, the middle ground terminated in 1815, leaving the impression that Indigenous agency had subsided and the complexity of the landscape had given way to some other narrative.

2. Borntreger, *A History.*

3. Schlabach, *Peace, Faith, Nation*; Yoder, *Tradition*; Good, "Lost Inheritance."

4. Comaroff and Comaroff, *Of Revelation*, 10.

5. Sleeper-Smith, "Women, Kin, and Catholicism"; Buss, *Winning the West.*

6. White, *Middle Ground.*

One of the ways scholars have picked up the narrative where the middle ground left off is by focusing on the dis-possessive impulse of settler colonialism. According to Patrick Wolfe, the compulsion for land is the essence of settler colonialism, which forges ahead until it acquires whatever territory it desires through whatever means are available.[7] Here again the narrative narrows to a linear flow in which the land lust of individual settlers and settler groups becomes reified, homogenized, and structured as though settlers were an indispensable cog in a machine set on a predetermined course. However, the unidirectional agency of settler colonialism skips over the liminality, diversity, and reciprocity of Indigenous-settler-government relations that existed throughout the Great Lakes during the nineteenth century. I suggest that this period of change and uncertainty in the Great Lakes region is best understood in terms of settlerscapes.

The term settlerscape draws attention to the way clearly recognizable Indigenous landscapes became transformed into distinctive, settled communities. Much as the middle ground did for the fur trade, the settlerscape recognizes the competition and complementarity of interests converging in particular places, only this time during the settlement period. It acknowledges the uneven transformation and attempted erasure of the Indigenous landscape, which insisted on bleeding through.

Theoretically, the term settlerscape relies on the British anthropologist Tim Ingold's dwelling perspective of a landscape.[8] From a dwelling perspective, a landscape is understood as the forms that emerge out of the human activity of dwelling, rather than simply the imposition of the imagination of humans through force upon the raw materials of nature. Culture, and for that matter, religion are not simply a matter of the mind, nor are they performed in thin air. Culture is embodied and emplaced within a landscape. In other words, humans do not build and cultivate to dwell; rather, as they dwell, they build and cultivate constrained by the resources available to them. Over time, humans embody particular ways of engaging the world in which they live, which generates what philosophers refer to as a way of being-in-the-world. As people engage in a landscape, they participate in an ongoing story that is never complete.

When nonindigenous settlers began to arrive in northern Indiana in the late 1820s and early 1830s, the Potawatomi had inhabited northern Indiana continuously for nearly one hundred and fifty years. The fertile drainage basin of the St. Joseph River, which attracted settlers from the east, provided an abundance of game, fish, berries, plants, garden plots, and fields

---

7. Wolfe, "Settler Colonialism."

8. Ingold, *Perception of the Environment.*

for the subsistence needs of Potawatomi. Recognizing these advantages, the US government negotiated a series of treaties with the Potawatomi beginning in 1789. By 1833, the Potawatomi had ceded a majority of their land to the United States, ending in their forced removal from northern Indiana by the US military in 1838.[9] The treaties leave the impression of a somewhat civil process between the US government and the Potawatomi; however, the journal of the proceedings to the negotiations details the collision of vastly different perspectives, values, and visions for the contested land.

What follows are excerpts from three discourses portraying three widely differing understandings of the region. They include the voices of a US commissioner, a Potawatomi headman, and an Amish Mennonite bishop.

As a result of the 1821 "Treaty of Chicago," the Odawa, Chippewa, and Potawatomi ceded a large portion of their territory in Michigan and northern Indiana to the United States. In filing his report on the details concerning the negotiation and terms of the treaty, Solomon Sibley had this to say to President Monroe:

> The treaty requires that all the lands reserved and granted shall be located in conformity with the principles of the public surveys. These locations must, of course, be suspended until the public surveys are completed. The reason which induced the commissioners to insert that provision, was a suggestion that the former mode pursued in designating the reservations in Indian treaties, was attended with inconvenience, by necessarily creating several fractional sections adjoining each location, and which it was desirable should be avoided.
>
> The country embraced by the treaty has been estimated at between four and five millions of acres. The quality of the soil in this tract of land is believed equal to that of any other country of similar extent. It possesses the advantages of a mild climate, and of being watered in its whole extent by large navigable rivers that traverse the country from east to west. The St. Joseph and Grand rivers open into lake Michigan, and contain at all times a sufficient depth of water for the admission of vessels from the lake some distance into the country, and good boat navigation nearly to their sources. Streams of less size and well calculated for mills and machinery, with numerous springs of the purest water, abound in every part of the country.

9. Though the focus of scholarship has been on the termination of the Potawatomi's presence in northern Indiana and southern Michigan through forced removal, a significant population of Potawatomi avoided removal while others continued to return to the region from Kansas for a number of years

> This purchase unites together the several tracts of land lying within the peninsula, and heretofore purchased from the Indians, and which, once settled, will effectually divide the northern Indians from those who inhabit the country to the south and west; and will also interpose a barrier to all foreign influence in that quarter. The commissioners cannot but consider this acquisition of primary importance to the future growth and prosperity of the lake country, and particularly that portion which is destined, on some future day, to form the state of Michigan; and they presume to hope, that it will be so received by the President, and that the proceedings of the commissioners, in relation to the negotiation, will meet his approbation.[10]

The exact terms of the treaty were to be delayed until the "public surveys" conducted by the deputy surveyors of the Land Office could be completed. Earlier treaties had reserved land for the Indians associated with their use. These lands were scattered and disconnected, disrupting any uniformity of the boundaries the United States wished to establish. The surveys would divide the land by section, township, and county, making it saleable for impending settlement. Waiting until the land was surveyed to designate reserved lands would insure that they fell within the arbitrary lines of the survey, and out of the way of settlement and progress.

Further, the newly acquired land would create a political wedge intended to weaken the alliance of the Odawa, Chippewa, and Potawatomi. The treaty consolidated land from several previous treaties into one land mass, which would, in Cass's words, "effectually divide the northern Indians from those who inhabit the country to the south and west."[11] The commissioners saw the purchase of land as essential to the expansion of the United States, not only for increased land base but also to strengthen their position politically in the region. Once settled, the land would create a "barrier to all foreign influence."[12]

Economically, the land was strategic in that it offered access to extensive waterways. The waterways would provide transportation, industry, and communication links between the east and the west. For the United States, the land was valued as a commodity to be bargained for, divided into arbitrary units, and sold. It had no meaning attached to it other than its economic and political value, which could be calculated, conquered, and controlled.

10. "Letter from the Secretary of War," 145–46.
11. Ibid., 146.
12. Ibid.

Not surprisingly, the Potawatomi had a very different understanding of the land and its usefulness. Their understanding of the Great Lakes region was based on having inhabited these places for many generations. This sense of rootedness is expressed in a speech by Awbanawben during the negotiations of an 1826 treaty. Being asked by Governor Cass to respond to the Commissioners' proposal to move west of the Mississippi River, Awbanawben replied:

> Father, what you are going to hear from me now is not from me, as an individual, but it is from my fellow young men, our war chiefs, our peace chiefs and from all, and not from me alone. . . .
> To us to smoke, was an emblem of peace and charity, but we find it was intended for our destruction and misery. Father, when you collected us here, you pointed to us a country, which you said would be better for us where [we] could live. You said we could not stay here. We would perish. But what will perish[?] But what will destroy us[?] It is yourselves destroying us, for you make the spirituous liquor. You speak to us with deceitful lips, and not from your hearts. It seems so to me. You trampled on our soil, and drove it away. Before you came, the game was plenty, but you drove it away. The Great Spirit made us red skins, and the soil he put us on is red, the color of our skins. You came from a country where the soil is white, the color of your skin. You point to a country for us in the west, where there is game. We saw there is game there, but the Great Spirit has made and put men there, who have a right to that game and it is not ours.[13]

This was not Awbanawben's commentary on biological race; it was a philosophical reflection on the ways subsistence and survival had become embodied and emplaced by his people. Leaving the land would in Awbanawben's words mean "destruction and misery," and ultimately they would be destroyed and perish, if not physically, then psychologically and culturally. The Potawatomi's very being depended on the places they inhabited.

Awbanawben was aware that his people were not unique in this regard. He was equally concerned with what would happen to the people they would displace should they agree to move west of the Mississippi. The Potawatomi's reluctance to move was based on their recognition that people are profoundly rooted in and shaped by the places in which they live. They understood the disruption that removal would bring to their own well-being, as well as the impact it would have on others. This notion of being rooted in the land stands in sharp contrast with that of the commissioners

13. "Treaty of October 23, 1826," National Archives Micropcopy T 494 Roll 1.

of the US government, and to some extent that of nineteenth-century Anabaptist settlers.

The complementarity of Amish Mennonite perceptions of land are demonstrated in a letter I came across early on in my research. Located in the Mennonite Church USA Archives in Goshen, Indiana, the letter is written by Friedrich Hage, an Amish Mennonite bishop living in Holmes County, Ohio. It is the only document written in the 1830s I have found that speaks directly to how Amish Mennonites in western Pennsylvania and eastern Ohio understood the land west of where they lived.

The letter was written on May 25, 1839, only a year prior to the initial exploration of northern Indiana by Amish Mennonite scouts from Somerset County. It was addressed to a relative in Europe and explains the conditions, experience, and life in North America from Hage's perspective. The letter is fragmented. Fortunately the passage containing Hage's description of the land remains largely intact. Translated from German, the passage reads:

> Afterward we moved to the State of Ohio because the land in Pennsylvania was [. . .]. An acre costs from 200 to 250 florins [. . .]. I bought 80 acres for 825 florins but the land is [. . .] in this vicinity that I could now sell it [. . .] reckoned according to this money. Two florins, 30 kroners are reckoned as a [. . .] in America. But whoever goes farther back into the country can buy land cheaply from the government, a dollar and a quarter or two florins, fifty-seven kroner for an acre. However, it is nothing except woods as it was purchased from the Indians or wild people. For the government purchased the land from them two to three hundred hours distance in one piece. So, if a man has youngsters or his own people, he soon has a nice farm. For the income from the land is very slight. For it is not as in Europe, but men servants and hired girls are expensive.[14]

Hage's letter is important in understanding how Amish Mennonites perceived the Great Lakes region. In a cursory reading, "it is nothing but woods" could lead one to believe these lands were considered undesirable by Amish Mennonite settlers. However, understanding the agricultural practices Amish Mennonites had developed over time in Europe brings a different perspective to this comment. The work of other scholars has shown how disenfranchisement throughout Europe gave Anabaptist farmers the opportunity to improvise outside the established subsistence farming and land inheritance practiced by mainstream society, particularly in France and Germany. The innovations Anabaptists introduced included

14. Mast Collection.

intensive livestock production, fertilizing fields with manure, clearing of forests, draining wetlands, revitalizing fallow grasslands, and a crop rotation system that depended upon legume production, particularly alfalfa.[15] These practices are what geographers refer to as land reclamation.[16] In land reclamation, swamps, woodlands, and fallow grasslands considered to be waste or unused land are turned into what is regarded as productive agricultural land.

Biologists Stinner et al. have shown how the symbiotic relationship between Anabaptist farmers and the land they farmed had developed into a way of being-in-the-world.[17] The ability of forage legumes such as alfalfa to produce *Rhizobium* bacteria, which fixates nitrogen from manure in the soil, increased crop production. Increased crop production allowed for more intensive animal husbandry, in turn creating more manure, and so forth. Anabaptists carried these practices with them wherever they were forced or allowed to live, turning abandoned or unwanted land into productive agricultural farms that became the envy of their neighbors. Stinner et al. believe that these practices grew deeper than the legumes they were growing and actually shaped Anabaptist perceptions of the world.

The insights of Stinner et al. align with and support the kind of interaction between humans and the land that Ingold proposes in his dwelling perspectives. Again, it is not the forms that people create within a landscape that are significant; it is the actual process of building and cultivating in which meaning is generated. Humans incorporate and embody these practices over time, forming a way of being-in-the-world. When viewed through the lens of the dwelling perspective, Anabaptists' rootedness was not linked to a particular place; it was linked to a particular way of interacting with the world that they lived in. Thus, the woods of northern Indiana beckoned to Amish Mennonites, not simply because it was cheap land but because the skills they embodied equipped them to deal with such land.

For Anabaptists, it was the activity of distinctive agricultural practices that rooted them in the world, not the particularity of place. They could set up shop anywhere and still be at home. This is significant because Anabaptism has also identified itself as a religious diaspora in which the meaning of place is found in placelessness. The agricultural practices described above sustained diaspora, but diaspora also sustained agriculture. According to Paul Johnson who has studied the diasporic religion of the Garifuna, *"If*

15. Correll, "Mennonite Agricultural Model"; Séguy, "Religion and Agricultural Success"; Reschley, *Amish*.

16. Curtis and Campopiano, "Medieval Land Reclamation."

17. Stinner et al., "Forage Legumes."

religions are sometimes the cause of diasporas, diasporas sometimes make religions" (italics in original).[18] Agriculture and diasporic religion had become dovetailed for Anabaptists, making it difficult to distinguish where one ended and the other began. Neither one depended on a particular place.

The same skills and abilities of Amish Mennonite farmers that had fostered land reclamation in France and Germany (in line with what the US commissioner had in mind in the Great Lakes region) resulted in landscape transformation in places such as northern Indiana. The difference between land reclamation and landscape transformation is a matter of cultural relations.

BIBLIOGRAPHY

Borntreger, Hans. *A History of the First Settlers of the Amish Mennonites and the Establishment of Their First Congregation in the State of Indiana: Along with a Short Account of the Division Which Took Place in this Church*. 1907. Translated by Elizabeth Gingerich. Sugar Creek, OH: Schlabach, 1992.

Buss, James Joseph. *Winning the West with Words: Language and Conquest in the Lower Great Lakes*. Norman: University of Oklahoma Press, 2011.

Comaroff, Jean, and John Comaroff. *Of Revelation and Revolution: Christianity, Colonialism, and Consciousness in South Africa*. Vol. 1. Chicago: University of Chicago Press, 1991.

Correll, Ernst H. "The Mennonite Agricultural Model in the German Palatinate." Translated by Marion Lois Huffines. *Pennsylvania Mennonite Heritage* 14, no. 4 (1991) 2–13.

Curtis, Daniel R., and Michele Campopiano. "Medieval Land Reclamation and the Creation of New Societies: Comparing Holland and the Po Valley, c.800–c.1500." *Journal of Historical Geography* 44 (2014) 93–108.

Good, E. Reginald. "Lost Inheritance: Alienation of Six Nations' Lands in Upper Canada, 1784–1805." *Journal of Mennonite Studies* 19 (2001) 92–102.

Ingold, Tim. *The Perception of the Environment: Essays in Livelihood, Dwelling and Skill*. London: Routledge, 2000.

Johnson, Paul Christopher. *Diaspora Conversions: Black Carib Religion and the Recovery of Africa*. Berkeley: University of California Press, 2007.

"Letter from the Secretary of War to the Chairman of the Committee of Ways and Means, Upon the Subject of the Appropriations for the Year 1822." In *Congressional Edition*, 67:139–48. US Government Printing Office, 1822. Digitized April 29, 2011.

Journal of the Negotiations of the Treaty of October 23, 1826. National Archives Record Service. National Archives Microcopy T 494 (Record Group 75). Documents Relating to the Negotiation of Ratified and Unratified Treaties with Various Tribes of Indians, 1801–1869. Roll 1. Washington, DC: National Archives, 1801/1869.

Reschley, Steven D. *The Amish on the Iowa Prairie, 1840–1910*. Baltimore: John Hopkins University Press, 2000.

18. Johnson, *Diaspora Conversions*, 42.

Samuel Mast Collection on Holmes County (Ohio) Amish and Amish Mennonites, 1824–1961. HMI-346. Mennonite Church USA Archives-Goshen. Goshen, Indiana.

Schlabach, Theron F. *Peace, Faith, Nation: Mennonites and Amish in Nineteenth-Century America*. Eugene, OR: Wipf and Stock, 1988.

Séguy, Jean. "Religion and Agricultural Success: The Vocational Life of the French Anabaptists from the Seventeenth Century to the Nineteenth Century." Translated by Michael Shank. *Mennonite Quarterly Review* 47, no. 3 (1973) 179–224.

Sleeper-Smith, Susan. "Women, Kin, and Catholicism: New Perspectives on the Fur Trade." *Ethnohistory* 47 (2000) 423–52.

Stinner, Deborah H., et al. "Forage Legumes and Cultural Sustainability: Lessons from History." *Agriculture, Ecosystems and the Environment* 40 (1992) 233–48.

White, Richard. *The Middle Ground: Indians, Empires, and Republics in the Great Lakes Region, 1650–1815*. Cambridge: Cambridge University Press, 1991.

Wolfe, Patrick. "Settler Colonialism and the Elimination of the Native." *Journal of Genocide Research* 8 (2006) 387–409.

Yoder, Paton. *Tradition and Transition: Amish Mennonites and Old Order Amish, 1800–1900*. Scottdale, PA: Herald, 1991.

19

Humanity from the Humus

Early American Mennonite Humility Theology as a Resource for a Grounded Theological Anthropology

Douglas D. H. Kaufman

But pride is of such a nature that it cannot and will not be hid: it likes to be seen and to make great display, in order to make itself "a name." It is far too prevalent and is clearly visible in the needless splendor, costliness, and magnitude of houses, barns, etc., which are sometimes highly ornamented, and painted in a variety of colors, merely to make a magnificent show . . . Even among non-resistant professors of Christianity, may be seen some very unsuitable ornaments such as portraits of military heroes and officers armed with the instruments of death![1]

This quote from John Brenneman appears in his booklet *Pride and Humility*. First published in the *Herald of Truth*, an Elkhart-based paper in Indiana distributed to Amish and Mennonites throughout North America, it was republished in 1867 as an independent booklet. The booklet is still in print for use by Old Order Mennonites and Amish and still stands as one

---

1. Brenneman, *Pride and Humility*, 8–9.

of the most sustained Anabaptist Mennonite treatments on the subject of humility.[2]

This essay explores an early American Mennonite theology of humility and suggests that this humility tradition can help us recover a proper understanding of humanity's role vis-à-vis the rest of creation. While Brenneman interpreted humility as "lowliness of mind," primarily in relation to God and other humans,[3] I will apply this lowliness of mind to our fellow creatures and, indeed, the earth itself. Humility is a resource for a grounded theological anthropology that keeps us rooted in creation. We are creatures along with all other creatures, yet we are also articulate—able to both speak to and listen to God. A proper understanding of humility allows us to celebrate fully our humanity and to live in a relationship of mutuality with one another and with our fellow nonhuman creatures.

I will explore both the promise that humility offers in construing the human relationship with the rest of creation as well as the peril it presents, when misunderstood, in its potential for undervaluing ourselves. I will first explore the Mennonite understanding of humility that came to fruition in the 1860s, looking especially at the work of Heinrich Funck and John Brenneman. Secondly, I will engage with the feminist theological critique of pride and humility, noting that pride is not the primary temptation for all humans. Finally, I intend to develop how humility can enhance a Christian understanding of our relationship to the rest of creation.

MENNONITE HUMILITY THEOLOGY

Mennonite historian Theron Schlabach argues that humility was not a central concern of early Anabaptists, the predecessors of Mennonites. But by the mid-nineteenth century in America, humility became central.[4] Furthermore, Schlabach argued, humility supplanted suffering as the primary motif of Mennonite theology.

Schlabach sees the first step of this development in the book *Restitution* by Pennsylvania Bishop Heinrich Funck, published posthumously in 1763. Funck describes the Passover feast as not just a meal of bread and wine but also Jesus's broken body and shed blood. Followers of Jesus keep the Passover by partaking of the Lord's Supper and, more importantly, by

---

2. See Liechty, "Humility"; and Schlabach, "Humility," for an overview of early American Mennonite humility theology.

3. Brenneman, *Pride and Humility*, 33–36.

4. Schlabach, "Humility," 401–2.

following Jesus in the way of suffering and even death. He describes Anabaptist martyrs as keeping "grim Passover feasts."[5]

Funck wonders why pacifist Christians are no longer persecuted as they were in the past. As an immigrant from Germany to Pennsylvania in 1717, he may have noticed this shift in his lifetime. While he recognizes a number of possible reasons for this change, such as God's mercy or God controlling the hearts of the authorities, he believes the primary reason is that nonresistant Christians themselves were taking great effort to prevent suffering. How? His reply: "Christian humility is disregarded. The ways of the world are adopted in a life of pride and ambition for worldly honor and wealth in order to be like the world, and thereby avoid being despised by the world."[6]

While Funck emphasizes humility in this passage, the most important sign for him of the regenerated life is suffering and death. Humility is presented as a means to a greater end. Humility is not yet the central theme that it will become in later writings.

Another Pennsylvania Bishop, Christian Burkholder, further develops the theme of humility in a book published in 1804. He writes: "For the heart of man by nature, is proud and conceited; but the heart of a penitent is humble and contrite; and, as the heart is, so is the fruit thereof." A humble person "cannot bring forth fruit that has externally the appearance of pride, whether it be in words, actions, or the 'putting on of apparel.'"[7] Here, humility becomes the most critical sign of regeneration.

The climax of Mennonite humility theology comes in the booklet by Ohio Mennonite Bishop John Brenneman quoted at the beginning of this essay, published as *Pride and Humility*. Brenneman not only continues patterns from earlier Mennonite writings but also solidifies and centralizes humility as a theme.

Like Funck before him, Brenneman sees the origin of pride in Satan: "[He] was the first that fell thereby." Yet Brenneman more clearly connects pride with the fall. "Here they fell through pride; for if they had remained steadfast in humility, they would not have fallen."[8]

Brenneman, like both Funck and Burkholder, emphasizes the embodiment of pride and humility. The inner disposition of pride and humility is important and even the root of the behaviors. But the reverse is also true: behavior demonstrates the inner disposition. Like Burkholder, Brenneman

5. Funck, *Restitution*, 268.

6. Ibid., 269.

7. Burkholder, "Addresses to Youth," 187.

8. Brenneman, *Pride and Humility*, 7.

uses the image of fruit to describe this: "Pride in a [person's] heart cannot remain concealed, but, like the fruit of a tree, will crop out, and manifest itself in look and gestures."[9]

All three emphasize what humility is not. In other words, there is much more described about the vice of pride than about the virtue of humility. This is evident in the opening quote of this essay. And while this quote goes into lavish detail about homes and their furnishings, Mennonite emphasis on humility increasingly focused on clothing, with about one-fourth of Brenneman's booklet focused on clothing alone.

But Brenneman's focus on the pitfalls of pride does not mean that he ignores the benefits of humility. While much of the booklet focuses on the first phrase of 1 Pet 5:5—that "God resisteth the proud"[10]—perhaps the last fourth is dedicated to the final phrase that God "giveth grace to the humble." He sees humility as the essential ingredient in turning from death to life. "Without humility we have no promise of the saving power of grace; and without this saving grace no one can be a child, and consequently neither an heir, of God . . . Without true humility of heart we have no promise of grace; but on the contrary we are threatened with God's resistance."[11]

This theology ebbed by the end of the nineteenth century as Mennonites experienced a "great awakening" of revivalism, missions outreach, and the building of churchwide institutions. The mark of the Christian became activism rather than meekness. Christian faithfulness was marked by active Christian service rather than a lifestyle forgoing pride.[12]

Andrew Martin has recently challenged several of Schlabach's premises regarding humility. Martin demonstrates that humility was a substantial theme within Anabaptist—and more broadly, Christian—literature. So its centrality in the 1860s was not as unprecedented as Schlabach might have us think. Rather than humility supplanting suffering as the primary motif, Martin shows that the two themes often functioned in tandem within Anabaptist writings.[13]

Suffering and humility worked together even in the 1860s. Brenneman's other significant publication at the time was in response to the Civil War. The title begins *Christianity and War: A Sermon Setting Forth the Sufferings of Christians*. In this 1863 publication, Brenneman describes the suffering that comes with refraining from participation in war. While Martin offers a

9. Ibid., 8.

10. Brenneman quotes from the *King James Version*.

11. Ibid., 32–33.

12. Schlabach, "Humility," 402.

13. Martin, "Mennonite Spirituality."

helpful corrective, it seems to me that Brenneman's booklet gives humility a centrality that is unprecedented and unrepeated among Mennonites.[14]

As we look especially at Brenneman's writings, what might we discover about humility as a way of construing theological anthropology? We see both the grace and disgrace of being human. Brenneman describes humanity as "created good and noble in the image of God, exalted and set over all other creatures, yet, by their fall through transgression, they became the poorest and most wretched of all creatures."[15] So for Brenneman, pride is a basic problem of humanity: "Pride exists, by nature, in [humans], in a greater or less degree, as long as [they are] not regenerated, and [have] not been changed from [their] old nature to a state of humility."[16]

What a stark transformation—from being exalted over all other creatures to becoming the most wretched. Yet the human predicament does not end there. Brenneman offers hope for humanity in the promise that though God resists the proud, God also "giveth grace to the humble." "Through grace we are . . . accepted . . . as children, and made heirs of [God's] eternal and heavenly kingdom . . . [God] gives grace to them even in this life, insomuch as [God] pardons their sins and blesses them in body and soul with all manner of good gifts; and in the life to come [God] bestows on them eternal and heavenly gifts and possessions, and eternal joy, rest, and happiness."[17]

So while we may think of humility theology leading to an abased view of humanity, we find here language of exaltation, blessing, and good gifts. We want to keep this in mind, because certainly an ongoing danger of making humility theology more central is the problem of self-abnegation, a problem raised especially by feminist theologians.

FEMINIST CRITIQUE OF PRIDE AND HUMILITY

In her essay "The Human Situation: a Feminine View," Valerie Saiving explores how male experience has shaped theology, and she wonders how taking account of female experience might change this theology. Saiving convincingly argues that temptation for women is different than temptation for men.

> The specifically feminine forms of sin . . . have a quality which can never be encompassed by such terms as "pride" and

14. Brenneman, *Christianity and War.*
15. Brenneman, *Pride and Humility*, 29.
16. Ibid., 8.
17. Ibid., 32.

"will-to-power." They are better suggested by such terms as triviality, distractibility, and diffuseness; lack of an organizing center or focus; dependence on others for one's self-definition; tolerance at the expense of standards of excellence . . . in short, underdevelopment or negation of the self.[18]

Thus, those theologians who assume that pride is the basic human sin have not adequately taken into account women's experience. It's not that this temptation of self-abnegation is only a problem for women but that it is more emphatically present among women than men.

Twenty years after Saiving's article appeared, Judith Plaskow developed her insights into a sustained critique of the theologies of Reinhold Niebuhr and Paul Tillich. While this critique is the primary purpose of her book, she is also interested "in a secondary way with the idea that women are closer to nature than men and the way in which this stereotype functions in women's lives."[19] She summarizes the article by Sherry Ortner "Is Female to Male as Nature is to Culture?," highlighting Ortner's contention that every culture distinguishes culture and nature, asserts its superiority to nature, and sees women as closer to nature than men.[20]

Plaskow examines the way that Jungian psychologists have brought together the traits of naturalness and passivity in feminine experience. She quotes Erich Neumann who relates receptivity and acceptance to the experience of bearing children: "In all decisive life situations, the feminine, to a far greater degree than the nothing-but-masculine, is subjected to the numinous elements in nature, or, still better, has these 'brought home' to it. Therefore, its relation to nature and to God is more familiar and intimate, and its tie to an anonymous transpersonal allegiance forms earlier and goes deeper than its personal tie to a man."[21]

Is this a paean to women's superiority to men? That depends on how much nature, the numinous, and God are valued. If this is praise, it can be a shallow praise that keeps a woman within carefully circumscribed boundaries where now, instead of inferiority, the reason to limit her role is because of her superiority.

18. Saiving, "The Human Situation," 37.

19. Plaskow, *Sex, Sin, and Grace*, 3.

20. Ibid., 12–13, quotes Sherry Ortner, "Is Female to Male as Nature is to Culture?," in *Woman, Culture, and Society*, ed. Michelle Zimbalist Rosaldo and Louise Lamphere (Stanford: Stanford University Press, 1974).

21. Plaskow, *Sex, Sin, and Grace*, 27–28, quotes Erich Neumann, "The Moon and Matriarchal Consciousness," in *Dynamic Aspects of the Psyche* (New York: Analytical Psychology Club, 1956) 62.

Ultimately, Plaskow considers the primary error of Niebuhr a certain one-sidedness. "The problem with Niebuhr and Tillich is not particularity *per se*, but the universality of their claims on behalf of the particular . . . If Niebuhr does not succeed in showing that pride is *the* human sin, he does establish it as an important temptation of human finitude, and in such a way that it can be recognized and named wherever it is found."[22] By considering men's experience to be universal, Niebuhr and Tillich discount women's experience of the opposite temptation of self-abnegation. If both pride and self-abnegation are temptations, then each requires a different remedy.

Unlike Brenneman and Neibuhr who assumed that pride was the universal sin and humility the universal remedy, Plaskow's critique allows us to be more nuanced in the remedies for temptation. Applying Plaskow's critique to Brenneman's humility theology, I propose that the remedy is different for different temptations: if a person's sin is pride, then humility would clearly be the antidote, but if a person's sin is self-abnegation, then a certain amount of pride would be the antidote.

HUMILITY IN JOB

The biblical tradition works with pride and self-abnegation. In the Magnificat, Mary sings that God "has brought down the powerful from their thrones, and lifted up the lowly" (Luke 1:52).[23] This proclaims that *already* God has taken action to lift the lowly. Not altogether different from this passage is the 1 Pet 5:5 verse (KJV) quoted by Brenneman: "God resisteth the proud, and giveth grace to the humble."[24]

A passage that brings together pride, humility, and human relationship to God and the rest of creation is God's enigmatic speech to Job in Job 38–41. Often interpreted as a humiliating reminder to Job of his finitude and mortality, it can also be read as a bracing call to glory in Job's ability to challenge God.

God's speech on creation in Job stands in contrast with Gen 1 where the climax of God's creation is humanity. In Job 38–40, God hardly mentions humanity and its role. The speech emphasizes God's sovereign and intimate relationship with all creation, quite apart from any human intermediation or intervention. We are reminded of the intrinsic value of all God's creatures whether humans have found a use for them or not.

22. Plaskow, *Sex, Sin, and Grace*, 174.

23. All Scripture quotations in this essay are from the NRSV Bible unless otherwise indicated.

24. *Pride and Humility*, 3.

Does this speech in Job leave humanity out of the picture? Not quite. After all, we are the ones whom God addresses. We are the ones who are engaged in a dialogue with God about the purpose and direction of creation. In particular, in Job 40:15 God says, "Look at Behemoth, which I made just as I made you."

Why compare us to this fearless, great and mighty, yet gentle plant-eating creature? God may be saying, "Buck up, Job. Be strong even in the midst of your suffering and weakness; take your place as one of God's great creatures."

Job's response to God's speech is as enigmatic. In Job 42:6, according to the *New Revised Standard Version Bible*, Job says, "Therefore I despise myself, and repent in dust and ashes." This follows the more traditional interpretation that would say that Job was too brazen in his complaints against God and so now he repents of all those strong words. The dust and ashes are symbols of his repentance.

But Carol Newsom has offered at least five legitimate translations of this text. In light of the ambiguities of the book of Job, she refuses to consider any single translation as the one most likely intended. One translation she offers is, "Therefore I retract my words, and I am comforted concerning dust and ashes." In this version, Job repents of his bitter words that being made in the image of God is a curse. And he takes hope in his role as dust and ashes.[25]

This phrase "dust and ashes" appears one other time in the Bible—in Gen 18 when God is dialoging with another human, this time Abraham. God is planning to destroy Sodom because of its sin, and Abraham is concerned about God overreacting. He negotiates with God, getting God to agree not to destroy Sodom if ten righteous people can be found in the city. In this context, Abraham calls himself but dust and ashes while calling God the judge of all the earth.

God listens to Abraham. Genesis 18 has a curious image of the judge of all the earth waiting to learn what dust and ashes will teach about God's justice. And so now too in Job, God listens to Job. A twelfth-century illumination dares to portray Job standing face-to-face talking to God. And even more clearly, God is portrayed as listening intently to what Job is saying. After a lengthy and magnificent speech, God silently waits to see what can be learned from Job.[26]

25. Ballentine, *Job*, 694–97, cites Carol Newsom, "The Book of Job," New Interpreter's Bible 4 (Nashville: Abingdon, 1996) 629.

26. Ibid., 694–99.

So we are dust and ashes, but we are articulate dust and ashes—those who can speak to and listen to God, praising God or even questioning God. Job portrays the glory and humility of human existence as the part of creation that articulates to the creator our predicament.

A DOWN-TO-EARTH THEOLOGY

The part of humility that emphasizes our lowliness, or what might better be called groundedness, is what leads me to think that humility is especially helpful in construing the human relationship with the earth. An interesting relationship exists between humans, humility, and the earth that is best expressed by noting the similarity between the words human, humble, and humus. The *Oxford English Dictionary* identifies the root of "humble" as the Latin word *humus*, which is "ground" or "earth."[27] This is also related to the roots of the English word "human."

The human-ground relationship is even clearer in the original Hebrew of Gen 2:7, when God creates the human from the dust of the ground. In this text, human is *adam* and ground is *adamah*. Another way to express this relationship is that God created the earthling from the earth.

Out of this complex of relationships, humility images our rightful relationship with the earth. We are a grounded people. We are called to keep our sights on the ground from which we came. There are several ways that humility would change our relationship with the rest of creation.

The first way that humility would change our relationship with creation comes most clearly from the Mennonite sources above. The embodiment of humility in our lives would mean living more simply and working to lessen the harmful effects of our lifestyle on the earth. I recognize that Brenneman focused more on personalistic and moralistic choices about clothing, and to a lesser extent housing, such as we see in my opening quote of this essay. Our decisions about simple living would need to extend beyond this to creating a lifestyle with less of a negative impact upon the earth.

The second way that humility would change our relationship with creation comes from interaction with the feminist sources above, especially Saiving. Humility causes us to more fully embrace the limitations and possibilities of our biological lives. Plaskow seems to argue against the tradition of a woman's role simply being an outgrowth of her biology and argue instead for women having the same right as men to live according to personal choices beyond biology.[28] I am concerned that this emphasis can lead to a

27. *Oxford English Dictionary*, 446.

28. Plaskow, *Sex, Sin, and Grace*, 28–29.

prideful lack of groundedness with our fellow biological creatures. While I agree with the intent of equality, I argue that the roles of both men and women should fully embrace their respective biologies rather than arguing that a woman's role should not be defined by her biology. Such a view would more readily accept our biological and ecological limitations and live within them.

Finally, a humble relationship with the earth would help us more fully understand the give and take of that relationship. We would more fully understand how our actions impact the ways that the rest of creation acts toward us. We are in a living relationship with the rest of creation. There is mutuality in this relationship.

Having suggested that humility is something that needs to be embodied, how might it be embodied today? Part of that groundedness would mean paying attention to our locality—the literal ground upon which we stand. We would buy local products and find ways to live and work locally. We would walk or bike short distances and avoid long trips as much as possible.

The Mennonite emphasis on simple living has at times devolved into an emphasis on spending as little as possible. Unfortunately, this can lead to practices that may be cheaper in the short run but ultimately unsustainable environmentally.

The Mennonite emphasis on simple living can also devolve into depriving ourselves. Deprivation is not necessarily a part of humility. Paying attention to our locality and our food can be tremendously rewarding. Meals prepared with homegrown foods and herbs are often superior to those eaten at all but the finest restaurants. Eating fresh food and highlighting its flavors with a variety of herbs and spices is far superior to eating food prepared long before it is eaten and flavored primarily with sugar and fat. As Henry David Thoreau discovered at Walden Pond, living humbly can be a way to "live deep and suck out all the marrow of life."[29]

CONCLUSION

Calvin Redekop, in his conclusion to the book *Creation and the Environment: An Anabaptist Perspective on a Sustainable World*, blames human hubris as the cause of our environmental crisis. He therefore calls for Christians to show more humility in their relationship with nature. Yet Redekop

---

29. Thoreau, *Walden*, 118.

does this in apparent ignorance of the historic Mennonite statements on the centrality of humility.[30]

A theology of humility is a part of the Mennonite tradition that has long been submerged but that can now provide a resource for confronting today's environmental crisis. Humility points toward both the glory and the shame of our human situation, of our situation as God's creatures. We are humanity, articulate humus, called to humbly listen to and address God. Humility reminds us to live in mutual submission to one another as humans and in mutual submission with the rest of creation. It reminds us that all of God's creatures are called to submit to God's will and way.

BIBLIOGRAPHY

Ballentine, Samuel. *Job*. Macon: Smyth & Helwys, 2006.

Brenneman, John M. *Pride and Humility: A Discourse, Setting Forth the Characteristics of the Proud and the Humble*. 1867. Hagerstown: Deutsche Buchhandlung, 1996.

———. *Christianity and War: A Sermon Setting Forth the Sufferings of Christians . . . by a Minister of the Old Mennonite Church*. Chicago: Hess, 1863.

Burkholder, Christian. "Addresses to Youth on True Repentance and Saving Faith in Jesus Christ." In *Christian Spiritual Conversation on Saving Faith for the Young, in Questions and Answers*, and a Confession of Faith, of the Mennonites. Ephrata: Committee of Mennonites, 1974.

Funck, Heinrich. *Restitution: Or, An Explanation of Several Principal Points of the Law: How it Has Been Fullfilled by Christ . . . According to the Teachings of the Old and New Testament Scriptures: Compiled in Twenty-five Chapters*. Elkhart: Mennonite, 1915.

Liechty, Joseph C. "Humility: The Foundation of Mennonite Religious Outlook in the 1860s." *Mennonite Quarterly Review* 54, no. 1 (1980), 5–31.

Martin, Andrew. "Mennonite Spirituality: A Reassessment of 'Humility Theology' in North America in the Nineteenth Century." *Mennonite Quarterly Review* 85 (2011) 293–323.

Oxford English Dictionary. Vol. 4. London: Oxford University Press, 1961.

Plaskow, Judith. *Sex, Sin, and Grace: Women's Experience and the Theologies of Reinhold Niebuhr and Paul Tillich*. Lanham, MD: University Press of America, 1980.

Redekop, Calvin, ed. *Creation and the Environment: an Anabaptist Perspective on a Sustainable World*. Baltimore: Johns Hopkins University Press, 2000.

Saiving, Valerie. "The Human Situation: a Feminine View." In *Womanspirit Rising: A Feminist Reader in Religion*. Carol P. Christ and Judith Plaskow, eds. San Francisco: Harper & Row, 1979.

Schlabach, Theron F. "Humility." *Mennonite Encyclopedia*, edited by Cornelius J. Dyck and Dennis D. Martin, 5:400–402. Scottdale, PA: Herald, 1990.

Thoreau, Henry David. *Walden*. New York: Crowell, 1961.

30. Redekop, *Creation*, 206–7.

20

They Were Right

Agrarian Voices of Mennonite Civilian Public Service Men

Rebecca Horner Shenton

It may seem as if theological interest in care of the land is only a recent response to secular agrarian and environmental movements. Indeed, prior to the first Earth Day in 1970, Christian books and periodicals dealing with environmental issues were rare. In the 1970s, with a greater awareness of pollution, acid rain, and other ecological problems, Christians began to formulate theological responses. However, until the mid-1980s, such books were few; in the 1990s they became more common. The journal *Ecotheology* started publication in 1996, and since 2000, a number of books, articles, and organizations have considered ecological and environmental issues from various Christian perspectives. The most significant Anabaptist contribution to this literature is a collection of essays titled *Creation and the Environment: An Anabaptist Perspective on a Sustainable World.*[1]

This dearth of published material creates the false impression that Christians were unaware of the dangers of environmental degradation prior to 1970—and worse yet, that they were unconcerned. While the publication of Rachel Carson's *Silent Spring* in 1962 certainly was an eye-opener

1. Redekop, *Creation and Environment.*

regarding the serious negative impacts of pesticides such as DDT,[2] Christians interested in rural life had already been thinking and writing about care of the earth for decades. One catalyst for their reflections was early twentieth-century research regarding the extent of soil erosion on US farmland, which prompted both agricultural and theological reflection on the role of farmers as responsible stewards of land belonging to God. Mennonites have had a long history of considering agriculture from a standpoint that is both agrarian and theological, and their writings reflect this. However, these reflections often go unnoticed because they are contained in small, popular publications rather than scholarly works.[3]

CIVILIAN PUBLIC SERVICE WRITINGS

The writings of Civilian Public Service (CPS) workers assigned to Soil Conservation Service projects during World War II are one important Mennonite source of such reflections. The CPS program was developed by the historic peace churches (Brethren, Friends, and Mennonites) at the beginning of World War II to provide a government-approved alternative for men called up to report for wartime military service. The vast majority of program participants were peace church members, although other conscientious objectors could, and did, participate.

Almost half of the US cropland under cultivation at the start of the war was already damaged by erosion: one hundred million acres had lost all topsoil, and another hundred million acres had lost more than half.[4] The Soil Conservation Service emphasized maintaining and improving soil fertility and productivity to meet the present and future food needs of humanity. Soil conservation work was therefore considered to be "work of

2. Carson, *Silent Spring.*

3. There were many of these publications throughout the twentieth century. For a survey, see Shenton, *Cross and the Plow*, chap. 2.

4. Gingerich, *Service for Peace*, 108–9. While the US government, farmers, and Mennonites had been aware of soil erosion since before World War I, the issue was brought to a critical level after the Dust Bowl of the 1930s. Some government officials, such as land-use planner Lewis Gray of the USDA Bureau of Agricultural Economics, took the position that some areas of the plains should never have been put under cultivation and should thus be returned to their native short-grass prairie. The Soil Conservation Service took the opposing viewpoint—that the problem had been caused by a lack of rainfall, which had been exacerbated by unwise farming practices. Farmers attributed the Dust Bowl to an unusual lack of rain, and hoped that this would be a temporary problem; they preferred the Soil Conservation Service's approach because it allowed them to continue putting their land into crops, rather than retiring it completely. "A Great Waste," 69; Danbom, *Born in the Country*, 224–28.

national importance" suitable for CPS workers, since preserving the fertility of the land was essential for ensuring a stable food supply for US citizens and allies. Men in the CPS program were assigned to different agencies for alternative service, including the Soil Conservation Service, Forest Service, Agricultural Experiment Stations, mental hospitals, and general hospitals; they also voluntarily served as "human guinea pigs" for research experiments. Each service location was called a "camp," and the men serving in that location were called "campers." In its early days, "over half the men in Mennonite [CPS] camps" were involved in soil conservation work.[5]

Many CPS camps printed newsletters to send back home to churches, family, and friends; the articles reported on camp activities and also reflected campers' views of the work itself. These newsletters are not the only example of Christian concern for the earth in the first half of the twentieth century. However, they reflect concern for the land's health beyond what was necessary for human survival, and they provide evidence that Mennonite CPS men recognized the value of the earth as God's creation and the Christian responsibility to steward it as a sacred trust—well before the advent of "environmentalism." This essay examines the themes of care for the land in a sampling of CPS materials and connects these reflections to contemporary Christian ecotheological and agrarian works. Thus, it situates the contemporary theological focus on land and community within a Mennonite historical trajectory of such concerns, demonstrating that concern for land care is more than a recent innovation.

Three CPS camps in Nebraska and Maryland offered Farm and Community School programs that involved lectures and study related to agriculture, community life, and the Mennonite faith. These programs were designed to prepare participants to be leaders in Mennonite rural life after the conclusion of the war.[6] One such program was based at Camp 138 in Malcolm and Lincoln, Nebraska. In 1946, Menno Koehn, a farmer from Halstead, Kansas, wrote about the importance of soil conservation in the camp's *Mennonite Farmunity* newsletter. He observed that differences in rainfall patterns between the United States and Europe required different farming practices to protect the soil from erosion. More than just protecting the soil's fertility, however, he stressed the importance of making the farm

---

5. Ibid., 108. A good source of both general and specific information regarding the CPS program is "Civilian Public Service Story." I obtained biographical details regarding specific campers from this website and from *Mennonite C.P.S. Directory* (1948).

6. Some camps were divided into subunits at different locations; some printed multiple newsletters over the lifespan of the camp. For simplicity, I have omitted reference to the subunits and refer to the newsletters by name and date.

"a pleasant place to live" and emphasized that the true reason for farming should not be to make money but because farming is a fulfilling way of life.[7]

CPS Camp 106 in Lincoln, Nebraska, also offered a Farm and Community School program. In *The Agrogram*, one camper elaborated on the goals for the program; his comments regarding the program's six standard aims are instructive. The first aim is "to live the life of Christian discipleship, stewardship, brotherhood, and nonresistance in all of our farm and community life." The author adds, "We need to be the true stewards we profess to be in our chosen field of agriculture. Only with genuine commitment and ever new search into our faith can we make it a living reality that our lives may be a witness."[8] Here, stewardship of the land is more than just maintaining soil fertility; it is one of many places that the Mennonite practice of convictional living might be displayed.

Something similar is seen in David H. Suderman's encouragement to take the "long view" of years or decades to best see the importance of soil conservation work. Suderman reminds his fellow CPS men at Camp 5 near Colorado Springs, Colorado, that they need to assess whether they are "discharging [their] responsibility according to [their] best efforts" and to ask themselves, "Do our efforts truly testify to those about us of this Jesus' Way of Life we profess?"[9] Done properly, the work would do more than restore the soil: it would also reflect the importance of a peaceful way of life, tending God's garden.

Ralph Beechy, a teacher and farmer from Apple Creek, Ohio, directed the Farm and Community School at Camp 24 near Hagerstown, Maryland. One of his articles connects stewardship of the land with Christian faith:

> Man . . . cannot exist . . . apart from the soil, the earth. It is the basic resource over which man, in cooperation with the Creator, makes his home, his bread, and his beauty, and, if used aright, his brotherhood. Out of the earth man came, upon it he lives, to it his body returns . . . As Christians, we may call her the Holy Earth, since she is the creation of God and has been entrusted to man's stewardship.[10]

In the same article, Beechy also comments on the significance of the rural setting of Scripture:

7. Koehn, "What We Think," 22.

8. "Aims of the Farm and Community Schools," 2.

9. Suderman, "The Long View," 2.

10. Beechy, "Rural Living," 1.

Scores of the loveliest sayings and parables of Jesus, which il-
luminate and clarify great spiritual values, are found in scenes
of the countryside. Nine-tenths of His sayings are drawn from
life and language of the farmer. He grew up and spent the years
of His ministry among a people predominantly rural. His soul
was nurtured in the teachings of men whose life's high passion
was social justice in terms of the will and purpose of God for a
people living on and of the soil.[11]

Beechy considers "the kingdom ideals" essential for a strong rural life.
These include "the practice and culture of community brotherhood based
on love among men . . . the holding of gifts of God as a sacred stewardship or
trust, and the way of self-sacrifice, even suffering love as the ultimate way of
life."[12] Practicing these ideals—and others taught by Jesus—is thus necessary for developing a meaningful, satisfying way of life. Beechy expressed
similar sentiments in a 1944 publication that collected many of the teaching
materials from the Farm and Community School program:

The farmer is more than a business man. He is a creature of God
who cooperates with God's precious gift of soil, plants and animals. Farming is his way of life. It enters into every part of his
day.[13]

He hoped that the program had inspired program participants and
readers of the publication alike to practice responsible stewardship of "God's
Good Earth."[14]

Lester Culp, from Tiskilwa, Illinois, served as farm manager at the
Camp 24 Farm and Community School. His article focuses on statistics
showing a negative correlation between soil erosion and financial giving to
church work. Culp concludes: "It is our duty as faithful stewards to take
good care of the soil, a part of our God's creation, by using such practices as
are necessary to conserve soil and water to keep the land fertile and productive. In so doing we shall enjoy a more abundant home and church life."[15]
Stewardship, for Culp, was required for Christians, but it also bore tangible
financial fruit. For those who considered soil conservation practices such
as farming on the contour, terracing, and strip-cropping to be a waste of
time and energy, this economic viewpoint would have been important: in

11. Ibid.

12. Ibid., 5.

13. Beechy, "Why the Farm," 3–4.

14. Ibid.

15. Culp, "Church and Soil Conservation," 82–83.

time, these practices—which seemed crazy to those who were accustomed to neat, straight rows of wheat, corn, and other crops—would pay off for family and church.

CONTEMPORARY ECOTHEOLOGIANS

Interestingly, the themes raised by CPS men also appear in the work of contemporary ecotheologians, and indeed, seem to prefigure themes that are now mainstays among theologians with such interests. By participating in the *practice* of land conservation, these humble Mennonites hit on the themes that others are now "discovering" through theory. The connections here are varied, but four themes in particular are parallel: the significance of the rural setting of Scripture, stewardship and care of the earth, the importance of community, and the missional implications of rural life.

The Agrarian Setting of Scripture

Ralph Beechy's recognition that the agrarian setting of Scripture was significant is emphasized by Fred Bahnson and Norman Wirzba, who write that Jesus's

> ministry took place not in the airless confines of the temple but in the open hill country of Galilee: mountaintops, olive gardens, lakes, rivers, wilderness. It is only we moderns who think of these physical places as quaint backdrops, interchangeable stage settings on which the real action takes place—the preaching and praying, the baptizing and converting, the healing and resurrecting. Yet the mystery of the incarnation means that these places are inseparable from the story itself.[16]

Further, Ellen Davis comments that "agrarianism is the way of thinking predominant among the biblical writers, who very often do not represent the interests of the powerful."[17] Thus, learning to read the Bible with agrarian eyes is a necessary step in living as faithful disciples.

16. Bahnson and Wirzba, *Making Peace*, 53–54.
17. Davis, *Scripture, Culture, and Agriculture*, 1.

Stewardship as Sacred Responsibility

Several CPS men wrote about the importance of stewardship as a sacred responsibility. Ecotheologians go one step further, arguing that because God delights in all of creation, because humans are *part* of that creation, and because humans have been given the ability and responsibility to be reflective caretakers of God's "garden," Christians need a broader ecological perspective that recognizes our *membership* in creation.[18] This view rests upon the theocentric understanding that the earth and everything in it was created by God, belongs to God, and is sustained by God; human worship of God properly includes respectful care for what God has created.[19] Thus, the relationships between humans and the rest of creation require attention.[20]

For ecotheologians, caring for the soil is far more than the prudent move that the term "soil conservation" suggests. Instead, as Wirzba notes, it is "the quintessential human vocation (Gen. 2:15), [which] introduces us to the fundamental grace and mystery that sustains our and every being." In caring for God's garden, we become partners with God in God's creative work. Even as our careful tending nourishes the soil, we are nourished through our contact with the soil as our understanding of God deepens.[21] This work recognizes that the aim of farming is not to maximize the harvest but to nurture the plants, animals, and soil in our care so that our work leads to the flourishing, not the suffering, of all creation. Human life requires the "continued integrity" of the natural systems of which we are a part; "if we are wise, then, we will recognize that the land rightly 'expects something from us.'"[22] Careful tending of the land is no less necessary for us than it was for the Israelites in the hills of Canaan[23]—indeed, perhaps it is more so, given that unbridled use of modern technology has the potential to harm the land much more quickly.

18. Wirzba, *Food and Faith*, xiv–xvi. Wirzba expands on the significance of human membership in creation throughout this book.

19. Wirzba, *Paradise of God*, 139; Mustol, *Dusty Earthlings*, 204n2.

20. Bauckham, *Living with Other Creatures*, 4–5.

21. Wirzba, *Paradise of God*, 22, 31.

22. Davis, *Scripture, Culture, and Agriculture*, 31.

23. Davis, "Just Food," 129–30. Davis notes here that although Egypt's agricultural lands were flat and irrigated by water from the Nile, Canaan was a land of "steep slopes and small valleys, and a thin layer of topsoil easily eroded by the strong winter winds and rain . . . [that] allowed little or no margin for bad farming." Farmers needed, therefore, to "be vigilant in guarding its fertility."

Strong Communities

Mennonite CPS men—and other mid-century Mennonites—recognized the importance of strong communities in sustaining rural life. Contemporary ecotheologians and agrarians remind us that our definition of community needs to be expansive and inclusive. A flourishing community is vital since "creatures cannot and were never meant to exist in isolation or separation from each other. Kinship and harmony, mutuality and intimacy are to be the rule of healthy life together."[24] The scope of our community transcends neighborhood and town, however. Truly, we are all members of the community of creation, and "as members we depend on the membership of the whole to feed and sustain us."[25] This is an active membership, "informed by mercy and care, fidelity and love. Our dwelling in creation is to be inspired by the God who dwelt among us, and in that dwelling showed us the ways of forgiveness and peace and joy."[26] This understanding does not neglect the reality of smaller communities where we live out our daily lives in fellowship with one another; in fact, it requires them. However, rather than insular settlements that divide Mennonites in their sameness from the rest of the world, true Christian community rejoices in God's creation in all of its difference, shows hospitality to others, and chooses to sacrifice for the flourishing of the whole. We are unique individuals, but membership in a community means that our own "needs, desires and enjoyments make no sense apart from the life we live *together*. Only then can people become the sort of community that functions like an organic body—no member or part alone, but all working together to be a healthy whole."[27]

While Wirzba helps us to see the big picture of membership in the community of creation, Mennonite S. Roy Kaufman focuses on the importance of local human communities. These are modeled after the alternative communities found in Scripture, where primary identity is formed by membership in the face-to-face community created by its members' common response to God's call. Prioritizing devotion to local community, place, and ecology will lead to the well-being of neighboring communities and larger groups.[28] God's alternative community is marked by complete trust in God and equal sharing of power and economic resources, through which the

---

24. Wirzba, *Food and Faith*, 39.

25. Ibid., 58.

26. Ibid., 79.

27. Bahnson and Wirzba, *Making Peace*, 126–27.

28. Kaufman, *Healing God's Earth*, 43–44, 114–16.

community discovers that all of its needs are met.[29] Thus, a contemporary Christian understanding of community attends to the particularity of local place and face-to-face relationships. It also situates those relationships within the broader context of all of creation.

Faithful Stewardship of the Land

CPS men at Camps 106 and 5 recognized that faithful stewardship of the land, including soil conservation and improvement and attention to one's relationship with God, had missional implications. Kaufman raises the possibility that North American Mennonites have been prepared in God's providence for this critical time in history. He recommends that "rural congregations . . . invest their lives in the subversive re-creation of self-sustaining rural communities in the midst of urban imperialism," embracing their agrarian heritage and leveraging it in making "rural revitalization and community formation" the church's primary missional work.[30] In so doing, North American rural communities will be able to stand "in solidarity with traditional cultures under siege around the world."[31]

CONCLUSION

The recent attention paid to ecological issues by Christian theologians is important, and we have much to learn from their careful analysis. However, as we consider how to live in harmony with the rest of creation, let us also pay attention to the words of rural people of the past century. They remind us that earth care is not a new idea; it is something that grows out of our relationship with God, each other, and all creation. They also remind us that attention to the land's health really only makes sense as one practice embedded within a set of practices that express our commitment to follow Jesus in *all* of life.

BIBLIOGRAPHY

"Aims of the Farm and Community Schools." *Agrogram*, February 9, 1945.
Bahnson, Fred, and Norman Wirzba. *Making Peace with the Land: God's Call to Reconcile with Creation*. Downers Grove, IL: InterVarsity, 2012.

29. Ibid., 179, 180, 182, 183.
30. Ibid., 117, 255.
31. Ibid., 5.

Bauckham, Richard. *Living with other Creatures: Green Exegesis and Theology*. Waco: Baylor University Press, 2011.

Beechy, Ralph. "Rural Living." *Green Pastures*, May 1944.

———. "Why the Farm and Community School?" In *Farm and Community School: Civilian Public Service Camp No. 24, Unit 4 (Clearspring, Maryland)*, edited by Sanford E. Miller et al., 1, 5. Akron, PA: Mennonite Central Committee, 1944.

Carson, Rachel. *Silent Spring*. Boston: Houghton Mifflin, 1962.

"The Civilian Public Service Story: Living Peace in a Time of War." http://civilianpublicservice.org/ (accessed August 6, 2014).

Culp, Lester. "The Church and Soil Conservation." In *Farm and Community School: Civilian Public Service Camp No. 24, Unit 4 (Clearspring, Maryland)*, edited by Sanford E. Miller et al., 82–83. Akron, PA: Mennonite Central Committee, 1944.

Danbom, David B. *Born in the Country: A History of Rural America*. 2nd ed. Baltimore: Johns Hopkins, 2006.

Davis, Ellen F. "Just Food: A Biblical Perspective on Culture and Agriculture." In *Creation in Crisis: Christian Perspectives on Sustainability*, edited by Robert S. White, 122–36. London: SPCK, 2009.

———. *Scripture, Culture, and Agriculture: An Agrarian Reading of the Bible*. New York: Cambridge University Press, 2009.

Gingerich, Melvin. *Service for Peace: A History of Mennonite Civilian Public Service*. Akron, PA: Mennonite Central Committee, 1949.

"A Great Waste." *Christian Monitor*, March 1909.

Kaufman, S. Roy. *Healing God's Earth: Rural Community in the Context of Urban Civilization*. Eugene, OR: Wipf and Stock, 2013.

Koehn, Menno. "What We Think about Soil Conservation." *Mennonite Farmunity*, First Anniversary Edition, 1946.

Mennonite C.P.S. Directory: A Supplement to the 1948 Mennonite Yearbook. Scottdale, PA: Mennonite, 1948.

Mustol, John. *Dusty Earthlings: Living as Eco-Physical Beings in God's Eco-Physical World*. Eugene, OR: Cascade, 2012.

Redekop, Calvin Wall, ed. *Creation and the Environment: An Anabaptist Perspective on a Sustainable World*. Center Books in Anabaptist Studies. Baltimore: Johns Hopkins University Press, 2000.

Shenton, Rebecca Gay Horner. "The Cross and the Plow: Fertile Soil for a Mennonite Ethic of Food and Farming." PhD diss., Fuller Theological Seminary, Center for Advanced Theological Studies, Pasadena, CA, 2014.

Suderman, David H. "The Long View." *Pike View Peace News*, March 18, 1944.

Wirzba, Norman. *Food and Faith: A Theology of Eating*. New York: Cambridge University Press, 2011.

———. *The Paradise of God: Renewing Religion in an Ecological Age*. New York: Oxford University Press, 2003.

Sustainable Agriculture as Conscientious Objection: Perspectives from Japan

Raymond Epp

Connecting fields and gardens to the tables of people living nearby provides new opportunities to live out our commitment to Jesus's way of nonviolence and peace.

The present food system of the developed world, when viewed from the perspective of the powerless, is a form of structural violence. Dominating corporations are undermining local food systems by shaping government policies and international trade rules in their own favor. They are creating a world in which small farmers and rural communities struggle for survival and the urban poor struggle to find good nutritious food. Meanwhile, the creation groans.

Conscientious objection to the structural violence of this system may be our only hope. For communities of resistance, this will mean "unmasking the powers" of the food system, reflecting on the biblical teachings on peace and justice, praying for the system to return to its intended vocation of praising God and serving the needs of life, and incarnating a new way that connects people and cares for land.

Menno Village in Hokkaido, Japan, has been growing vegetables and other foods for a Community Supported Agriculture program for nearly twenty years. We make our own fertilizers using Japanese traditional knowledge and locally available waste products. We have also developed vegetable storage that is suitable to the Hokkaido climate and requires no energy. We have learned about the importance of appropriate scale processing equipment that allows us to make our own vegetable oil, mill our own flour, and bake our own breads on a village scale.

It needs to be made clear that this kind of life is not utopian dreaming. The only way to challenge the domination system is to work together to create real, local, more ecologically sound and stable communities of caring that feed people whom we love. This simple but difficult work is a witness to the *missio Dei*, God's desire to reconcile all humanity and all creation back to Godself. It is hard work, but it is possible because God is with those who hunger and thirst for justice.

The present system of economic injustice places ecological strains on soil, air, land, and water; exploits small farmers; and results in anomie, loneliness, and insecurity. The system wants us to believe that the problems we are confronting are just the "cost of progress" or that it is impossible to change. But believing that this system can continue forever is utopian dreaming. When we expose the contradictions and strains the system is causing, continuing in this approach is an indefensible default option. It is solidarity with death.

Jesus's resurrection points us to the possibility of new beginnings. New life is possible not in some purely mystical or spiritual sense but in relation to real flesh and blood people rooted in real soil in this time.

"Cultures of caring" demonstrate what an economy could be like if its guiding principles were love and justice. We invite others to the table of plenty that is part of the new economy of God. We practice imaginative acts as a means of expressing hope in what God will do. This is our way to witness to a culture of peace by refusing to cooperate with the violence of the existing system and by affirming our desire to follow God's way of justice. It is a way of creating a "new life within the shell of the old."

Subject Index

Scripture Index

Author Index

Printed in the USA
CPSIA information can be obtained
at www.ICGtesting.com
CBHW072211120924
14476CB00010B/258

9 781498 235549